Corruption and
American Cities

# Corruption and American Cities

*Essays and Case Studies in Ethical Accountability*

*Edited by*
JOAQUIN JAY GONZALEZ III *and*
ROGER L. KEMP

McFarland &amp; Company, Inc., Publishers
*Jefferson, North Carolina*

ALSO OF INTEREST AND FROM MCFARLAND: *Privatization in Practice: Reports on Trends, Cases and Debates in Public Service by Business and Nonprofits*, edited by Joaquin Jay Gonzalez III and Roger L. Kemp (2016); *Immigration and America's Cities: A Handbook on Evolving Services*, edited by Joaquin Jay Gonzalez III and Roger L. Kemp (2016); *Urban Transportation Innovations Worldwide: A Handbook of Best Practices Outside the United States*, edited by Roger L. Kemp and Carl J. Stephani (2015); *Global Models of Urban Planning: Best Practices Outside the United States*, edited by Roger L. Kemp and Carl J. Stephani (2014); *Town and Gown Relations: A Handbook of Best Practices*, Roger L. Kemp (2013); *The Municipal Budget Crunch: A Handbook for Professionals*, edited by Roger L. Kemp (2012); *Cities Going Green: A Handbook of Best Practices*, edited by Roger L. Kemp and Carl J. Stephani (2011); *Cities and Adult Businesses: A Handbook for Regulatory Planning*, edited by Roger L. Kemp (2010); *Documents of American Democracy: A Collection of Essential Works*, edited by Roger L. Kemp (2010); *Cities and Sports Stadiums: A Planning Handbook*, edited by Roger L. Kemp (2009); *Cities and Water: A Handbook for Planning*, edited by Roger L. Kemp (2009); *Cities and Growth: A Policy Handbook*, edited by Roger L. Kemp (2008); *Museums, Libraries and Urban Vitality: A Handbook*, edited by Roger L. Kemp and Marcia Trotta (2008)

LIBRARY OF CONGRESS CATALOGUING-IN-PUBLICATION DATA

Names: Gonzalez, Joaquin Jay. | Kemp, Roger L.
Title: Corruption and American cities : essays and case studies in ethical accountability / edited by Joaquin Jay Gonzalez III and Roger L. Kemp.
Description: Jefferson, North Carolina : McFarland & Company, Inc., Publishers, 2016. | Includes bibliographical references and index.
Identifiers: LCCN 2016033667 | ISBN 9781476665771 (softcover : acid free paper) ∞
Subjects: LCSH: Misconduct in office—United States. | Political corruption—United States. | Fraud—United States. | Contracting out—Corrupt practices—United States. | Transparency in government—Law and legislation—United States. | Ethics—United States.
Classification: LCC KF9409 .C67 2016 | DDC 364.1/3230973—dc23
LC record available at https://lccn.loc.gov/2016033667

BRITISH LIBRARY CATALOGUING DATA ARE AVAILABLE

**ISBN (print) 978-1-4766-6577-1**
**ISBN (ebook) 978-1-4766-2714-4**

Front cover image of payout © 2016 Kritchanut/iStock

Printed in the United States of America

*McFarland & Company, Inc., Publishers*
*Box 611, Jefferson, North Carolina 28640*
*www.mcfarlandpub.com*

Jay:
To my parents,
Benny and Agnes

———⊷⊶———

Roger:
To my granddaughter, Anika,
the best and the brightest

# Acknowledgments

We are grateful for the financial support of the Mayor George Christopher Professorship, the Russell T. Sharpe Professorship at Golden Gate University, the Bibbero Trust, and GGU's Pi Alpha Alpha Chapter. We appreciate the encouragement from Dean Paul Fouts and our wonderful colleagues at the GGU Edward S. Ageno School of Business, the Department of Public Administration, and the Executive MPA Program.

Our heartfelt "THANKS!" goes to the contributors listed in the back section and the individuals, organizations, and publishers below for granting permission to reprint the material in this volume and providing research assistance. Most waived or reduced fees as an expression of their support for practical research and information sharing that benefits our community.

American Society for Public Administration
Association of Local Government Auditors
Beth Payne
California City Management Foundation
Center on Wage & Employment Dynamics, University of California, Berkeley
*Charlotte Observer*
Elise Borbon Gonzalez
e.Republic
*Governing*
Government Auditors Association
Government Finance Officers Association
Greater Good Science Center, University of California, Berkeley
International City/County Management Association
John Wiley & Sons
Karen Garrett
National Civic League
*National Civic Review*
National Institute of Governmental Purchasing
National League of Cities
nj.com
*PA Times*
*PM Magazine*
*Police Chief*
State of Connecticut
*The Times-Picayune*
U.S. Department of Justice
University of Illinois, Chicago
Zach Patton

# Table of Contents

## Part III: Caveats and the Future

## Appendices

# Preface

Corruption is a serious chronic public concern that afflicts America's cities and other municipalities. Human greed, ethical lapses, and lack of accountability have drained millions of dollars in precious tax revenues. The court proceedings to investigate and prosecute perpetrators have also become budget-busters. These corrupt practices range from outright theft, bribery, kickbacks, extortion, embezzlement, graft, nepotism, patronage, to the misuse of public funds, vehicles, equipment, supplies, and other public resources. Citizens and businesses do not wish to have to deal with corrupt government.

Exposés broadcast 24/7 news on mainstream and social media have magnified the visibility of abusive and unethical actions locally, regionally, nationally, and globally. Thus, we could not help but notice these disturbing headlines enumerating the inappropriate behavior by elected and appointed city officials in the State of Connecticut:

- "Middlebury Fire Chief Allegedly Stole $70,000 from Municipal Funds,"
- "Winstead Finance Director Stole $2.5 Million in Municipal Funds,"
- "Tolland Public Works Director and Wife Accused of Stealing from Town,"
- "Norwich Assistant Town Clerk Allegedly Steals $3000,"
- "Plymouth Finance Director Misappropriated Town Money,"
- "Oxford Tax Collector Steals $243,000,"
- "Shelton Assistant Finance Director Stole $478,000 over Several Years," and
- "Former Hartford Cop Stole $30,000 from Concealed Weapons Permit Fees."

Similar glaring news stories forwarded via Twitter, Facebook, and thru other electronic media going viral are probably the main reason why "corrupt government officials" emerged as the top fear among 88 topics in Chapman University's "2015 Survey of American Fears." These unethical acts have also tainted America's global reputation. Examine, for instance, the highly reputable Transparency International (TI)'s "2015 Corruption Perception Index," where you might not be surprised to discover that the United States is only ranked 16th out of 168 countries as the least corrupt. America's TI ranking has been struck in the unimpressive 16th to 22nd range for more than a decade.

Sadly, America has year-after-year been out performed by the "clean government reputations" of Canada, the U.K., New Zealand, Denmark, Germany, and even by tiny Singapore. To some scholars and practitioners, this satisfactory grade of a "B+" equivalent is okay but not to citizens who expect a better ranking from the country leading the advocacy for open and transparent government.

What is hindering the U.S. from joining

the top ten countries in the list? What continues to fuel the American public's fear of government abuse? What are America's cities doing to clear the smudges?

## What's in America's Anti-Corruption Toolbox?

Let's answer the last question first. A closer look at the available executive, legislative, and judicial actions, processes, procedures, and ordinances, reveal that America's cities have a wealth of classic and contemporary practices on preventing and combatting corruption to choose from, including (see Appendix V for glossary definitions):

- background check;
- campaign finance reform;
- check and balance system;
- civil service commission;
- civil service exam;
- closed-circuit television camera (CCTV);
- compliance officer;
- conflict of interest law;
- district attorney, city attorney;
- eGovernment transaction;
- election;
- ethics commission;
- FBI sting operation;
- Form 700: Statement of Economic Interest;
- grand jury;
- inspector general;
- internal affairs unit;
- internal and external audit;
- law enforcement officer;
- media exposé;
- merit-based recruitment, selection, promotion, and retention system;
- oath of office;
- ombudsman;
- 1-800 toll free anonymous tip hotline;
- open bidding system;
- openness and transparency;
- sunset law;
- sunshine law;
- watchdog group; and
- whistleblower policy.

Then why does America have a less than stellar reputation, domestically and internationally, even with all of these anti-corruption programs, processes, laws, and institutions?

To find answers to this question, we performed a national literature search. As anyone would have imagined we got an enormous amount of "hits" on this topic. But we narrowed our finds down to 60 practical, straightforward, and easy-to-read cases representing experiences, reports, and possibilities about cities and other local jurisdictions from all over the United States of America. They were penned by practitioners, scholars, journalists, and organizations who want to see a less corrupt America and a better world for all. We are one with their hearts and minds.

## Part I: The State of Corruption

From this collection of 60 articles (chapters), we developed our story.

A large part of the blame for America's lingering "bad rap" could be attributed to the issues that go along with applying "New Public Administration" principles and practices. In other words, while the trendy moves toward deregulation, privatization, downsizing, performance measurement, and market competition have benefited many cities, some have had mixed results due to mismanagement and abusive acts. As one of our contributors aptly quoted, "Today's problems are yesterday's solutions."

Five chapters in our compilation elaborate on this dilemma, starting with two revealing *Governing* essays. The first chapter, Daniel C. Vock's "The Town That Can't Seem to Govern Itself," dramatizes the contempt, crime, and collusion between borough council members and public employees in the tiny town of Colwyn, Pennsylvania. While in Chapter 2, "Drained," Josh Goodman delves into the noxious cocktail of mismanagement, political paralysis, corruption, and bad luck that led to the fiscal collapse of Jefferson County, Alabama. Meanwhile in Chapter 3, "Dilemmas Faced When Contracting Out Public Services," Andrea Headley argues that unethical behaviors could be traced to the overly creative use of corporate techniques, especially outsourcing, when delivering city services.

But topping Colwyn and Jefferson in terms of illegal acts many times over is Chicago—nicknamed the Capital City of Corruption—by University of Illinois Professor Dick Simpson and his colleagues in their Chapter 4 contribution, "Chicago and Illinois, Leading the Pack in Corruption." Another revelation from management expert Ken Miller in Chapter 5, "The Dark Side of Awards and Accountability," is the appalling story of how Washington, D.C., school district teachers and administrators tailored the results of their performance tests to show that they hit or even exceeded national standards, leading to the resignation of their top school official.

Nonetheless, the dysfunctions of private sector practices creating issues in public service applications are on the outer layer of America's ethics and accountability core. Beneath the surface are deeper concerns about the public servant's ethical values, self-interest, proper behavior, and negative experiences, according to our contributors from chapters 6 to 9.

From boroughs to cities, citizens have grown quite wary of the ethical values of government officials according to Dulce Pamela Baizas in "Public Corruption: An Ethical Challenge." But as Ravi Subramanian observes, because of human desire and inherent imperfection, corrupt action could be rooted in people's "enlightened self-interest." Or does the public really know if their leaders are behaving badly as Alan Ehrenhalt's appropriately titled essay asks:

"When Does Politicians' Unethical Behavior Become a Crime?" All of these negative experiences with government accumulate to create citizen's fear of abusive authority which Brynne VanHettinga elaborates on in "Managing Public Mistrust of Government."

What about our cities' vanguard of justice—their police? Citizens assume that police vigilance in this evolving new public administration context is still crucial. After all, on a daily basis they have to make judgments on whether or not citizens are committing a crime or public officials are doing something illegal. However, recent headlines have shined the light on serious missteps and shoddy behavior by members of the law enforcement community, which have also tarnished their credibility. Thus, we decided to devote two thoughtful chapters, 10 and 11, on them.

In "Coffee and Doughnuts: Building Accountability," John J. Carroll writes that even our friends in blue who are supposed to be highly visible defenders of justice have "bad apples" within their ranks who taint an otherwise respectable profession. Oakland Assistant Chief of Police Paul Figueroa admits in "Can Police Departments Reduce Implicit Bias?" that these unscrupulous officers have only deepened the chronic and pervasive distrust, especially between communities of color and cops.

## Part II: Practices and Possibilities

At the heart of this volume are 34 colorful cases—14 chapters on the classic tactics and 20 chapters illustrating contemporary practices and possibilities.

**Classic:** Our long list of tried and tested anti-corruption practices are filled with classic measures—many of which are still in use, with modifications—up until the present day as illustrated by chapters 12 to 25.

In Chapter 12, Josh Goodman details how Cuyahoga County near Cleveland, Ohio, moved to hiring professional administrators instead of electing politicians and complementing this arrangement with the classic system of checks and balances. Next, long-time East and West Coast city manager Roger L. Kemp shares his experience-informed thoughts on the continuing need for public officials to be politically neutral. In his Los Angeles case study in Chapter 14, Bob Stone suggests that high-ranking authorities should learn to use the old-school test "How would your action as public officials look in the morning paper?" as a test on the propriety or impropriety of their deeds. In the meantime, reporting from North Carolina, Mark Washburn, Jim Morill, and Michael Gordon write in Chapter 15 about an FBI sting operation which caught the Charlotte mayor red-handed.

Informed by his Illinois experience, former U.S. Attorney Patrick Fitzgerald, in Chapter 16, recommends vigorous prosecution of public corruption to challenge and transform the culture of acceptance. Sustainability writer Tom Arrandale, in Chapter 17, discusses the success of a City of Helena-based whistleblowers organization's monitoring campaign aimed at ensuring strict implementation of Montana's environmental policies. In Chapter 18, G. Edward DeSeve makes the case for going back to the basics to regain the people's sagging trust in government. Meanwhile, in Chapter 19, professor Chelsea A. Binns updates readers on how New York City's more than one-hundred-year-old Department of Investigation works in tandem with the newly created state's Commission to Investigate Public Corruption to effective mitigate illicit acts in America's largest city. Over in neighboring Newark, New Jersey, community reporter Dan Ivers points out that better oversight procedures could easily prevent gross mismanagement, particularly at the city's water agency, in Chapter 20.

Next, *Governing's* eloquent publisher Mark Funkhouser reiterates the importance of financial auditing to winning the war on corrupt accounting practices. In Chapter 22, Kevin Litten reports on how legislative audits helped uncover misuse of funds in Louisiana. Then in Chapter 23, Kevin Duggan warns public officials what basic probing interview questions the media would ask to hold them accountable. ICMA's ethics director, Martha Perego, encourages public organizations to consider steps to promoting and enforcing an ethical culture in Chapter 24. From California, Tracy City Manager Troy Brown adds, in Chapter 25, that renewed attention should be given to adopting the International City/County Management Association (ICMA)'s prescribed code of ethics not only by its members but all municipal officers.

**Contemporary**: Many of the contemporary practices and possibilities were crafted to reinforce the use of the classics. Hence, the application of new public administration techniques are better protected from associated deviant behavior and illicit actions. Hopefully, strengthening America's antibodies through these new immunizations would help exterminate this dreaded disease, so when the next corruption perception surveys are administered the nation's results would show less public fear in corrupt government domestically and a better corruption image internationally.

In Chapter 26, City Ethics researcher Robert Wechsler discusses how to take the ethics theme to the next level by not just focusing on a culture of ethics and a code of ethics but also a proactive ethics reform program that implements training, advice, disclosure, and enforcement. More specifics about this newer anti-corruption possibility come from JoAnne Speers, Jan Perkins, and Arne Croce in Chapter 27, who endorse the utilization of California's Institute for Local Government (ILG) and ICMA's three-part ethics assessment tool. In chapters 28 to 30, professors Michael W. Manske and H. George Frederickson suggests a four-pillared comprehensive ethics program, ICMA specialists Elizabeth Kellar and Jan Perkins underscore the importance of not just the ethics training per se but complimenting good applications and actions thereafter, and professor Alicia Schatteman explains the critical importance of integrating ethics in public management education at universities.

Increased transparency has been one of the contemporary actions for fighting corruption in the United States and globally, based on chapters 31 to 33. Taking the lead, as usual, ICMA provides public officials with straightforward guidance on building transparent communities. Penelope Lemov cites FloridaCompareCare.gov, which publicizes comparative healthcare information on the best city and county hospitals for Floridians seeking general and specialized care. Next, Paul Blumenthal's "Cycle of Transparency" elaborates on the actors and actions that need to blend together to create open, transparent government.

According to the California City Management Foundation and the ICMA, in Chapter 34, citizens and cities should seriously consider the council-manager model, which is the fastest growing form of government in the United States because of its built-in check and balance features to deter abuse. In Chapter 35, Jim Sullivan advocates for an independent monitor to keep a watchful eye on private contractors and slam the door on unscrupulous vendors before they have an opportunity to engage in fraud. Similarly, in Chapter 36, *Governing*'s executive editor Zach Patton reports the possibility of using joint city-state oversight on New York nonprofits that perform public services to prevent abuse. For this era of big data and hacking of confidential information, professor Chelsea A. Binns says that New York City employees must be ever vigilant to reduce data breaches, in Chapter 37.

*National Civic Review* editor Michael Mc-Grath, in Chapter 38, describes the new "never again" atmosphere of public engagement in corruption-ravaged Bell, California. To reinforce this initiative at the City of Bell, Kevin Duggan details how ICMA members and their allies stepped up to help in the rebuilding of the public trust and better institutions, in Chapter 39. In Chapter 40, professor-practitioner Roger L. Kemp proposes the innovative idea of using both balanced budget and public service impact statements to prevent impropriety. Then, in Chapter 41, Liz Farmer suggests avoiding the deadly sins of public finance.

In his second contribution, Oakland, California's assistant police chief Paul Figueroa pushes for data-driven accountability using body-worn cameras, in Chapter 42. Another creative idea put forth by Mike Maciag, in Chapter 43, proposes real-time tracking of how taxpayer dollars are spent. In Chapter 44, award-winning California city manager Brian A. Moura prescribes using new tools and technologies to ramp up access and increase transparency. In Chapter 45, Mattie Quinn suggests an accreditation system for government agencies, starting with state and local public health departments.

We conclude this book with some caveats from contributors on why some of these latest antidotes to corruption work while others do not work, and where municipal ethics and accountability are headed.

Although exposing your public employer for wrongdoing is a noble option, Brynne VanHettinga warns, in Chapter 46, that whistleblowers should be careful since laws meant to protect their noble actions are at times confusing and ambiguous. Professional facilitator Dana K. Lee, in Chapter 47, "Dealing with Public Mistrust," shares key strategies on compartmentalizing, minimizing, eliminating, deflecting, or otherwise ignoring the negative attacks on public officials' integrity, motives, and competence.

In Chapter 48, "When Transparency Fails

to Produce Accountability," Pospere Charles elaborates on the inherent dilemma between transparency and accountability, pointing out that one does not necessarily trigger the other, and so tight connections must be incorporated into any anti-corruption approach to achieve effectiveness. Stuart C. Gilman and Howard Whitton, in Chapter 49, "When Transparency Becomes the Enemy of Accountability," identify major issues that practitioners must think about when linking transparency and accountability. In Chapter 50, Jusil Lee and Erik W. Johnston dispense advice on "How to Embed Transparency into Collaborative Governance." In Chapter 51, "Corruption, Ethics and Accountability," Rod Erakovich, et al., argue that moral accountability should be included in everyone's anti-corruption toolkit.

States and cities are connected at the hip in terms of ethics and accountability. So we also provide some state reports affecting cities. Citiscope founder Neal Peirce writes, in Chapter 52, "Anti-Corruption Effort Targets All the States," that the Pulitzer Prize winning Center for Public Integrity found that most of the United States' anti-corruption and transparency safeguards are filled with loopholes. To rub more salt on America's wounds, Mike Maciag adds, in Chapter 53, "States Disclose Economic Development Subsidies," that even in this day and age of the internet some states still lag far behind others in disclosing information on their websites. Moreover, Liz Farmer writes in Chapter 54 in support of legislation like the MADOFF (Making All Data Open for Financial) Transparency Act, which would standardize how data is reported at the state and local government levels.

Chapters 55 and 56 discuss public employee pay following the Bell, California, scandal. First, University of California, Berkeley, researchers Sylvia A. Allegretto and Jeffrey Keefe, in "The Truth about Public Employees in California," find that most are neither overpaid nor overcompensated. And yet, as *Governing*'s Data Editor Mike Maciag points out, "Disclosing Public Employee Pay Troubles Some Officials."

## *Appendices*

Our appendices yield important lessons, too, featuring a number of resources which we believe citizens, advocates, and decision makers will find useful.

These documents include the Government Finance Officers Association's "Professional Code of Ethics," the International City/County Management Association's "Code of Ethics with Guidelines," the State of Connecticut's "Code of Ethics for Municipal Officials," and the National Institute of Governmental Purchasing's "Transparency in Government Procurement: Position Paper." We end the compilation with Joaquin Jay Gonzalez III's "Glossary of Anti-Corruption Practices."

We hope you have an insightful and inspiring read on this dynamic and evolving topic. Our goal is to try to improve ethics and accountability at all levels of our government—local, regional, state, and federal. Please help us spread the world about these findings and good practices.

# 1. The Town That Can't Seem to Govern Itself*

## *Daniel C. Vock*

Not many people have heard of Colwyn, Pennsylvania. It's a tiny Philadelphia suburb of about 2,500 people that covers just 0.3 square miles. But this spring, it gained notoriety when it was declared "financially distressed" by the state. Local Philadelphia stations had already been airing chaotic council meetings, complete with screaming matches, swearing, and even occasionally pushing and shoving. But the declaration brought even more attention. One TV station created a recurring segment called "Chaos in Colwyn" to cover the many resignations, firings and scandals that are ongoing. All this news coverage, along with state audits, have revealed just how poorly managed, and possibly corrupt, Colwyn is.

Colwyn, pronounced "call-win," entered in May the state's Act 47 program, a near last-resort option for towns declared financially distressed. Under the program, city leaders work with a state-appointed coordinator to develop a recovery plan. Colwyn is the 29th Pennsylvania municipality to be declared financially distressed since 1987. Only nine of those municipalities have emerged from the program.

Many question whether Colwyn can be one of the nine. When the Act 47 team initially tried to draft a financial rescue plan for the borough, they had to start from scratch. The town had no ledger and no budget to speak of. The team had to piece together how Colwyn had been spending its money by using bank statements, cancelled checks and tax records. "The Borough of Colwyn has not been a functioning representative democracy for years," the team warned in October. "The citizens lack the basic information required for them to cast meaningful votes. And the elected officials lack accountability to the citizens."

Indeed, Colwyn's elected officials have been more consumed with infighting than running the government. The fire department, police department and building code enforcement divisions have all been enmeshed in scandal. The widespread chicanery is apparently keeping the district attorney very busy. A grand jury is digging into Colwyn's finances, and prosecutors twice raided the local fire company. On Monday, the district attorney issued arrest warrants for three fire company employees on charges of theft.

Colwyn is a perfect example of what happens when virtually every aspect of local government breaks down. The state inter-

---

*Originally published as Daniel C. Vock, "Colwyn, Pennsylvania: The Town That Can't Seem to Govern Itself," *Governing*, December 22, 2015. Reprinted with permission of the publisher.

vention, scrutiny and criminal prosecutions have created some hope that Colwyn can be pulled out of its quagmire. But given the borough's seamy past and the deep-seated divisions that remain among its council members, no one is taking that for granted.

Colwyn lies just outside Philadelphia, about 10 minutes from the city's airport. It is almost entirely residential, with block after block of run-down brick houses. Economically, it's stagnating. The median income is $33,000, and no new buildings have been built there since 2007.

But while the economy has played a role in the borough's troubles, local observers say the drama has been exacerbated by Colwyn's elected and appointed leadership. Anthony Williams, a Democrat who represents the area in the Pennsylvania Senate, says he once backed candidates running for the borough's council but stopped any involvement in local politics there several years ago. "All I saw was a bunch of people screaming and hollering at each other at council meetings and making decisions that were pretty narrow in the focus and were hurting the town," he says. "I don't care if they're Democrat or Republican. I don't care if they're my friend or not my friend. A long time ago, when they were making decisions about how to spend money, they made the wrong decisions."

Many of those choices came to light in 2014, when a new majority took over the borough council and installed a full-time manager. The manager, Paula Brown, had served eight years as the mayor of Darby, a larger neighboring town, before coming to Colwyn. Brown knew right away that she had her work cut out for her. "When I walked into the office," Brown says, "it was strewn with trash and papers and files. Nothing was filed. Nothing was organized. It was two feet thick on the floor of just files and records, mixed in with cigarette butts that were stamped out on the rug and rat poop. It was disgusting."

What she eventually found in the files disgusted her too. The borough had issued debit cards to council members and city employees for expenses. Bank statements showed they had been used for hair salons, cellphone bills and restaurants. One employee, Brown says, bought gas on the borough card and then sold the gas to other customers at a discount. Brown found dozens of empty envelopes marked with dollar amounts, dates and written notes. She alleges that the envelopes held cash from residents paying their parking tickets and fines. But the money was never deposited in the bank. Instead, it was kept in a safe accessible only to certain council members.

Brown immediately started collecting information to turn over to the district attorney's office. She also started posting information on the borough's website and alerting the local media to her findings.

Meanwhile, the borough continued to fall behind in paying its bills despite having the second-highest property taxes in its county. By this year, it had $634,000 in outstanding bills for a government with an annual budget of $1.4 million. The vast majority of its debt was to the local sewer authority and to its pension funds.

As a result, the council took several steps to right its fiscal ship earlier this year, not least of which was to seek relief from the state government under Pennsylvania's Act 47. Despite all these positive strides, however, Colwyn remains embroiled in turmoil.

This spring the balance of power on the council shifted again, when then-Council President Fred Lesher, who held the crucial swing vote on the seven-member body, switched his allegiances from the group that took over in 2014 to the group that controlled the council previously. One of the first things the new majority did was fire Brown and replace her with part-time employees.

Brown had been a controversial hire from the outset. While her supporters praised her experience in government, her critics chafed at her confrontational tactics. When she served as Darby mayor, for example, she repeatedly parked her car on train tracks because of an ongoing conflict with the railroad that owned them. Ultimately, it was her approach that led to her dismissal. "I personally couldn't deal with her any more, and the people in the community couldn't deal with her," Lesher says. "She always ran to the media and caused trouble. And she wasn't an elected official. If the council voted on something, she would decide on her own that it's not what we wanted to do."

Perhaps unsurprisingly, Brown's exit was dramatic. After the council voted to replace her, Brown returned to her office, locked the door and waited until all the council members left the borough hall. Then she started packing boxes of documents for the district attorney's office. The next day, a TV camera crew caught a friendly council member handing her a McDonald's breakfast through her office window. Brown said she simply didn't want to leave her office until she could compile all of her records. She feared council members would destroy them after she left.

After all, Lesher's new partners on the council include some of the same members—Patricia Williams and Martha Van Auken—whom Brown accused of abusing the borough's expense accounts. But the biggest abuses were not the petty charges to borough accounts, according to Lesher, but the padding of the borough's payroll. Lesher dismantled much of the borough's professional staff. "It's a four-block town," Lesher says. "You have to run a one-horse town with one horse."

Jesse Brundage quit his position on the council this fall, saying he could no longer handle the constant stress. He cites several altercations at polling places in both the primary and general elections, including one in which he got in a pushing match with the husband of a council opponent on election day in November. "I typed my resignation letter that very night and emailed it the next day. I'm a 66-year-old senior with heart conditions. I have risked both life and limb with these council persons and their hangers-on. This was the tipping point," he says. "My other motive was to call on the state to pay closer notice to the culture of illegality present in the borough."

Brundage was allied with Brown and the faction that controlled the council last year. He hoped his resignation would convince the Act 47 team to recommend that Colwyn be placed in receivership because of its financial conditions. But the team, led by Stephen Mullin, a former top budget official for St. Louis and Philadelphia, did not go that far. With all the money accounted for, the borough could dig itself out of its financial hole by 2019, says Mullin, now a president of Econsult Solutions. "This is an extremely manageable issue if borough and council want to manage it."

But Mullin made clear that his plan, which was turned in to the state in November, would only work if Colwyn agreed to empower a strong borough manager. Otherwise, his team said, the state should consider "more drastic remedies."

Lesher, then the council president, was initially opposed to the team's plan because of its recommendation for a full-time manager. He relented, however, because the state required the borough to come up with its own plan it if rejected the state blueprint. But Lesher hinted at the time that he would fire the manager down the road—once Colwyn was back on track.

Those plans may ultimately be moot. Mayor Michael Blue, a Brown ally, told the council last week he vetoed the ordinance because he feared the new manager would take away many of his duties. He did so without informing the council, however, an apparent violation of Pennsylvania law. The council has rejected the mayor's veto, leaving the future of the Act 47 intervention murky. Amid this back and forth, the council also replaced Lesher as chair with Patricia Williams, who led the council before 2014.

Meanwhile, Delaware County District Attorney John Whelan says his lawyers are still combing through Colwyn's finances to investigate possible crimes. There's no doubt money is missing, he said at a press conference Monday, but proving that crimes occurred is difficult because of the lack of records for the cash transactions.

Paula Brown, who is still thoroughly enmeshed in Colwyn's politics and elections, remains hopeful that charges will come. "I can't go away until the handcuffs are put on these individuals and justice is brought back to this town," she said. "I live five blocks away. If Colwyn doesn't survive, if you don't have the right kind of services, if the houses start declining because there's no code enforcement, if they don't hire enough police officers, then that affects my town too. I can't turn my back on them."

# 2. Drained[*]

## Josh Goodman

These days, Bettye Fine Collins doesn't talk like a power politician. "It's not easy being me," she complains. It's not hard to understand why. As president of the County Commission in Jefferson County, Alabama, she's the top elected official in one of the nation's most financially troubled jurisdictions. The county of 660,000, anchored by Birmingham, has teetered on the brink of bankruptcy since April 2008. That's when Jefferson County ceased making payments to creditors holding bonds that paid for its sewer system. "It's a long, terrible situation," Collins says. "I don't think there's another situation in this country that would compare."

Despite the downbeat tone of her rhetoric, Collins is a powerful presence. The sewer crisis has served only to highlight the clout that she and the rest of the Jefferson County Commission possess—and their ability to use that power to dance around pressure points. To wit: Since the crisis hit, the commission has neither filed for bankruptcy nor raised sewer rates nor found other revenue to help pay its debt. Despite court hearings, endless debate over bankruptcy and pleas to state and federal officials for help, the county has managed not to do much of anything. In the midst of that inaction, creditors have been powerless to force the county to pay. If Jefferson County does file for bankruptcy soon, it's likely to be because of an unrelated fight with the Alabama state legislature over taxes—not its mountain of sewer debt.

Jefferson County's problems stem from a noxious mix of incompetence, political paralysis, corruption and bad luck. While a possible solution is in the offing, the tale is a cautionary one—for municipalities across the country, as well as anyone who is owed money by a local government.

Jefferson County's saga began in 1993, when members of the Cahaba River Society complained that the county's sewer system was discharging raw sewage into waterways. Federal officials issued a consent decree in which Jefferson County promised to upgrade the system.

To do so, the county issued $3 billion in bonds, an incredible amount for a sewer system with only 150,000 customers. As sewer rates rose to meet those costs and Jefferson County struggled under its debt, county officials looked for a way to lessen its loan payments. In 2002 and 2003, they refinanced their bonds with variable-rate and auction-rate securities. Auction-rate securities are bonds where the interest rate is reset by auctions conducted by brokerage firms every few weeks. "It's a little like some-

*Originally published as Josh Goodman, "Drained," *Governing*, July 31, 2009. Reprinted with permission of the publisher.

one buying a house and getting a pretty good 30-year fixed-rate mortgage," says Christopher "Kit" Taylor, former executive director of the Municipal Securities Rulemaking Board. "Then somebody says, 'Why don't you get an adjustable-rate mortgage?'"

Auction-rate securities were supposed to be safe, but the auction-rate market collapsed in February 2008. That wasn't the county's only misfortune. The bond insurance companies that were backing the county's debt suffered their own fiscal problems and their credit was downgraded. All of which caused the county's interest rates to skyrocket, much like a homeowner whose subprime mortgage has just reset. Revenue from sewer fees could not keep up with the borrowing costs. On April Fools' Day 2008, Jefferson County couldn't make its payment on its debt. Instead, it reached an agreement with its creditors to pay the interest and get an extension on the principal.

These forbearance agreements have continued ever since. Last September, creditors took the case to federal court, hoping a judge would appoint a receiver to force the county to pay the nearly $4 billion it now owes. It wasn't until this June that the judge ruled that federal law prevented him from appointing a receiver. In other words, Alabama's most populous county simply hasn't been paying its sewer debt for the past 16 months.

Why not? For one thing, Jefferson County's choices are truly unappealing. The county could raise sewer rates again, but they already are among the highest in the country. The county could file for bankruptcy, but elected officials worry that such a move would be a black eye for the county with potential long-term fiscal consequences.

County commissioners and other Alabama political players have conceived a variety of creative ideas to solve the sewer mess—to no avail. Governor Bob Riley spent last fall negotiating with creditors but, despite winning concessions, he couldn't find a plan that the county would accept.

The county's most promising solution was to tap excess sales tax revenue intended for school construction and use it to pay off the sewer debt. Riley supported the idea as part of his deal with creditors. Collins and other county commissioners were in favor of it, too. However, those efforts were rebuffed this spring by the state legislature, which has the final word in Alabama, where counties lack robust home rule. Jefferson County and state legislators have a long history of not getting along.

That political tension is also at the heart of Jefferson County's other fiscal crisis. In January, a state judge overturned the county's occupational tax, which had accounted for one-quarter of its general-fund budget. The legislature could have reinstated the tax this spring but didn't.

While a legislative special session still could do so, the county has made massive cutbacks—reducing department budgets by one-third, cancelling road maintenance contracts, closing courthouses and laying off hundreds of county workers. But the county still is on the brink of bankruptcy. "We're having to downsize this government," Collins says, "to the point that it may not be able to operate."

The difficulty of the dual crises that Jefferson County faces is only one of the reasons the county hasn't paid its sewer debts. There's another one: No one has been able to force it to do so.

The county issued revenue bonds, not general obligation bonds, which limits the creditors' claim to revenue other than from the sewer system. The federal judge who heard the creditors' case chastised the county for being irresponsible but also acknowledged that he couldn't appoint a receiver: Under federal law, federal receivers can't set local utility rates.

Some of the creditors now are pursuing their case in state court. Jeffrey Cohen, a municipal bankruptcy expert, doesn't think they'll get far. Although other experts disagree, his reading of Alabama's constitution rules out a state-appointed receiver who could force the county to raise rates. "It's a stalemate," he says. "Debt isn't being repaid and bondholders can't do anything about it."

Nor do all the bondholders necessarily deserve a generous remedy. The creditors include the bond insurance firms, which helped sparked the crisis when their credit ratings were downgraded. They also include investment banks, such as J.P. Morgan, which Jefferson County officials say pushed the county to make risky financial decisions. The Securities and Exchange Commission is investigating J.P. Morgan's role in the sewer bonds.

That's not the only hint of wrongdoing. Some 20 people, including three county commissioners, have been convicted of crimes involving the construction and financing of the sewer system. That has given Jefferson County's current commission the will to resist paying. Why, they argue, should taxpayers or ratepayers be punished for the greed of Wall Street banks and lawbreaking by local officials?

Jefferson County's particulars are not all that different from other insolvencies: Chapter 9 bankruptcy, which covers municipal defaults, is kinder to debtors than other forms of bankruptcy. There's no risk, for instance, of Jefferson County being forced to liquidate, the way a Circuit City or Linens n Things are. "When you're dealing with a municipal debtor," says Kenneth Klee, a law professor at UCLA, "the law does not allow you to take a park or a bridge or a city hall."

As a result, creditors are just as eager as local government officials to avoid a bankruptcy filing. They may even be more eager. In May 2008, Vallejo, California, filed for municipal bankruptcy. Yet Vallejo's unions, knowing that Chapter 9 would work against them, fought unsuccessfully to win a court ruling saying the city wasn't actually insolvent and wasn't eligible for bankruptcy.

This dynamic gives cities nearing default a tremendous amount of leverage. They can threaten bankruptcy and demand that creditors make allowances. In Jefferson County, the creditors already have offered $1.3 billion in concessions, but the County Commission hasn't taken the deal.

Variations on the situation in Jefferson County could play out elsewhere. The recession has put local governments on vastly weaker financial footing. According to Richard Lehmann, publisher of a newsletter that tracks bond defaults, there were only 29 municipal defaults in 2007 totaling $300 million. In 2008, those numbers skyrocketed to record highs: 150 defaults, totaling $7.8 billion.

Many of the defaults have been in what are known as "conduit bonds," where municipalities issue bonds on behalf of private companies, without any obligation for the government to guarantee the debt. Other municipal defaults are concentrated in nonprofits or small limited-purpose governments. Dozens of Florida's Community Development Districts, for instance, went into default last year as a result of the housing bust.

Some of the problems affecting these entities are buffeting general-purpose governments, too. Soon, other large jurisdictions may be unable to pay their bills. In this context, Jefferson County is serving as something of a test case. How far can a municipality go in not paying its debts? How long will it let a dangerous situation linger until it takes action?

This summer, the county commission took action to counter the loss of the occupational tax by slashing the budget. More remarkable, though, was a newfound unanimity on the sewer crisis. The commission voted unanimously in support of restructuring its debt. New bonds would be issued that would, in effect, turn back the clock. Jefferson County would owe what it would have owed had it issued bonds with a fixed interest rate of around 3.5 percent. Creditors would be responsible for the exorbitant costs from the auction-rate debacle. A new oversight board would supervise the sewer system. Unused money from the county's sales tax for school construction would be dedicated to paying the sewer creditors.

Creditors still have to agree to the deal, as does the state legislature. A positive outcome is not a sure or quick thing. "Most likely, there will be deal at some point," Klee says. "The only question is when."

# 3. Dilemmas Faced When Contracting Out Public Services[*]

## Andrea Headley

"Today's problems are yesterday's solutions." In 1999, Frederickson predicted that there would be a realization that the solutions of the time (e.g., deregulation, privatization, downsizing and market competition) would result in the ethical problems of the year 2008. Six years after 2008, this prediction has not ceased to be more than true. Privatization refers to government outsourcing of ownership, functions or services by the public sector to the private sector. While many arguments for privatization are centered on quality of service and cost-effectiveness (both looking at outcomes), much of the implementation process has been forgotten, as well as the ethical values and morals that fuel behavior in privatized contexts and the increased chance of opportunities for maladministration.

In a 1998 book titled *Public Administration Balancing Power and Accountability*, McKinney and Howard stated that "the goal of public service" is about utilizing "government resources to achieve publicly determined ends." Thus, it is not about profit-maximization, seeing as that is a predominately private sector goal. Each sector, public and private alike, is characterized by a set of ethical standards that define appropriate behavior

and guide decisions, albeit there are different standards of ethics for the respective sectors. In a 2004 *Journal of Public Administration Research and Theory* article titled "Privatization and its Reverse: Examining the Dynamics of the Government Contracting Process," Amir Hefetz and Mildred Warner noted that when privatizing services the ethical values that are inherent to the public sector such as public service, fairness and equality, are compromised to values of efficiency and profit-maximization.

According to the principle-agent theory agents are self-interested and seek to maximize their own benefit, rather than the benefit of their principal. In the public realm, the government, also known as the agent, is to act on behalf of the citizens, who are the principals. On the other hand, according to Ann Florini in a 2002 *International Journal on World Peace* article titled "Increasing Transparency in Government," in the private realm, managers are agents and the principals are the corporate stockholders. So, when contracts and partnerships come into play between the public and private spheres, there are two incompatible and often competing goals: to act on behalf of the citizenry and to act on behalf of stake-

[*]Originally published as Andrea Headley, "Dilemmas Faced When Contracting Out Public Services," *PA Times*, September 12, 2014. Reprinted with permission of the author and publisher.

holders. When the latter wins, private agencies seek to increase profit even if it means risking the government's goals and forfeiting the public good, as alluded to in a 2009 The *Public Sector Innovation Journal* article titled "Information Asymmetry and the Contracting Out Process." When public services become privately operated, actors are no longer subject to the same laws and regulations that govern public employees and that benefit the public at large. Specifically, private companies facilitating public services are not subject to transparency and accountability standards as public organizations and employees are.

Moreover, private companies providing public services are obliged to operate within two distinct environments: the public and the private sector. Hefetz and Warner also noted that an institutional environment governs the public sector, whereas the private sector operates by the economic/market environment. Both environments have different principles, values, beliefs and operating procedures, which can conflict with each other. If companies conform to the institutional environment alone then they suffer financially, if they conform to the economic market-based environment they suffer socially, legally and politically. Thus, they cannot conform to one without sacrificing the other. On the other hand, publicly governed organizations do not have to conform to the economic environment of the market, so they are able to maximize their opportunity within the institutional environment.

Even when the government chooses to contract certain services out to private companies, there are still obligations that the government has to the general public to be accountable and operate accordingly. However, where there is this lack of accountability and transparency due to contracting out, and the goal is money, then there is an open door to maladministration, which can include corruption, manipulation, bribery, scandals and maltreatment.

Furthermore, it is important for public servants to emphasize service above all else, thus by valuing public service this would serve as a driving and guiding force of all behavior. Conversely, if a private company is seeking to maximize profits, ultimately the firm will consider options that minimize costs, potentially at the risk of public service.

In a 2004 *Public Integrity* article titled "Professional Ethics in a Postmodern Society," David Schultz mentioned the call for the ethical values and morals of the public sector to be transferred to the private sector as well, thus suggesting that the constitutional limits that apply to the public sector should also apply to those performing governmental functions. Despite this need, there is a more impressing need for the realization that values still conflict, leaving higher-order values to take precedence. So, even if the ethical and moral values of the public sector are instilled in private companies, these companies can never escape the need to maximize profits and to answer to their shareholders.

Overall, it matters who provides the service when the goals change and the behaviors of the employees change accordingly. It matters who provides services when the public is impacted negatively, yet restricted from acting, such as in the case of private prisons. Private prisons function by maximizing profits at the expense of inmates and the greater society, due to the sensitive environment of prisons. Any minute factor can either hinder or facilitate rehabilitative aims. Also, the pursuit of profit can impede correctional goals of safety and protection.

When the pursuit of justice crosses paths with the pursuit of profit, there are conflicting interests. What is just is not always profitable and what is profitable is not always just. Therefore, there must be some restrictions on which services are outsourced, specifically as it relates to services that touch the very nature and being of humanity such as the administration of justice from courts, sentencing, policing, all the way to corrections.

# 4. Chicago and Illinois, Leading the Pack in Corruption*

## Dick Simpson et al.

For a century and a half, public corruption has been a shameful aspect of both Illinois and Chicago politics. The Governor's mansion and Chicago City Council Chambers have long been the epicenters of public corruption. The extent and pervasiveness of bribery, fraud, stealing from the taxpayers, and illegal patronage have made the city and state national leaders of corruption. Our notorious reputations have provided fodder for scores of comedians and late night talk show hosts. But corruption is a serious problem that hurts all citizens who put their trust—and tax dollars—in the hands of politicians who abuse the power they are given.

New public corruption conviction data from the U.S. Department of Justice shows the Chicago metropolitan region has been the most corrupt area in the country since 1976. In addition, the data reveal that Illinois is the third most corrupt state in the nation. The latest information, just released by the Justice Department, provides new evidence of the need for reforms to reduce rampant corruption in Chicago and Illinois.

## A State of Corruption

Since 1970, four Illinois governors have been convicted of corruption. Yet only seven men have held this office in this time, meaning more than half of the state's governors have been convicted in the past forty-two years. Otto Kerner, who served from 1961 until his resignation in 1968 to accept a federal judgeship, was convicted in 1973 of mail fraud, bribery, perjury, and income tax evasion while governor. Dan Walker, who served from 1973–1977, was convicted in 1987 of obtaining fraudulent loans for the business he operated after he left office.

George Ryan, who served from 1999–2003, was found guilty in 2006 of racketeering, conspiracy and numerous other charges. Many of the charges were part of a huge scandal, later called "Licenses for Bribes," which resulted in the conviction of more than 40 state workers and private citizens. The scandal involved unqualified truck drivers receiving licenses in exchange for bribes that would ultimately end up in Ryan's campaign fund. The scandal came to

*Originally published as Dick Simpson, James Nowlan, Thomas J. Gradel, Melissa Mouritsen Zmuda, David Sterrett, and Douglas Cantor, *Chicago and Illinois, Leading the Pack in Corruption*, University of Illinois at Chicago Department of Political Science and the Illinois Integrity Initiative of the University of Illinois' Institute for Government and Public Affairs, 2012. This chapter also appears in an expanded form in Thomas J. Gradel and Dick Simpson, *Corrupt Illinois: Patronage, Cronyism, and Criminality* (Urbana: University of Illinois Press, 2015). Reprinted with permission from the authors.

light when a recipient of one of these licenses crashed in to a van and killed six children. But perhaps the most famous of all Illinois corrupt officials is Rod Blagojevich, who served from 2003 until his impeachment in 2009. Blagojevich was ultimately convicted in 2011 of trying to sell the U.S. Senate seat vacated by Barack Obama. Other charges included his attempting to shake down Children's Memorial Hospital for a campaign contribution in return for funding and his trying to extort a racetrack owner.

## Capital City of Corruption

Not to be outdone, the City of Chicago has seen its share of convicted officials. The first conviction of Chicago aldermen and Cook County Commissioners for accepting bribes to rig a crooked contract occurred in 1869. Since 1973, 31 more aldermen have been convicted of corruption. Approximately 100 aldermen have served since then, which is a conviction rate of about one-third. In 1973 and 1974, four aldermen were convicted of bribery, income tax evasion and mail fraud in a scandal involving zoning changes. In the 1980s, three aldermen pleaded guilty or were found guilty in Operation Incubator, a major FBI investigation into Chicago corruption. The convictions included bribery, racketeering, extortion, mail fraud and tax evasion. Less than 10 years later, seven more aldermen were convicted as part of Operation Silver Shovel, another major FBI investigation into corruption in Chicago in the 1990s. Between 1996 and 1999 these seven were convicted of bribery, money laundering, fraud and tax evasion.

But not all of the convictions were part of larger FBI stings. In 1974, Thomas Keane, former 31st ward alderman and Mayor Richard J. Daley's floor leader, was convicted of conspiracy and 17 counts of mail fraud in connection with questionable real estate deals. In 2008 Ed Vrdolyak, former 10th ward alderman, was also convicted of fraud in a real estate sale involving the Chicago Medical School.

Corruption sometimes occurs multiple times in the same ward. Joseph Potempa and his successor Frank Kuta, aldermen of the 23rd ward, were both convicted in the same zoning scheme in 1973. After Thomas Keane, the 31st ward saw two more of its alderman convicted. In 1987 Chester Kuta pleaded guilty to fraud, income tax evasion, and violation of civil rights stemming from a payoff scheme. In 1997, 31st ward Alderman Joseph Martinez was convicted as part of Silver Shovel. The 13th, 20th, and 28th wards have seen multiple convictions as well. One has to wonder if certain wards especially breed corruption.

Corruption can even run in the family. In 1983 William Carothers, Alderman of the 18th ward, was found guilty of conspiracy and extortion. In 2010, his son Isaac Carothers, 29th ward alderman, pled guilty to accepting campaign contributions from an FBI agent posing as a developer seeking zoning changes. They were convicted for almost the same crimes twenty years apart.

## Patterns and Statistics

There are patterns to these crimes. All of the governors and 26 of the aldermen were guilty of bribery, extortion, conspiracy, or tax fraud involving schemes to extract bribes from builders, developers, business owners or those seeking to do business with the city or state. The bribe-payers either assumed or were told that payment was necessary to receive zoning changes, building permits or similar city or state action. In the case of Rod Blagojevich, an attempt was made to extract payment or campaign donations in exchange for appointment to a United States Senate seat. He also created a culture of corruption involving appointments to boards and commissions, campaign contributions and permits to expand hospitals. While Blagojevich represents the most egregious case, at the heart of most convictions is a payoff for something that is a sweetheart contract or a law or permit necessary to do business. This has been the main pattern of corruption in the city and the state for over 150 years.

Recent conviction data shows that the Chicago is the most corrupt area in the United States, and the State of Illinois is the third most corrupt state.

Since 1976, a total of 1828 elected officials, appointees, government employees and a few private individuals have been convicted of public corruption in Illinois—an average of 51 per year. Illinois is surpassed only by California with 2345 convictions (65 per year) and New York with 2522 convictions (70 per year). Rounding out the top ten are (from most convictions to least) Florida, Pennsylvania, Texas, Ohio, D.C., New Jersey and Louisiana. Both California and New York have much larger populations than Illinois. It is important to look at corruption per capita. Illinois, with about 12.8 million residents, averages 1.42 convictions per 10,000 residents. California, with about 37.25 million residents, averages 0.63, and New York with about 19.38 million residents averages 1.30. Per capita, Illinois among large states easily ranks above them all.

Although ranking higher than New York and California, Illinois is not the leader in per capita convictions, it ranks seventh. Coming in first is the District of Columbia, which with only 602,000 residents has a per capita conviction rate of 16.02 per 10,000 residents. Second is Louisiana, which with 4.5 million residents, has 2 convictions per 10,000 residents. Following them are several other states with smaller populations—Mississippi, Alaska, South Dakota and North Dakota. They have between 1.89 and 1.75 convictions per 10,000 residents. Among

the large states Illinois is the most corrupt with 1.42 convictions per 10,000 residents, followed by New York and Pennsylvania, with 1.30 and 1.23 convictions per 10,000 residents respectively.

These statewide numbers belie important regional factors. For federal jurisdictional purposes, states are divided up in to districts to handle caseloads. If we examine the districts that contain the bulk of the population, or the largest cities, the numbers tell a different story. The Illinois Northern District, which contains the entire Chicago metropolitan area, accounts for 1531 of the 1828 public corruption convictions in Illinois. Therefore, almost 84% of the state's federal public corruption conviction took place in the Northern District. This makes it the federal district with the most public corruption convictions in the nation since 1976.

A distant second is California's central district, headquartered in the City of Los Angeles. This district has had 1275 public corruption convictions since 1976. Third with 1202 convictions is New York's southern district, encompassing Manhattan, the Bronx and a few nearby northern counties. Rounding out the list are (in order of most to least): the southern district of Florida (includes Miami), the northern district of Ohio (includes Cleveland), the eastern district of Pennsylvania (includes Philadelphia), the southern district of Texas (includes Austin, San Antonio), the middle district of Florida (contains Orlando), the eastern district of California (including Sacramento, Fresno), the eastern district of Louisiana (including New Orleans) and the southern district of Ohio (including Columbus).

## Curing Corruption

Can corruption be cured? Attacking corruption starts with a comprehensive program of mutually reinforcing reforms. These should include a mix of corruption prevention and enforcement measures along with public involvement and education.

To pass these reforms and to implement them requires the development of a broad coalition of support. Reform efforts are needed at all levels and within all units of government and should move forward quickly while public support—following the recent conviction and sentencing of former Governor Rod Blagojevich—is at such a high level. There is indeed a possibility of building a broad coalition around a much more comprehensive reform program than existed in the past.

Governor Pat Quinn's proposal to allow Illinois citizens to adopt ethics reforms by referendum should be supported and passed.

Additionally, the following reforms should be adopted:

1. Amend the City's Ethics Ordinance to cover aldermen and their staff;

2. Give the Inspector General access to all city documents including those held secret by the Corporation Counsel;

3. Ban all gifts to all elected officials and public employees except those from family members;

4. Bar all lobbying of other governmental bodies by elected officials and city employees;

5. Prohibit double dipping, patronage and nepotism with real penalties including firing; and

6. Improve the city's ethics training and bring it up to at least the State of Illinois level.

## Conclusion

Corruption is not funny and it is not free. It costs the taxpayers of Illinois more than $500 million per year. Governor Blagojevich's well-publicized corruption antics led to a lowering of the state's bond rating, which cost the state more than $20 million during its last bond issue. Corruption also takes time and resources away from police and prosecutors. Blagojevich's first trial cost tens of millions of dollars to investigate and prosecute, and after a hung jury resulted in a retrial, the taxpayers footed the bill for Blagojevich's new attorneys. And so it goes—in a time of deep budget deficits, we are wasting taxpayer money and raising taxes and fees on citizens who can ill afford to pay for corruption any longer.

What has come to be called "The Chicago Way" or "The Illinois Way" of public corruption has undermined the voters' sense of political efficacy. Why apply for a city or state job if you know only patronage employees or politician's relatives will be hired anyway? Why report corrupt officials, if you know they won't be punished and they may turn the powers of the government on you? Voters may laugh at times at the antics of public officials, but in the end, they feel powerless, lose their faith in government and vote less often because they believe the "fix is in."

There are some signs of change. After Governor Blagojevich's impeachment, Governor Quinn's Ethics Reform commission held hearings and issued an excellent report. While most of its recommendations haven't been enacted, some have. Mayor Rahm Emanuel has appointed a Mayor's Ethics Taskforce to whom this report is being presented. Chicago, which didn't even have an ethics ordinance until 1987, may now finally get serious about reform. It is time to end the culture of corruption that has saturated the governments of the City of Chicago and the State of Illinois. There are many specific reforms to be enacted. But beyond all the individual reforms is the commitment to change. After more than a hundred years of graft and corruption, it is time truly to become the Land of Lincoln and the City that Works rather than "Where's Mine?"

# 5. The Dark Side of Awards and Accountability[*]

### Ken Miller

On March 28, *USA Today* published a scathing exposé of the seemingly miraculous test score gains of students in the Washington, D.C., public school system. Under former chancellor Michelle Rhee, schools that previously had underperformed on standardized tests began making remarkable gains. So remarkable, in fact, that Rhee became a national poster child for school reform. She graced the covers of *Time* and *Newsweek*, and appeared on countless TV programs touting her simple cure for the district's education malady: accountability.

Measure performance, set a target, reward those who meet it and fire those who don't. High-scoring teachers and principals received bonuses of $8,000 to $10,000. Low performers were dismissed—Rhee replaced nearly 45 percent of the teachers and principals in the system. Test scores improved markedly. Some schools posted gains of more than 40 percent, meriting national awards and federal incentive grants. When the city's mayoral administration changed last fall, Rhee left to start a billion-dollar foundation to replicate the accountability model nationwide.

So how exactly did all these incentivized, accountable educators improve their test scores? According to *USA Today* and CTB/ McGraw-Hill, the two organizations that scored the tests, they cheated. The high-performing D.C. schools had alarmingly high instances of wrong-to-right erasure rates on test answers. That is, someone was erasing wrong answers and replacing them with correct answers before the sheets were machine-graded.

Rhee, of course, denies any wrongdoing. And no one accuses her of ordering the schools to cheat. But critics say she didn't have to. Creating a climate of fear was enough to make these actions inevitable.

"The pressure on principals was unrelenting," Aona Jefferson, a former D.C. principal, told *USA Today*. Jefferson is now president of the Council of School Officers, representing principals and other administrators. Every year, Jefferson says, Rhee would meet with each principal and ask what kind of test score gains he or she would post in the coming school year. Jefferson says principals told her that Rhee expected them to increase scores by 10 percent or more every year. "What do you do when your chancellor asks, 'How many points can you guarantee this year?'" Jefferson says. "How is a principal supposed to do that?"

It would be easy to point the finger at the educators who cheated. But the real ques-

[*]Originally published as Ken Miller, "The Dark Side of Awards and Accountability," *Governing*, June 2011. Reprinted with permission of the publisher.

tion is, what would cause these good people—teachers and principals who love educating children—to make these unethical choices?

The problem is the system. When governments design and implement a system based on accountability and results, public employees—logically—start to tailor their results accordingly. Yelling at systems doesn't improve systems; bribing systems doesn't improve systems. Fixing systems improves systems. When we don't do the hard work to fix the systems, the only option is to game the measurement system.

It's a perfectly rational reaction: The smart choice when faced with being held personally accountable for a broken system is to game the measurement system. That's exactly what the D.C. principals and teachers did. Faced with being fired for low test scores—and with little control over the complex variables that make up student success, including class size, curriculum, socioeconomic conditions, the education level of parents, availability of quality food and the compound performance of all the previous teachers—what choice did they have?

It's OK to want results. It's OK to focus on results. But when managers move from desiring a better outcome to demanding a better outcome, unhealthy behavior occurs. It was perfectly acceptable for Rhee to want better test scores. It was OK for her to expect improved performance from her principals and teachers. But instead of telling educators, "Give me a number that I will hold you accountable for," Rhee could have been asking, "What systems in our district must improve in order for you to improve your learning outcomes? What methods need to be improved, adopted or removed to improve student performance?"

The entire carrot-and-stick accountability movement is predicated on the notion that the only variable that matters is effort. Front-line public employees simply must not be trying hard enough. With the right goals, incentives and constant monitoring, managers can finally get workers to use all that effort they've been withholding all these years. In that mentality, results come from people simply trying harder to get a carrot or avoid a stick.

The real truth is that we have good people trapped in complex, broken systems that they did not create. Performance improves when these good people in the system get together with those affected by the system to build a better system.

Management-by-fear has been the fad in the public sector for more than a decade. Across the country, in conference rooms of every size, governors are looking at cabinet members' performance measures and demanding to know why the curve isn't bending. There are city managers berating department heads because the trend line is going in the wrong direction. There are federal appointees making up excuses for why the green light turned yellow on their dashboard. Of course, nobody calls it management-by-fear. It's called accountability, managing for results, dashboards, scorecards or STAT. Different names, same assumption: The way to get better results is to hold people accountable for measurable goals. Unfortunately not only do these accountability systems rarely work (affixing blame instead of fixing systems), they also produce devastating side effects (gaming the measurement system and increasing fear).

As a management consultant to states and localities, I used to believe very strongly in accountability systems. I created and implemented dashboards, scorecards and every other one of the buzzwords. None of them made a bit of difference. Not because we didn't do them right. Rather, it's because we got the notion of accountability all wrong.

My own view on accountability was greatly changed by the stories of soldiers from World War II. My grandfather had fought in the war, but like so many of his generation, he had chosen not to speak of it. I had no idea what he went through until I saw the incredible work of Stephen Ambrose, Steven Spielberg and Tom Hanks in the HBO mini-series *Band of Brothers*. This graphic, eye-popping series followed Easy Company from the storming of Normandy Beach through the liberation and the eventual end of the European conflict.

Each episode of the 10-part series showed a key battle through the eyes of one of the true-life characters. Viewers saw what the soldiers saw and felt what they felt through some amazing acting and directorial magic. The most memorable part of each story, though, was the final five minutes, when the show interviewed the actual soldiers depicted. Seeing the gentleness in their faces, the wisdom in their eyes, the bottled-up pain and their lifelong quest for a peaceful place to live out their days brought me to tears. I appreciated my grandfather as I never had before.

If you've seen the series or know about the events, you know that these men displayed acts of unthinkable courage. They ran headlong into a hail of bullets. They dived on grenades and ran across enemy lines with little regard for their own lives. How? How did the military breed that kind of dedication? How do they continue to do that? Why does a soldier give his life? Surely it's because he is accountable to his sergeant and doesn't want to let him down. The sergeant, in turn, is accountable to his major, and the major to his colonel. All the way up the chain, everybody is accountable to someone above them.

Right?

Of course not. What the military knows, and what the soldiers in Band of Brothers revealed, was exactly the opposite. The frontline troops didn't feel accountable to their commanding officer. Heck, they didn't even like their commanding officer, and couldn't care less about his commanding officer. They were accountable to one another. They would

rather take a bullet than see their friend take one. They risked their lives to save the man next to them, knowing full well that man would do the same. True accountability is shoulder-to-shoulder. It's horizontal. Yet we keep trying to make it vertical.

True accountability looks like love and respect; we keep making it feel like fear.

Rather than creating a band of brothers (and sisters), rather than cultivating teamwork and togetherness, we continue to divide, separate and force competition. We incentivize the chain of command but do little to cultivate the foxhole. We keep trying to "re-form" government, thinking that another accountability form or scorecard will create excellence. That type of accountability only breeds compliance—doing just enough to avoid punishment. We can't comply our way to excellence. Excellence is a pursuit of the heart.

So how do we create shoulder-to-shoulder accountability? Create more foxholes. Continually cultivate ways for people to work together for a common good. Create organizational puzzles to solve and use teams to solve them. Good leaders don't have all the answers. Rather, they frame puzzles and challenge their people to solve them. The best way to do this is to form a team of people who work in a system to come together with people who are affected by the system to create a better system. Much like real foxholes, these team projects are harrowing and intense at the time, but create bonds that last a lifetime.

These foxhole moments not only create shoulder-to-shoulder accountability as the team members struggle, fight, coalesce and transcend, these moments also create the other powerful accountability: over-the-counter accountability. That is, accountability to the people that government serves. A child-abuse caseworker may loathe her supervisor and may not particularly enjoy her co-workers, but just try to get between her and what is best for the kids she is trying to protect. No top-down accountability system can produce even a fraction of the motivation, passion and creativity that comes from accountability to one's team and one's customers.

Vertical accountability perpetuates the parent-child relationships that so permeate public-sector agency cultures. Management author Peter Scholtes laments that most of our organizational cultures, rather than being populated by adult-to-adult relationships, instead are dominated by parent-child relationships. When we see others as children, we treat them accordingly. We try to direct them and control them. We punish them and praise them. If they please us, they get a reward. If they displease us, they get a talking-to. With this mentality, all organizational progress takes the same energy as getting a 3-year-old to put his shoes on.

Government managers have two options. They can keep trying to goad workers into putting forth more effort and punishing them for results that are beyond their control. Or they can create a system that fosters true accountability. They can foster the kind of horizontal accountability that arises when men and women form a band of brothers and sisters. That's the kind of meaningful accountability—and results—that can never come from a carrot and a stick.

Five Steps to True Accountability:

1. Define your system. Where does it start? Where does it end? Who is it for?

2. Measure the system. How long does it take? How much does it cost? Is it achieving its purpose? Are the customers happy?

3. Form a team of people from all aspects of the system and study it.

4. Radically redesign the system to get better results.

5. Continuously improve the system by communicating the measures and soliciting ideas.

# 6. Public Corruption: An Ethical Challenge*

## Dulce Pamela Baizas

There have been numerous, highly publicized episodes of corruption at all levels of government that raise serious questions about public service ethics. The number of cases involving corruption has many people wondering if public servants can be trusted. Public servants have the responsibility to uphold the public's trust in everything they do. When a public servant breaches that trust by committing a deceitful or illegal act, it can lead to wasted resources and reputational damage.

During my graduate studies, my ethics professor defined corruption as the misuse of power by government officials for private gain. It is a dishonest or illegal behavior that destroys people's trust. Most people equate corruption with bribery. However, there are other forms of corruption such as kickbacks, extortion, mail and wire fraud, money laundering, embezzlement, among others. These activities have something in common: personal enrichment and private gain.

When a public official is accused or convicted of corruption, the consequences include removal from office, impeachment, prison time and fines. Corruption is a serious crime, and when these crimes are brought to light, it tarnishes the reputation of public servants. Regardless of who committed the crime (elected, appointed, uniformed service or civilian employee), the harm done is the erosion of public trust in government. The fabric of government is tainted, resulting in society's increasingly pessimistic view of public servants as a whole. Unfortunately that view is reinforced each time the media covers yet another story of a disgraced and corrupt official.

As reported earlier this month, a former Virginia governor was convicted of public corruption charges for accepting bribes and was sentenced to two years in prison. And who remembers former Illinois Governor, Rod Blagojevich, who tried to sell or trade President Obama's old Senate seat? Blagojevich was the first Illinois governor to be impeached and involuntarily removed from office. He was convicted of numerous corruption charges and was sentenced to 14 years in prison in 2011. Blagojevich's predecessor, former Illinois Governor George Ryan, was also found guilty of public corruption and was sentenced to six years in prison. Illinois governors are infamous for corruption charges. In fact, four of the previous seven Illinois governors have ended up going to prison.

---

*Originally published as Dulce Pamela Baizas, "Public Corruption: An Ethical Challenge," *PA Times*, January 27, 2015. Reprinted with permission of the author and publisher.

Then there was the shocking story of how thousands of children in Pennsylvania were jailed by two corrupt judges who received $2.6 million in kickbacks from the builders and owners of private prison facilities. The scandal, dubbed as "Kids for Cash," sent thousands of children to juvenile detention facilities for minor infractions in exchange for kickbacks. It was an abuse of power, and the two judges were eventually tried and sentenced to long prison terms in 2011. The first judge, Mark Ciavarella, Jr., was sentenced to 28 years in prison. The second judge, Michael Conahan, was sentenced to 17.5 years in prison. In 2013, the "Kids for Cash" scandal was featured as a documentary film.

These corrupt officials, and many others, betrayed the trust and faith that the general public placed in them, feeding public frustration, cynicism and disengagement among citizens. The public has the right to expect that their leaders will honor the oath they swore to. Instead, these corrupt officials deprived the public of honest service. They used their positions to pursue illegal and unethical schemes motivated by power and greed.

Although there are millions of government employees who are ethical and hardworking, one scandalous act negatively impacts the entire government workforce. Corruption demoralizes and unfairly stigmatizes the dedicated work of honest public servants. So how can government rehabilitate its reputation to win back the public's trust and confidence in light of these scandals? How can public virtue be restored? Should ethics training be taken more frequently than the recommended annual training? Should the government offer hefty rewards to whistleblowers to encourage more reports of inappropriate and unethical activities?

It is unlikely that we will see an end to corruption scandals. We don't live in a perfect world. Humans have flaws and have failed in judgment time and time again. Ending corruption is like finding a cure for cancer. Corruption is the cancer in government in which we have no cure. But if it's detected in time, it won't spread its malignancy throughout all of the segments of government.

Is it wrong to think that a total cure for corruption is not a realistic goal? This question is like asking every single public servant to uphold the highest ethical standards. Yet, no one person is alike. Ethical decisions are made individually, based on a person's integrity, character, values and beliefs.

Collectively, public servants have the duty to be open, fair, honest and impartial in their dealings with society. Public servants are expected to use their office to further the public interest and not to enrich themselves or others. The public good should take priority in all circumstances, not personal self-interest. After all, public service is about duty and responsibility, not a personal benefit or right. That is the true essence of public service. Unfortunately the ethical challenge of corruption is here to stay. However, our greatest defense is to show the public that such acts of deceit and fraud will not go unpunished.

# 7. Corruption— An Enlightened Self-Interest?[*]

## Ravi Subramanian

More than a hundred years ago, our profession found legitimacy through two channels. The first was as a solution to fight the corrupt spoils system in government. The second was through President Woodrow Wilson.

During his terms in office, President Wilson was instrumental in signing significant legislation to address corruption like the Underwood Tariff, the Federal Reserve Act and the Clayton Antitrust Act. However, a few years before the end of his second term, he succumbed to illness resulting from strokes. His death resulted in the 25th amendment to the Constitution, which deals with presidential disability and succession. However, his refusal to compromise on the Treaty of Versailles after the First World was voted as the fourth worst blunder in a 2006 survey of presidential historians organized by the University of Louisville's McConnell Center.

Subsequent to World Wars I and II, 20th century politicians waged wars on drugs, poverty, homelessness and other causes of human suffering. Corruption has suffered the same limited success as these wars, probably because we keep fighting it or because we forget that it is as complex as we

are. Alternatively, is it because we often think we are fighting corruption in other people but seem to forget that the struggle is within each one of us? How many times have we read or watched the news and said, "Can you believe this?" as though corruption only applied to someone else. We are quick to justify our thoughts, behaviors, actions and habits and absolve ourselves.

The trifecta of our modi operandi is often selective focus, confirmation bias and self-interest. Behavioral science researchers like Nobel Laureate, Daniel Kahneman have tackled these subjects and offer valuable guidance. The premise of Kahneman's book *Thinking, Fast and Slow*, is that it is easier to recognize other people's mistakes than our own. According to Kahneman, confirmation bias has primarily to do with cognition. Kahneman states that biases cannot always be avoided because System 2—which is the part of the mind that "allocates attention to the effortful mental activities that demand it" like complex computations or those tasks "associated with the subjective experience of agency, choice and concentration,"—may have no clue on how to handle them. Apparently, System 1 "operates automatically and quickly, with little or no

*Originally published as Ravi Subramanian, "Corruption—An Enlightened Self-Interest?" http://patimes. org/corruption-enlightened-self-interest/, 2013. Reprinted with permission of the author and publisher.

effort and no sense of voluntary control." Therefore, when biases or errors of intuitive thought occur automatically they are often difficult to prevent. Kahneman says that such "errors can be prevented only by enhanced monitoring and effortful activity of System 2." Questioning and evaluating every instance of System 1 would not only be "impossibly tedious" but also counterproductive for "making routine decisions." Kahneman argues that the best we can do is learn to recognize the potential for pitfalls well in advance and work hard to avoid significant mistakes.

As Dan Ariely states in his book *Predictably Irrational,* we often believe that we are capable of making the appropriate decision for ourselves and this belief clouds our judgment and decision-making because our reasoning abilities are imperfect. Ariely argues that "recognizing where we depart from the ideal is an important part of the quest to truly understand ourselves, and one that promises many practical benefits." He posits that these "irrational behaviors" are "neither random nor senseless," but "systematic and predictable."

Robert Wright, in his book *Nonzero, the Logic of Human Destiny*, says that we are instinctively wary. It does not help that we are constantly bombarded with spam emails, dubious offers, false advertising and examples of bad behavior on the news, TV shows, social media and the Internet. Wright states there are two reasons—the free rider and the cheat—that "have given people an innate tendency to monitor the contributions of others, whether consciously or unconsciously." Therefore, the wariness is vital to "try to get the best deal possible." Wright argues that the "instinctively enlightened self-interest is the seed that has grown into modern society." Along the same lines, Ariely confirms that "we've become more distrustful—not only of those who are trying to swindle us, but of everyone."

Acting in our self-interest and getting into trouble is not new, but the fact that we continue to face the consequences, misunderstand the reality and often repeat the same mistakes seem to suggest that we are in a Pavlovian loop or just do not understand how to learn from our mistakes and the mistakes of others. We also forget that when we act selfishly, trust erodes and everyone ends up losing. The public good of trust or other resources become unsustainable when we act in our self-interest. Ariely states that every year:

- The retail industry loses $16 billion to customers who buy clothes, wear them and return the secondhand clothes for a full refund.
- Individuals add a bogus $24 billion to their claims of property losses according to the insurance industry.
- The IRS estimates a loss of $350 billion, representing the gap between what people should pay in taxes and what they do pay.
- Employees' theft and fraud at the workplace are estimated at about $600 billion.

Organizations and companies are no different.

All this sounds hopeless, but we know there are numerous examples of how we tend to trust each other, even when the evolutionary, scientific and behavioral odds are against us. There are also many examples of when public trust was lost and restored through proactively addressing complaints, transparency, accountability, sacrifice and in Ariely's words through "vulnerability," where consumers can talk freely with organizations about "products and services, warts and all." It is often harder to escape the consequences of dishonorable actions when we publicly pronounce our commitment to behave in a trustworthy manner. Maybe our war cry should be, "We value your trust and will not squander it!"

# 8. When Does Politicians' Unethical Behavior Become a Crime?*

## Alan Ehrenhalt

Many years ago, I spent a morning in the Pima County courthouse in Tucson, Ariz., talking politics with Conrad Joyner, one of the county supervisors. Joyner was running for Congress. I asked him if he expected to have any trouble raising money for his campaign. Joyner looked at me as if I had been born yesterday. "Are you kidding?" he said. "With all the zoning cases I've got coming up on the county board?"

I walked out of that courthouse trying to make sense of what I had just heard. Joyner seemed to be telling me he planned to extort campaign money from real estate developers who wanted his vote. Or maybe he just wanted the developers to think his vote was for sale so that he could pocket the money for his campaign and then vote his conscience. Either way, there was something sleazy about it. But if there were no conversations about a deal and no quid pro quo, the law couldn't touch it. That didn't seem quite right.

I remembered that morning in Tucson a couple months ago when Sheldon Silver, the speaker of the New York State Assembly, was arrested and charged with five federal counts of mail and wire fraud, conspiracy and extortion. According to the U.S. attorney who is prosecuting him, Silver collected large legal fees from patients suffering from asbestos-related illnesses, all of them sent to him by a prominent New York doctor. In return, Silver helped the doctor out by steering $500,000 in state grants to his research organization. He also stands accused of steering real estate developers to a law firm in which he had an interest in exchange for helping the developers with their legislative priorities in Albany.

What Silver is alleged to have done bears a resemblance to what passed for politics as usual in Chicago in the 1950s, when I was growing up there. Richard J. Daley, who was mayor at the time, used to offer a succinct piece of ethics advice to newly elected aldermen. "Don't take a nickel," Daley told them. "Just show them your business card."

Even the greenest of political newcomers understood exactly what Daley meant. He was telling them that people with an interest in city council decisions would be happy to throw an alderman a little cash on the side to help bring about a favorable outcome. They just had to find an acceptable way to do it. A law office was a good place. Petitioners who needed a favorable council vote could be depended on to pay generously for

*Originally published as Alan Ehrenhalt, "When Does Politicians' Unethical Behavior Become a Crime?" *Governing*, April 2015. Reprinted with permission of the publisher.

a little legal work. An insurance agency was even better. Aldermen who had insurance licenses could earn a handsome income writing up policies on buildings owned by politically needy landlords. Alderman Harry Sain, who represented the Skid Row neighborhood just west of downtown Chicago for 35 years, collected the insurance premiums on just about all the flophouses that stood there. And somehow those flophouses managed to pass code inspection year after year.

This was a couple of steps sleazier than the scheme I had heard about in Arizona. But it was all considered quite legal, at least in the ethical climate that existed in Chicago at the time. There was no quid pro quo, or any need to discuss out loud what the petitioners might want the city council to deliver for them. That part was understood. If a landlord or a building contractor or a labor union wanted to flatter a public official by doing business with him, they had every right to do so.

The rules are different now at all levels of American government. Public officials run the risk of being prosecuted for the things Sain did in Chicago, or even, in some cases, for the kinds of things Joyner boasted to me about in Tucson. The age of laissez-faire political tolerance has been replaced by something almost as disturbing in its own way. It has been replaced by a system in which the law is convoluted and the rules have been written to satisfy the ambitions of the public prosecutor.

Consider for a moment Sheldon Silver's case, or at least the portion of it that has been made public so far. Did Silver commit extortion? You wouldn't think so at first. As it turns out, though, federal law has for many decades stretched the meaning of extortion far beyond any common appreciation of the word. The Hobbs Act, passed by Congress in 1946, says that perfectly voluntary transactions can qualify as extortion as long as one of the parties is acting "under color of official right." Silver held the official

position of Assembly speaker, so under the terms of the Hobbs Act he could be an extortionist even if he never asked for anything.

And in case the charge of extortion doesn't stick, prosecutors could try Silver for "honest services fraud," a concept that lacks any precise meaning at all. A public official can be indicted and convicted on federal mail fraud charges if prosecutors can convince a jury that he or she deprived the public of "the intangible right of honest services."

Honest services fraud was written into federal law in 1988 to help federal prosecutors put away shady public officials who could not be found to have committed any tangible criminal offense. If that strikes you as disturbingly vague, you are not alone.

In 2010, the U.S. Supreme Court finally decided that prosecution for vague honest services fraud was wrong. It ruled unanimously that the concept could be used in court only in cases that involved actual bribery or kickbacks. In theory, this should have put an end to prosecutorial abuse. In practice, it can be an invitation for prosecutors to extend the definitions of "bribery" and "kickback" beyond normal human understanding.

My purpose in bringing all this up is not to induce sympathy for Silver or to suggest that he is innocent of all his alleged offenses. If he used his public office for improper personal gain, he should be punished. The point is that high-profile cases like this one demonstrate the rickety character of criminal law as applied to the behavior of public officials. Once largely blind to the subtle misdoings of those in office, it has been tilted to give prosecutors an added advantage when it comes to obtaining convictions for public corruption. Sometimes it serves to put greedy criminals behind bars. Other times it is used to manufacture crimes where they do not exist.

The most blatant example of flimsy prosecution involves former Alabama Gov. Don

Siegelman, who has spent most of the past decade in prison on charges that he violated the honest services law and committed bribery by offering a job to a man who contributed to his statewide campaign for a lottery. Siegelman didn't demand or accept any money for his personal use. The smoking gun, if you want to call it that, was Siegelman's comment to an aide that the lottery contributor would probably want to be rewarded with a seat on a state health-care regulatory board and that such an appointment would not be difficult to arrange.

Common sense tells us that Siegelman's recorded conversation amounted to nothing more than an acknowledgment of the way campaign finance works in this country and that if he committed a crime, a substantial portion of Congress and the nation's state legislators should be tried and convicted as well. A large cadre of members of Congress, legal scholars and prominent journalists have asked President Obama to pardon Siegelman, but as of this writing he remains incarcerated in the Oakdale federal prison in Louisiana.

Siegelman has been caught in the jaws of a legal system that lurched in a couple of decades from laughable leniency to vindictive and dubious intolerance. It may be unfair to put Siegelman and Silver in the same category, but the upcoming legal proceedings against Silver will still place the nation's anticorruption laws on display for everyone to look at.

Is there a way to police the conduct of elected officials that doesn't put prosecutors in the role of either inept bystanders or avenging zealots? Some would-be reformers think there is. Zephyr Teachout, a Fordham University law professor who ran unsuccessfully for governor of New York last year on an anticorruption platform, argues

that the real scandal in the system isn't the number of public officials who act illegally but rather the vast array of ethically questionable behaviors that are perfectly legal. Teachout would ban outside income for elected officials, provide generous public financing for candidates and undo the Supreme Court decisions that allow virtually unlimited campaign contributions from private corporations.

None of those things are going to happen anytime soon. The Supreme Court is not disposed to reverse itself on campaign finance, nor are the states going to accomplish that by constitutional convention. Public campaign financing is an experiment that the public has consistently said it doesn't want. And while barring outside income for legislators might sound like a promising idea in New York, where an Assembly member earns $79,500 a year plus a per diem, it would be completely unrealistic in some of the smaller states, where legislators who take in nothing beyond their salaries would be flirting with the poverty line for a family of four.

Impractical as Teachout's remedies seem, however, she makes one fundamental point that is hard to escape: Unethical behavior in any realm of American politics—maybe in politics anywhere—is essentially a structural problem, not a legal one. Drawing a nearly invisible line in the sand and then pouncing on a few who seem to cross it serves mainly to disillusion the public about the soundness of democratic government. "Whether influence is bought through a bribe, outside spending, outside income or campaign contributions," Teachout writes, "the public suffers in the same way. Until we move past scandals toward structural change, our democracy will suffer too." I'm afraid she's right about that.

# 9. Managing Public Mistrust of Government[*]

## Brynne VanHettinga

The American National Election Studies (ANES) biennially conducts a poll of electoral attitudes and behavior. The ANES survey captures trends in public opinion through a series of questions about trust, efficacy and responsiveness of government. Between 1980 and 2008, the percentage of citizens who believed government benefits a few big special interests as opposed to everyone, ranged from 61 percent—76 percent. Those who indicated that "quite a few" government officials are crooked ranged from 30 percent—52 percent. The percentage of citizens who agreed that people don't have a say in what government does ranged from 29 percent—56 percent, and those who believed that public officials don't care what people think ranged from 31 percent—66 percent.

The ANES survey results follow no particular pattern and citizen cynicism has not generally increased from year-to-year. However, the data indicate a persistent problem with public trust in governing officials and institutions. The consequence of low levels of citizen trust in public servants and public institutions can actually operate to hinder government performance, thereby aggravating perceptions of bureaucratic ineptitude. Public servants are increasingly constrained by strict rules and procedures that are intended to insure impartiality and accountability, yet they are denied the flexibility that enables them to address the individual needs of the citizens they serve.

There are a number of reasons that citizens develop a mistrust of government. Citizens tend to become aware of government action during negative experiences, such as payment of a tax or fine or long waits for administrative services. Citizens are also likely to become aware of government or official action only in instances of failure. This is abetted by a media that thrives on sensationalism. Media stories, such as the latest corruption scandal or the complete breakdown of services following Hurricane Katrina, can fuel perceptions that government is corrupt and/or incompetent. The more mundane experiences, such as roads, schools, water, sewer and trash services, tend to be either ignored or taken for granted.

Not surprisingly, the degree of public cynicism is correlated with general social and economic conditions. According to Evan Berman, in a 1997 *Public Administration Review* article, cynicism is lower in geographic areas with above average economic growth, lower crime rates and higher educational

---

*Originally published as Brynne VanHettinga, "Managing Public Mistrust of Government," *PA Times*, April 7, 2015. Reprinted with permission of the author and publisher.

levels. Voting patterns, an indicator of citizen engagement, also have a socioeconomic bias. In 1990, 86 percent of those in families with incomes over $75,000 reported voting compared to only 52 percent of those in families with incomes under $15,000. Whether governments are more responsive because voter participation is higher has not been conclusively established. However, the pattern of increasing income inequality over the past several decades will likely aggravate citizen distrust.

Researchers who have explored ways to increase public trust in government generally suggest the implementation of a broad range of strategies: greater transparency, engagement of citizens in the decision process through incorporation of citizen input and public information campaigns that inform the public about the good that government does. While governments can disseminate information through their own infrastructures (mailings, websites, etc.), these strategies also call for tactical use of the media. This approach recommends the use of positive press releases as well as developing relationships with print and broadcast journalists. In essence, governments are urged to utilize the same public relations strategies that corporations do. However, in a free democracy, the promotion of government by the media runs contrary to its traditional role as government watchdog.

Trust (or lack of it) runs both ways and some researchers have examined the degree to which political appointees and senior-level public administrators trust citizens. From the time of the Federalists, elites have promoted the notion of representative (rather than direct) democracy on the basis that the "masses" were unqualified to govern themselves. Today, some civil servants are reluctant to promote citizen participation because they regard the general public as being focused on short-term personal gains rather than long-term community interests, as well as being untrained in necessary technocratic knowledge.

Trust is often described in terms of social capital. Putnam has demonstrated the relationship between social capital and civic engagement, as well as a decline in both over the past several decades. This suggests that declining trust in government could, in part, be attributed to declining trust in general and not exclusively to failure on the part of government. While governments can certainly do more to promote trust by increasing transparency and citizen engagement, they may be relatively powerless to address larger social trends that are undermining trust.

Perhaps the most disturbing aspect of citizen mistrust is the "us versus them" view of government. Indeed, the very notion that public trust should be "managed" implies that citizens can be manipulated into correct behavior in the same manner corporate employers "manage" employees to forego self-interest in the pursuit of organizational objectives. The constitutional premise of government as "we the people" seems to be fractured. Overcoming citizen mistrust will require a long-term strategy and commitment.

# 10. Coffee and Doughnuts: Building Accountability*

## John J. Carroll

Most of the "mom and pop" doughnut shops are gone now. Thankfully, there is a coffee shop on every corner. Our main topic, Militarization of Law Enforcement, is an interesting take on an old topic and strikes me as a "no good deed goes unpunished" issue. With my first cup of coffee, I will look at accountability.

My perspective will probably be viewed as slanted. My service in law enforcement began in 1978 and continued until 2010. After my time in the Air Force, I went to work for a sheriff's office that grew into one of the largest in the nation. I served six sheriffs (five elected) from wide political persuasions and philosophies.

I learned firsthand how to balance the political and administrative (as well as the regular "crises du jour"). I was directly involved in crafting and implementing policies that affected all of our April topics (building accountability, managing community mistrust and skepticism). I hope this lends a bit of legitimacy to my view. The reader is of course free to agree or disagree.

According to the most recent Bureau of Justice statistics, there are almost 18,000 local police departments and sheriffs' offices, employing over 1.13 million people (including 765,000 sworn personnel). Like it or not, American law enforcement agencies are the embodiment of our layered and diffused federalist structure. Building accountability throughout so many agencies is not only essential, but when done properly, a continuous and ongoing process. It is also nothing new.

The "professional model" of policing that developed from the Progressive Era is still evident today. An accountability "arc" can be drawn from the famous Knapp Commission that investigated corruption in the New York Police Department in the 1970s to the current Commission to Combat Police Corruption within city government. This arc is also national, whether internally or externally imposed (courts, state or federal monitors). Since 1993, law enforcement agencies have been at the forefront of embracing the outcome/results oriented management style (i.e., NYPD's CompStat), which has accountability as the core element.

Law enforcement agency employees, particularly sworn ones, go through an incredibly rigorous hiring process. After hiring, the candidate must complete long and often

---

*Originally published as John J. Carroll, "Coffee and Doughnuts: Building Accountability," *PA Times*, April 10 and 17, 2015. Reprinted with permission of the author and publisher.

stressful training before they begin to serve the public. As an example, an officer or deputy in Florida is required to hold a statewide certification, undergo regular training in high liability (driving, use of force, etc.), ethics and other important subjects. There is also opportunity for additional career enhancements and formal education.

Do people get through that who should not? Yes.

The agencies are also supposed to have detailed policies that outline actions and behaviors, court decisions and statutory requirements. Agencies are also supposed to have mechanisms in place to handle complaints against employees along with a process to correct behaviors and root out the bad apples. Agencies may avail themselves to external accrediting bodies and leadership development programs (FBI National Academy, Southern Police Institute, etc.).

Does this guarantee accountability? No.

Building accountability comes from leadership. Taking a leadership role in the public sector is an incredible balancing act between interests, resources and time. A leader has to balance internal factors (such as worker demographics, behaviors, processes, organizational structure and culture) and external ones (market/economic, technology, political, demographic shifts) that affect the agency. Many of these the leader has no direct control over although he/she is responsible for the actual service responsibilities of the agency.

Commissioners Bill Bratton, Raymond Kelly, Charles Ramsey, along with Chiefs Cathy Lanier, George Turner and Kathleen O'Toole have been leaders in their agencies during unprecedented events and are well-known for showing accountability.

Law enforcement agencies have added citizen review boards to help oversee them. Elected officials have become particularly sensitive to race, culture and other important aspects of relationships and behaviors in their agencies. There is discussion about deploying body cameras to all patrol officers—another technology that is not new—as an accountability effort. Early indications are that deploying this tool reduces use of force incidents and complaints against officers.

The continuous media drumbeat of a handful of high profile events may lead the public at large to believe there is a lack of accountability in its law enforcement agencies. This is simply not true. Hundreds of thousands of men and women go to work every day, like their millions of counterparts in other government agencies, believing they are doing their best to serve the public in an honest way. Enlightened leaders across the public sector know that building accountability is a continuous task, not a new one.

Time for that second cup of coffee! A doughnut is an exceptionally rare event these days. More likely, I will have a bagel (usually dry) with my coffee. This is the 21st century after all and we are supposed to be eating healthier.

If you did not catch my first piece on these topics earlier this month, a caveat is in order. I may be a full time academic now but that followed a career as a law enforcement executive. I posit that the topic offered this month—militarization of law enforcement—may be what people are discussing, but is by no means new.

Assaults/murders of law enforcement officers and reported crimes are at record lows. In 2013, there were 27 officers killed in the line of duty and 49,851 were assaulted. Compare that to 1987 where 74 officers were killed and 63,842 were assaulted.

Is this because of militarization of law enforcement? No.

Is it better staffing, equipment, training and management? I would like to think so. I remember the whole "cops are outgunned" argument. I remember wearing bulky body armor, carrying a "six shooter" revolver and a baton.

As with anything else, knowledge and technology advanced. Revolvers became automatics. Batons became expandable. Non-lethal technology also evolved from Mace to pepper spray to electric stun weapons. Use of force policies and self-defense training got better. Shotguns are still around, but patrol rifles appear more widely deployed on patrol (not to say that I am a patrol rifle supporter). Riot gear and tactics seem largely unchanged over the years.

A number of agencies have always leaned toward a more militaristic appearance and demeanor (particularly state highway patrols). During times of emergency, law enforcement becomes more command structured to better manage an event. Yet, I have never heard a citizen or an elected official complain about police militarization.

A 2011 National Institute of Justice study revealed that 81.5 percent of respondents were either satisfied or very satisfied with the police—the unique aspect here is that all of the respondents were selected from people who had encounters with the police. This follows a stream of studies that show similar results. Internal community surveys over the years were very similar.

*Governing* reports that from 2008 through 2012, police (fire and EMS too) received 80 percent or better satisfaction ratings and had the highest ratings of all local government services. I will admit that Fire and EMS probably helped the ratings because everyone loves them! Could this level of satisfaction exist in the face of mistrust and skepticism?

Contrary to what is viewed in the entertainment media (dramatic programs and news), the vast majority of what law enforcement officers do every day is not crime related. Most time spent is handling service calls or interacting with the community. There might be a little coffee and doughnut time in there too.

How does the community feel about the media? According to a 2014 Gallup Poll, 60 percent of respondents record distrust of the media to accurately, fairly or fully report the news. In a 2011 Pew Center study, news organizations equaled or surpassed the all-time lows in performance indicators since 1985. This is exactly the opposite of what it should be.

Law enforcement officers should take responsibility for reducing crime and treating people in a civil and ethical way—period. Law enforcement agencies should work every day to improve services and enhance trust. The community should hold their police accountable for unjust acts of use of force and mistreatment. The community must be skeptical, yet trust its public servants. A typical shift is not the continuous parade of chases and violence shown in the news. Perhaps the media can focus more on building trust.

# 11. Can Police Departments Reduce Implicit Bias?*

## Paul Figueroa

Oakland's assistant police chief says that law enforcement must work hard to reduce implicit bias and create a new path for police-community relations. But the problem is not intractable.

This chapter explores the effects that unconscious racial biases have on the criminal justice system in the United States.

"In too many communities around the country, a gulf of mistrust exists between local residents and law enforcement," said President Obama in a recent speech at the Congressional Black Caucus Awards Dinner. "And that has a corrosive effect—not just on the black community; it has a corrosive effect on America."

These are powerful words from the President of the United States. In discussions around the country with other law enforcement and community members, I know the issue of police and race has reached a level of intensity that must be actively addressed. These conversations have taken place for many years, yet we don't seem to be making much progress on the core problem—chronic and pervasive distrust between communities of color and police.

The continued deficit in trust is a bitter pill to swallow, because I believe the vast majority of law enforcement began and remain committed to service of others. I have seen first-hand the sacrifice of police personnel and their willingness to accept high levels of risk in the performance of their duties. I have had the honor to know officers who have served the community in trustworthy ways and even paid the ultimate price to protect others.

Community trust in law enforcement isn't just nice to have—it's essential to the success of police work and the safety of residents. When trust in the police is low, community members don't call the police, they don't cooperate with the police, they don't testify, they don't provide information, and, sometimes, they may take matters into their own hands.

We have all dropped the ball, from the level of the office of the President to the halls of academia to the streets that police try to keep safe. This isn't to say there is never probable cause for arrests or that many of the people arrested don't need to be brought to justice. But enforcement strategies and tactics have often been a breeding ground for conflict, even where

*Originally published as Paul Figueroa, "Can Police Departments Reduce Implicit Bias?" http://greater good.berkeley.edu/article/item/can_police_departments_reduce_implicit_bias, August 5, 2015. Reprinted with permission of the author and publisher.

there is legal justification for law enforcement to take action. In addition, the staggering incarceration rates and the costs of incarceration have had measurable and devastating effects for many communities, particularly communities of color.

Those are not outcomes that most officers want. But the research highlighted in *Greater Good*'s implicit bias series has raised serious concerns about the effects implicit bias can have on policing decisions. The work shows how our unconscious biases can undermine our consciously held beliefs. This is true for all people, and even for people making decisions affecting their same racial group. Implicit bias isn't the only factor driving disparities of enforcement and unacceptable incarceration rates, but it certainly has an impact. The only way to determine and address the impacts of implicit bias—and address them—is to do the following: have direct, open, and honest conversations with the community, rigorously collect and study the data, and implement enforcement strategies and training programs focused on fairness and equity, particularly for communities of color.

Can policy help to challenge bias? To begin the trust-building conversation, law enforcement, elected officials, and all community stakeholders must start by recognizing that racial disparities have had terrible consequences for our society—and that we are ready to do something about it.

This is, in fact, the starting point for racial reconciliation efforts underway by the National Network for Safe Communities and other trust-building conversations around the country. I strongly believe this position is a key element for building lasting trust with communities of color, who are looking for tangible signs that police agencies are doing what they say they will do. These conversations also allow law enforcement to talk about the realities they face in deciding where and when to conduct enforcement efforts to reduce crime.

## Getting the Facts Raises Awareness

Data collection can play a critical role in helping law enforcement to recognize that there is a problem—and in shaping the response. Professor Jack Glaser, in his 2014 book *Suspect Race*, outlines the latest scholarly research and provides compelling evidence for the presence of racial bias in many policing practices—and he argues how racial profiling exacerbates incarceration rates among affected populations. Stanford professor Jennifer Eberhardt's groundbreaking work continues to illustrate how race can impact decision-making—which can lead to negative outcomes for African Americans.

Though there is debate about how and why evidence should be collected and analyzed, efforts should be made by all police agencies. Collecting and sharing data is, at a minimum, a significant step toward transparency; unfortunately, efforts over the years to collect and analyze data have generally been localized because of inconsistent collection methods across agencies. Fortunately, there is a nationwide effort underway by the Center for Policing Equity. These efforts will involve data collection from agencies around the country and normalize how the data is compared across categories. This is a particularly encouraging innovation for law enforcement research.

On the cutting edge of the research, there are efforts underway by Professor Eberhardt to look at the extensive amounts of body camera footage collected by a police agency. The goal is to analyze the quality of the interactions in order to identify themes during police stops and engagement with the community. It may identify if and how bias plays a role in the encounter, and allow agencies to design interventions to address the problem.

But it can also provide feedback regarding positive and negative interactions. This approach can go a long way toward informing training and policy with a constant eye on improving interactions with the police. The goal is always to move toward increased positive interactions, even during difficult circumstances, as a way of building trust with the police. This is one of the first systematic and large-scale efforts to use footage captured by body-worn cameras for this purpose.

## Building a New Culture

Of course, facts will not be helpful without a culture of fairness and inclusion in police agencies. The Chicago Police Department has pioneered and implemented training that emphasizes four key elements of procedural justice, all of which can help build trust in the police and may have positive impacts at addressing effects of implicit bias: Voice, Neutrality, Respect, and Trustworthiness.

There are three agencies in California also providing this training. If we take the research on procedural justice seriously, it gives us a clear framework to shift our policies and procedures toward building legitimacy. The legitimacy can be earned, day-by-day, by changing the nature of the interactions between police and communities of color so that instead of reinforcing distrust and tension, they begin to build trust and cooperation. This training is now being adapted for application in at least two states.

## Programs That Shift Bias

Given the importance of trust to public safety—and the ongoing coverage of negative, often tragic encounters between police and community members—I strongly believe law enforcement leaders must openly advocate and implement strategic polices and

enforcement strategies to focus on increasing trust and lowering crime at the same time. This will go a long way toward signaling their commitment to a new way and a new type of relationship with the communities they serve.

One excellent example is the Cease Fire strategy, which recognizes that a very small number of people are responsible for shootings and homicide—and they themselves are often the targets of violence. These people can be identified and communicated with in a direct and respectful way. The communications to them explain the risks of continued participation in violence and offer services available to them. It is made clear that the community and law enforcement want something different for them: for them to be alive and free. But this is not a Pollyannaish approach, for it also makes clear that violence cannot be tolerated. Those who continue to make their communities unsafe will face enforcement action and prosecution.

This approach has proven far more effective in reducing violence and building community trust than stopping large segments of a population, a strategy sometimes equated with racial profiling, which only exacerbates tensions between police and the community. There are additional promising strategies related to restorative justice and re-entry programs which lower recidivism rates.

The evidence of low trust of the police in communities of color is disheartening. Law enforcement leaders are in the unique position to implement programs to address the low levels of trust.

There is no magic wand—and building trust is hard work. It begins with an honest conversation about the effects of policing in the past. Law enforcement leaders must recognize that key members of the community may not even sit at the trust-building table until they observe law enforcement leaders making concrete efforts to address the issues. The President's Task Force Report on 21st Century Policing is a great place to start when considering the best steps forward to building trust in your community. It's hard work, but the problem is not intractable. I am grateful to the UC Berkeley's Greater Good Science Center's implicit bias series for offering thoughtful discussion and research on this critically important topic for society today.

• *A. Classic* •

# 12. Cuyahoga County's Road to Recovery from Corruption*

## *Josh Goodman*

When federal officials indicted Cuyahoga County Commissioner Jimmy Dimora on corruption charges in September, it was the latest indication that the government in Ohio's most populous county was broken. That wasn't news to the citizens of Cuyahoga County, though—they approved a plan a year earlier to fix it. As a result, the form of government is changing in Cuyahoga County, which spans Cleveland and many of its suburbs.

Under the old system, county commissioners and a multiplicity of other offices, including county coroner and county engineer, were elected countywide. The result was a government that was simultaneously fragmented and lacking in checks and balances, says Martin Zanotti, a former mayor of Parma Heights and architect of the reform plan. Each elected official ruled over an independent fiefdom. Hiring decisions were decentralized, creating inefficiencies and opportunities for patronage and corruption.

People in positions of power took advantage of those opportunities. That reality started to become clear in July 2008, when federal agents conducted a massive raid of county offices. Since then, more than 30 county officials and contractors have pled guilty to a variety of corruption charges. County Auditor Frank Russo faces more than 20 years in prison after admitting to accepting bribes and kickbacks. And Dimora, who doubled as head of the county Democratic Party, stands accused of using his elected office for personal gain. He says he's innocent.

But corruption isn't the only thing ailing Cuyahoga County. Cleveland has long suffered from all the familiar problems of the industrial Midwest: population loss, poverty and economic stagnation. Even wealthier suburbs aren't immune. "Cuyahoga County is having to grapple with some of the problems that have affected Cleveland for years," says Jennifer Bradley, co-director of the Brookings Institution's Great Lakes Economic Initiative.

Starting in January, Cuyahoga County will have a single county executive as its top elected official who, proponents hope, will provide energetic leadership and serve as a focal point for much-needed economic development. It will have an 11-member County Council with members representing distinct districts, giving the county a legislative branch to check the executive. Most of the

*Originally published as Josh Goodman, "Cuyahoga County's Road to Recovery from Corruption," *Governing*, November 2010. Reprinted with permission of the publisher.

old countywide elected offices will become appointed positions, which will be filled by professionals instead of politicians. The changes are similar to ones made a decade ago in Allegheny County, Pa., where Pittsburgh is showing signs of economic rebirth.

Still, no one in Cuyahoga County is naive enough to think a change of government structure is a comprehensive solution to the region's problems. The system's success may hinge on who county voters pick as the new first county executive in an election this month. "Any form of government," Zanotti says, "is ultimately only going to be as good as the people you elect."

# 13. How Public Professionals Stay Politically Neutral

## *Roger L. Kemp*

Early in my city management career, a council person said that he thought that I was a "liberal," since I seemed overly concerned about certain segments of the public in the policy-setting process when I made staff recommendations.

Later in my career, another council person said that he had heard that I was a "conservative," and this is why all of my staff recommendations were fiscally conservative in nature. These were comments made by elected officials on governing bodies that hired me by majority vote to serve as the city manager of their community.

Even later in my city management career (more like by my mid-career) I got tired of elected officials trying to politically categorize me because of my personal political party affiliations over the years. After all, I was their hired city management professional, and my staff recommendations had nothing to do with my personal partisan political party affiliations. I only made, as their city manager, professionally responsible and politically neutral staff recommendations.

During my mid-career as a city manager, I changed my personal political party affiliation to be an "unaffiliated" voter. After all, I did not professionally care what political party a mayor or council member belonged to since they were all my bosses, collectively speaking. Each one of them received a ma-jority vote, either at-large or in a district, and they individually and collectively "held the trust" of the people that they represented. Their personal election was a result of our nation's democratic election process, which is used to elect public officials at all levels of government (i.e., municipal, county, state, and federal).

I've worked in both liberal communities and conservative communities, and I never searched out or preferred one political type of a community over the other. I liked one community where council members ran for office and the political party they belonged to was not even on the ballot (out West). Later on, in another city, every candidate for office had their party affiliation listed after their name on the ballot (back East). Out West when council members were elected to office I did not even know about their personal political party affiliation. Nor did I personally or professionally care. Back East I knew of every candidate's political party affiliation, since it was on the ballot.

I would always tell elected officials, primarily mayors and city council members, that they collectively hired me and that I worked for them. All of my recommendations were always professional in nature, and there was no politics involved in the staff recommendation process. I also told them that I did not care what political party that they personally belonged to. They were all elected by the people, by majority vote, and they all held the trust of the people in the area that they were elected to represent. Regardless of their personal party affiliation, they were all my bosses, collectively speaking.

This is the professional role of a city manager. City Managers should be politically neutral, and tell elected officials wherever they work that all of their recommendations are always professional in nature. After all, the folks elected by majority vote hold the trust of the people, and they are collectively your boss, and they should all be treated with equal respect by their professional management staff.

I have also worked in cities where you see, at election time, signs for political candidates along party lines. All of the Democrats (D's) are listed on some political signs, and all of the Republicans (R's) are listed on other political signs. Each party wants you to vote for its party's endorsed political candidates. In the real world, it is a politically mixed group of candidates that usually get elected and, as a City Manager, the elected officials are collectively your boss regardless of their respective personal political party affiliations.

I've known some city managers that, and if they were a "D," they only wanted to work in liberal communities, and if they are an "R" they only wanted to work in conservative communities. I always had twice as many jobs to apply for than they did, since I did not care which party that my bosses (the elected officials) belonged to, and I told them this during the job interview process.

This is the political role of a true city management professional.

During job interviews, at the end, when I was allowed to make a comment, I would explain this philosophy to the elected officials that I could wind up working for/with. I'd also always tell them that "doing the right thing meant more than my job"—professionally speaking.

Lastly, I would also say that I applied for this job because I liked their community, I felt that I could help them improve it, both fiscally and operationally, and that I welcomed the opportunity to work for/with them during the coming years as their city manager.

I usually wound up as one of the "top three" candidates that applied for the city manager position during a city's respective recruitment, selection, and hiring process. On average, I would get a job offer for one of the three city manager positions that I applied for, since I usually wound-up as one of their "top three" candidates during their respective city manager selection processes!

My public service career started when I was appointed as an assistant to the city manager in the City of Oakland, one of the largest cities with the council-manager form of government in the State of California. I was later the city manager of the City of Clifton, the largest city with the council-manager form of government in State of New Jersey. I also served as the city manager of the City of Meriden, the largest city with the council-manager form of government in State of Connecticut.

Taking extra efforts to be politically neutral in local governments is the wave of the future.

# 14. How Would It Look in the Paper?*

## Bob Stone

Appearances matter. Where there's smoke there's fire. If it looks like a duck and quacks like a duck, it's probably a duck.

We're continually warned to avoid the appearance of impropriety. Many state and local ethics codes advise us to judge the ethics of a proposed action in part by how it will look in the newspaper. Machiavelli explained, "The great majority of mankind are satisfied with appearances, as though they were realities, and are more often influenced by the things that 'seem' than by those that 'are.'"

Those of us with a long history in the public sector can recall urging our employees to avoid doing things they would not want to read about in the morning newspaper. Bob Stone and Mike Ukjela suggest that the "newspaper question" remains a reasonable one for today's public managers to ask, but caution against its customary use as an ethical test. Innovation and good ethical decisions may in fact lead to negative newspaper articles; sometimes it's worth the risk. Bad ethical decisions, likewise, can stem from a desire to avoid bad press. Bob and Mike call attention to both scenarios.

But appearances are not realities, and, "How will it look in the newspaper?" is not related to ethics. It might be, if newspapers adhered to the highest ethical standards we aspire to, but sadly, newspapers slip up like the rest of us. Newspapers—and other media—rake in readers by reporting scandal. When real scandal is in short supply, they may have to invent some, and then ethical behavior can be made to look very bad indeed.

Readers of the *Los Angeles Times* picked up their paper on June 7, 2006, to see this lead to a story splashed across the front page of the California section.

"One recent Friday, while thousands of motorists were suffering through freeway traffic from the San Fernando Valley to downtown Los Angeles, Police Chief William J. Bratton skipped the congestion and made the trip in a fraction of the time, buzzing from Van Nuys to Parker Center [police headquarters in downtown Los Angeles] in a city helicopter."

The headline read, "Chief Says LAPD Flights Save Time, Money," but any reader would have assumed that the chief must have done something wrong, or else why would the paper have printed the story?

Bratton's behavior looked very bad in the newspaper. But the only ethical violation

---

*Originally published as Bob Stone, "How Would It Look in the Paper?" *Governing*, August 19, 2009. Reprinted with permission of the publisher.

that day belonged to the paper itself. Bratton wasn't getting any personal benefit from his exhausting travel schedule. He was furthering his extraordinarily successful work to cut crime and to change the culture of the LAPD. His intensive travel let every cop see him and hear firsthand what the new chief demanded of the department

Had Bratton applied the "how would it look" test, he would have done much less traveling and been a much less successful chief.

Even though appearances aren't reality, and even though ethical behavior can appear unethical and vice versa, appearances do matter, for business reasons if not for ethical ones. Unfavorable publicity like the Los Angeles Times story on Bill Bratton can inhibit bold-but-proper behavior.

So it's not a bad idea to ask yourself, before making a decision, "How would it look in the newspaper?" But that's a business decision, not an ethical one. Our guess is that Bill Bratton would willingly have risked the unfavorable story rather than give up his style of leadership-by-presence.

There is sometimes, however, a valid connection between the appearance of ethical behavior and the reality of ethical behavior. For example, a position requiring impartiality, like a judge, also requires the appearance of impartiality. If the arresting officer appears to be buddy-buddy with the court bailiffs, the scales of justice are tipped because the defendant's expectation of a fair trial is diminished.

Similarly, when a person in a leadership position does something ethical that appears unethical, her followers may get the idea that they're part of an unethical organization, or worse, that unethical behavior is all right. The ethical leader has an obligation to explain herself when she takes an action that might appear ethically wrong or questionable.

This obligation is widely misunderstood. Leaders often avoid explaining their behavior to subordinates for a variety of reasons. They don't want to appear defensive, or they don't have a satisfactory explanation, or they may just belong to the "never explain" crowd. But since leaders teach by everything they do—walking, talking, standing still, or being silent—it's important that they explain questionable-looking behavior.

Explanation is especially important because leaders are in the business of changing things, and many people's ethical grounding is based on what is. "That's the way it's always been done" is often a simple and comfortable guide to what's permissible or ethical. Since leaders are in the business of not doing things the way they've always been done, their behavior is easily misunderstood. Indeed, leaders are often in the business of smashing organizational norms of behavior. When they do, they'll need to make it clear that breaking the norms is part of the new way of doing business, not just an attitude of "the rules don't apply to me."

The "never explain" school of leadership doesn't work when the leader's action may appear unethical. Neither does the "watch what I do, not what I say" school. Absent a clear explanation, people are left to infer that the leader is a law unto herself—a particularly bad lesson in ethics.

While "How would it look in the paper?" is a good question to ask before making a business decision, "How would it look to the staff?" is the more important question affecting the ethical health of an organization. A better test of the ethics of a hypothetical action is "Can I explain it to my mother (or to my child)?" If either of those questions makes you uncomfortable, you can be pretty sure that in your gut you believe the action is unethical. For ethical people like us, that may be the best of all tests.

# 15. Charlotte Mayor Resigns After Arrest on Corruption Charges*

## *Mark Washburn, Jim Morrill and Michael Gordon*

Charlotte Mayor Patrick Cannon was arrested Wednesday on public corruption charges, with the FBI alleging he took tens of thousands of dollars in bribes—including $20,000 in cash delivered in a briefcase last month to the mayor's office where he also solicited $1 million more.

Cannon resigned Wednesday evening. He was arrested that morning at a South-Park apartment used by undercover FBI agents after the mayor turned up expecting another payment, sources say.

The case against the former mayor alleges that in return for money, trips, hotel rooms and access to a luxury SouthPark apartment, Cannon promised to help agents posing as potential commercial investors with zoning, parking and other city-related issues.

According to officials, Cannon turned himself in to federal marshals after learning of a warrant for his arrest. He was immediately taken before U.S. Magistrate Judge David Keesler of Charlotte.

Cannon was charged with theft and bribery after the FBI sting operation, said Anne Tompkins, U.S. Attorney for the Western District of North Carolina. He was released on $25,000 unsecured bond, pending indictment, which could come as early as next week. The court file shows Charlotte attorney James Ferguson is representing Cannon. Ferguson did not return a phone call Wednesday afternoon.

If convicted on all charges, the 47-year-old faces up to 50 years in prison and $1.5 million in fines. The case is part of an ongoing investigation, according to the U.S. Attorney's office.

Cannon was the longest-serving elected official in Charlotte, having joined the city council in 1993. He is the region's highest-ranking official to be charged in a corruption case since former N.C. House speaker Jim Black of Matthews, also a Democrat, pleaded guilty in 2007.

Cannon's arrest follows a four-year investigation, which stretched from a Las Vegas resort to the mayor's office on the 15th floor of the Government Center, which Cannon has occupied for only five months.

Authorities said Cannon took bribes from undercover FBI agents five times—the most recent on Feb. 21 when he collected $20,000 in cash in the mayor's office.

Tompkins said undercover agents showered Cannon with more than $48,000 in

---

*Originally published as Mark Washburn, Jim Morrill and Michael Gordon, "Charlotte Mayor Resigns After Arrest on Corruption Charges," *The Charlotte Observer*, March 26, 2014. Reprinted with permission of the publisher.

cash, airline tickets, a trip to Las Vegas, and use of a luxury SouthPark apartment in exchange for "the use of his official position," Tompkins said.

FBI agents searched the mayor's office, his home at Cumnor Lane and his offices at E-Z Parking Inc. at 312 West Trade St. They seized financial records, phones, computers and other electronic devices. They were also searching for a leather briefcase that agents say they stuffed with cash for the February visit to the mayor's office.

Cannon made a brief court appearance Wednesday at the federal courthouse in uptown where he was told, among other things, that he could not be in possession of firearms.

Cannon declined to comment when approached by a WCNC-TV reporter as he left the building. "At this point, there's nothing to respond to," Cannon said.

### Fanning the Cash

The federal investigation began in 2010. Originally, the FBI focused on other Charlotte targets but focused on Cannon in 2011, according to an affidavit from Eric Davis, an FBI special agent who specializes in public corruption cases.

At the time the probe began, Cannon was a city council member and mayor pro tem.

An undercover agent passed himself off as a business manager for a venture capital company based in Chicago. According to the affidavit, he met Cannon in November 2010, telling the city council member he and his investors were interested in opening a nightclub and bar in Charlotte.

Ultimately, the agent chose a property in uptown that had parking problems and required zoning changes. In subsequent meetings, Cannon described his relationship and influence over certain city departments and employees, including the zoning board.

On a Dec. 12, 2012, Cannon met an un-

dercover agent at Capitol Grille, an upscale steakhouse on North Tryon Street—and the same restaurant where Black was accused of accepting bribes from a group of chiropractors years earlier.

Cannon asked the undercover agent if he'd be interested in investing in a business Cannon planned to start called HERS, which would sell a feminine hygiene product nationally. The agent agreed to give Cannon a $12,500 "zero-percent return on investment" loan in return for his assistance in getting approval for the zoning needed for the nightclub.

But Cannon said he needed $40,000. "I can do something for around $12,500. Any ideas how I can close the gap and get me some of that capital to get me started to pull this thing in?"

In exchange for the money, the agent asked Cannon to "make sure I don't run into any problems," the affidavit said.

Cannon replied: "I will definitely help you out. So you just want me to help you out on that front?"

At a Jan. 17, 2013, meeting in SouthPark, the undercover agent gave Cannon the $12,500 in cash by putting it on a coffee table in front of him. Cannon, according to the affidavit, looked nervously toward a window and covered the money with a folder.

After the agent closed the blinds, Cannon put the bills to his ear and fanned them.

### "That's not how I flow"

In a later conversation with the undercover agent, Cannon tried to characterize his acceptance of the money as a business investment unrelated to his public office, the affidavit says.

In laying out his philosophy as a public official, Cannon told the agent that he would have helped him even without the $12,500. "I'm not one of those Chicago- or Detroit-type folk. That's not how I flow."

In an ironic aside during that same meeting, Cannon said that he looked good "in an orange necktie, but not in an orange suit."

Agents said they gave Cannon ample opportunity to return the money, but he never did.

When Cannon announced his candidacy for mayor on May 21, 2013, he invited the undercover agent to attend, the affidavit says.

That month, the city council approved a streetcar line to west Charlotte. Weeks later, a second undercover agent approached Cannon and said his company was interested in investing along the streetcar's path. He told Cannon he needed his help persuading potential investors, and he'd fly Cannon to Las Vegas to do it.

## Las Vegas: Lies for Cash

As part of a trip with the agent, Cannon agreed to create "the false impression with the investors" that Cannon had had a long relationship with the undercover agents, the affidavit says.

In June, during discussions before the trip, Cannon raised the question of how he would be compensated for his role. When the agent replied, "I want to take care of you on this," Cannon immediately suggested a contribution to his ongoing mayoral campaign. But the agent refused to pay Cannon before they took the trip. Cannon, according to affidavit, continued to press for the money up front.

In the end, the agent flew Cannon and his wife to Las Vegas on July 1 and paid for hotel room. He also gave Cannon $1,000 in cash at the hotel.

During the subsequent meeting, four FBI agents posing as businessmen promised to invest up to $25 million each for commercial property along the streetcar line.

Again, Cannon boasted of his ability and willingness to make things happen. "Being around for 20 years has helped me a little bit, I think. I've gone through probably four police chiefs, five city managers, three mayors, something like that."

Asked by one of the investors how long and often Cannon could assist with the project, Cannon replied: "As long as I'm elected."

## A Second Vegas Payoff

Afterward, the second undercover agent had a private meeting with Cannon. The affidavit says they reached Cannon's wife, Trenna, by speakerphone, and she personally thanked the agent for the $1,000 from the day before. After the call, the agent paid Cannon another $5,000 in cash for his presentation to the investors. Cannon put the envelope containing the bills in the breast pocket of his suit.

Then Cannon asked whether he could work with the second agent "on some private deals," the affidavit says. "Your value to us, obviously, is the position that you're in and that you can pick up the phone and make things happen for us that, from our perspective, is absolutely invaluable There's no reason why it can't be a win-win relationship for both of us," the agent told him.

After returning to Charlotte, Cannon met with an undercover agent in a SouthPark apartment rented by the FBI for $2,100 a month and equipped with hidden cameras. Agents gave Cannon an additional $10,000 for his work in Las Vegas.

Throughout the investigation, authorities said, Cannon had asked for keys or access to the apartment. The agent told Cannon that he was about to drop the lease on the apartment but would continue to pay rent if Cannon wanted to use it. When Cannon got his own key, he told the agent excitedly, "Aw man!"

## Payoff in February

On Feb. 21 this year, an undercover agent brought one of the phony Las Vegas investors to Cannon's office in the Government Center. During that meeting, the affidavit says, Cannon received a leather Fossil briefcase containing $20,000 in cash. Then, Cannon asked for substantially more.

"I told Trenna she has a point," Cannon told the agents.

"She has what?" the agent responded.

"A point, one percent," Cannon replied.

According to the affidavit, Cannon was asking for a 1 percent payoff from the potential $125 million project, or $1.25 million in all.

Then the mayor and the agent grappled for the best way to get the $20,000 out of the office. Since the briefcase had passed through security when the agent arrived, they talked about how it would be best if he took it out, and perhaps meet near the airport for the hand-off. In the end, the briefcase stayed in Cannon's office, the affidavit says.

"I just got to be conscious about that kind of stuff here," Cannon said.

Cannon had scheduled a meeting about the payments for Wednesday with the agent, according to the affidavit.

## Trial Likely

On the morning of his arrest Wednesday, Cannon spent about an hour on the phone with Gov. Pat McCrory, himself a former Charlotte mayor, to discuss the city's airport, according to McCrory.

Cannon then drove to SouthPark, where federal agents were waiting, a source confirmed.

If Cannon is indicted next week as expected, prominent Charlotte defense attorney Jim Cooney says he expects the case to go to trial.

"If he takes a felony or pleads guilty, it's over for him. Everything he has always worked for is lost," Cooney said.

If Cannon alleges entrapment by the FBI, Cooney said his attorneys face a difficult legal task.

"You've got to show that you wouldn't have done it otherwise," Cooney said. "Here, the issue is, how did you target him to begin with? Was he having financial problems? Did you know that? Were you playing to a weakness? The defense attorney may argue that he tried to give some of the money back.

"In the end, it depends on what the jury feels about what the government has done." Did they catch a felon, Cooney said, or "take an otherwise law-abiding person and convince him to commit a crime that he normally wouldn't have committed."

If convicted, Cooney and other Charlotte attorneys expect the former mayor to spend a significant amount of time in prison.

"I know very few judges who consider a conviction like this anything else than a very, very serious matter," Cooney said.

# 16. The Costs of Public Corruption*
## Patrick Fitzgerald

Vigorous prosecution of public corruption has always been vital to our country. Public corruption takes a heavy toll on our communities. Corruption gives unfair advantages to those willing to break the law: public officials, their relatives and friends, and those who willingly pay bribes to gain public contracts and other government actions. But there are many victims: both those who are shaken down for bribes and kickbacks, and the members of the general public, who pay for corruption through inflated costs and loss of faith in government. With tightening budgets throughout all levels of government, vigorous enforcement is even more important than ever.

The residents of the Northern District of Illinois in particular have suffered many consequences as a result of generations of corrupt state and local government officials. Illinois roads were made more dangerous when state employees issued drivers licenses to truck drivers in exchange for bribes, intended to finance campaign contributions to former Gov. George Ryan's political war chest. Some of the unqualified truck drivers given licenses as a result of that corrupt scheme caused serious accidents, the most horrific resulting in the death of six children whose family van exploded when it ran over a piece of equipment that fell off a truck driven by a bribe-paying driver.

There are also financial consequences to corruption. Millions of taxpayer dollars are paid out on contracts and other government benefits steered by public officials to insiders who, in turn, shower financial benefits on those public officials and their associates. Recently, Chicago taxpayers saw hundreds of thousands of city dollars funneled to sham minority-owned trucking companies under a program that served to enrich city workers with kickbacks.

Corruption can also change the face of a community. Over and over, for several decades, some Chicago aldermen have given away public benefits, like zoning rights and city-owned land, to real estate developers who, in turn, have lined the aldermen's pockets and campaign purses.

Undoubtedly the most harmful consequence of endemic public corruption in a community is the apathy that it engenders—the culture of acceptance. Over many years of seeing corruption in almost every facet of government, many residents of a community begin to simply accept corruption as the immutable status quo. They come to assume government is broken and

*Originally published as Patrick Fitzgerald, "The Costs of Public Corruption—and the Need for the Public to Fight Back," http://www.justice.gov/usao/priority-areas/financial-fraud/public-corruption (July 8, 2015). Reprinted with permission of the author.

ineffective and destined to function corruptly. The consequences of this culture of acceptance in a community are many. Some residents simply disengage from the political process and no longer trust their government to function well or in their interest. Other residents may come to believe they must engage in corruption in order to gain government benefits themselves. Still others will begin to look the other way when they witness corrupt transactions. And honest folks are discouraged from entering politics or suffer from the skepticism engendered by others' misdeeds.

The culture of acceptance makes it very difficult to detect, investigate and prosecute corruption. Although there are a variety of federal statutes that we use to prosecute corruption, including fraud, bribery and extortion statutes, as well as RICO, prosecutions cannot be successful without truthful witnesses and willing cooperators. Because voluntary assistance from the public in corruption cases is often hard to come by, we use many investigative techniques that assist us in gathering evidence and requiring cooperation, such as the use of grand jury subpoenas, grants of immunity, consensual recordings, and wiretaps. Using a wide range of these tools to vigorously investigate corruption can lead to convictions of corrupt officials once thought to be above the law, which, more effectively than anything else, demonstrates that the public need not accept corruption. Successful prosecutions that show that no one is beyond the reach of corruption statutes serve to encourage, empower and mobilize members of the public to work to change the culture of acceptance. We are grateful in the Northern District of Illinois that juries time and time again have rejected the argument that corruption is acceptable because it is the "Chicago way."

In addition to the need for effective prosecutions, federal prosecutors must engage in community outreach to ensure that all residents of a community know that they can have a voice in stopping corruption and that they need not accept corruption in any degree—at any level of government. In the Northern District of Illinois, we try to send the message as often as we can that community involvement is critical in rooting out corruption. We regularly communicate that residents must take an active role in their government so that it properly functions for them. We also emphasize that the vigorous efforts of law enforcement should not be used as a rationale for the community to stay silent. The public's refusal to accept corruption is the first line of defense in the fight against it.

While corruption will never be eliminated from our communities, vigorous investigation and prosecution of corrupt officials can serve to reduce its harmful effects and, most importantly, greatly diminish the culture of acceptance.

# 17. Whistleblowers Anonymous*

## Tom Arrandale

Kevin Keenan's epiphany came on an October morning six years ago. At the time, he was Montana's chief water-quality regulator and had worked in the state's water-pollution program since earning his chemistry degree in 1972. He knew, going into a meeting with the Montana Environmental Quality Council that state legislators and other members of the panel expected the rote testimony he'd delivered many times before. Instead, he says, "I decided while I was standing in front of them that I would tell them the truth about the corruption in the program I was administering."

He told the startled advisory council that although environmental statutes required that penalties be calculated to fit the crime, his bosses preferred to give big polluters a slap on the hand. After corporate executives asked the governor's office to inquire about a case, Keenan's supervisors negotiated lenient settlements. When a Bozeman developer openly defied the state's subdivision regulations, two successive pollution-control directors misplaced the file after Keenan recommended prosecuting. As he recalls it now, he told the board that "the political people who control state environmental agencies think environmental law is something you wink and nod about."

Keenan then called his bosses to alert them to his revelations. That was the beginning of the end of his government career. During the next two years, he says, supervisors took away his staff, left him out of meetings and forbid him to meet with legislators. Finally, thoroughly frustrated, he decided to take early retirement at age 46. "They forced me out of something I'd wanted to do all my life," he says. "By the time I retired, I thought we would have cleaned up the entire country."

Despite all of his disappointments, Keenan remains as militant about Montana's environmental issues as he ever was. He stayed in Helena and set up the first state capital office for a feisty whistleblowers' organization called Public Employees for Environmental Responsibility. Keenan says he took the PEER job in 1996 "to give ethical employees still inside the agency a way to get information into public hands" without making the sacrifice that he himself endured when he could no longer hold his tongue.

The organization, which was founded a decade ago by a former U.S. Forest Service employee and is based in Washington, D.C., has opened chapters in Helena, Sacramento, Austin, Tallahassee and five other state capitals, as well as popped up in other states from time to time to work with dissident employees. PEER's stealthy brand of advocacy

*Originally published as Tom Arrandale, "Whistleblowers Anonymous," *Governing*, June 2000. Reprinted with permission of the publisher.

is increasingly alarming pollution-control commissioners around the country.

In the past few years, top-level administrators have concluded that governments need to do more to help businesses comply with emission standards, so they've shifted resources away from relying primarily on old-school, command-and-control-type enforcement. The way many of their lieutenants still look at the world, however, that's getting too close to the polluters they should be cracking down on. Every state agency has still got gung-ho regulators on its staff. Most are lawyers, engineers, biologists and other scientific specialists who came to work for pollution control agencies in the 1970s and '80s as governments geared up to enforce newly enacted environmental statutes. Some have risen to become bureau and division chiefs, and they share Keenan's deeply held conviction that tough by- the-book enforcement of pollution control laws is the only way to clean up the environment.

And that's whom Keenan and his PEER colleagues say they speak for. Its operatives usually oppose "customer friendly" regulation in apocalyptic good-versus-evil terms, contending that it stands with righteous public servants to combat sleazy political manipulators. In Rhode Island, Jan H. Reitsma, the state's Department of Environmental Management director, says, "people trying to make changes have been attacked in a very ferocious way" by PEER.

Although PEER doesn't compile membership lists, Jeff Ruch, the national executive director, says its supporters tend to be veteran employees "who have gone through a journey of disillusionment and are motivated by what's happening to their life's work." To enlist these regulators in the cause, PEER guarantees them confidentiality. It's just too easy, PEER's leaders explain, for agency managers to devastate a subordinate's career through transfers, formal rebukes and more subtle personnel decisions. "These people are scared to death," Ruch

says. "What happened to Kevin Keenan is emblematic of the problem."

But the clandestine methods that PEER practices to provide allies with cover are irksome to their superiors. Sometimes PEER passes mid-level state regulators' complaints along to the U.S. Environmental Protection Agency in the hope that the feds will intervene. In other cases, state workers have turned internal agency documents over to PEER, which then gives them cover by filing federal Freedom of Information Act requests to obtain the same papers itself. PEER officials frequently pass damaging documents along to major newspapers in a state, helping reporters research investigative stories built around employee allegations. The organization also drums up controversy by publishing snappily titled "white papers," often authored anonymously by agency workers. PEER draws considerable public attention by distributing surveys that invite employees to vent dissatisfaction without giving out their names.

So far, however, PEER has generated far more public controversy than real change in environmental policy. "PEER hits the headlines, but they never follow up and pinpoint things that are illegal," says Mark Simonich, director of Montana's Department of Environmental Quality and Keenan's former boss. "The other thing they never do is bring forward proposed solutions."

In Connecticut, PEER conducted what turned out to be brief assaults on Governor John G. Rowland's environmental policies. Two years ago, with Rowland up for reelection, the group published an anonymous white paper, authored by Department of Environmental Protection employees and called "A Friend in High Places." It contended that the agency was going easy on big polluters who were important Rowland supporters. Among other charges, PEER alleged that the governor had assigned a former campaign fundraiser as the DEP commissioner's executive assistant to watch out for corporate interests. The group contended that agency directors refused to pass cases along for Connecticut's Democratic attorney general to prosecute.

A month after Rowland was reelected, a state General Assembly investigations committee released a report concluding that the DEP had been indifferent to "staff confusion and concerns." The report didn't confirm the most sensational charges, however, and PEER thereafter "departed the same way they arrived, in the dead of night," says Arthur Roque, Jr., Rowland's environmental commissioner.

More recently, PEER has jumped into an ongoing fray in neighboring Rhode Island. PEER attorneys are now representing Beverly M. Migliore, the former chief scientist in the state's hazardous waste program, in an acrimonious legal case against the Department of Environmental Management, where she's worked for 13 years. After Migliore objected to a 1996 reorganization that split Rhode Island's enforcement and permitting operations, she contends that superiors excluded her from meetings, denied travel requests and threatened disciplinary action for disclosing agency data to PEER.

"I thought I was doing a good job, but all of a sudden everything I did was being second-guessed or just sitting on the shelf," Migliore says. Last summer, a U.S. Department of Labor administrative law judge awarded her $843,000 in damages for the harassment she alleges, although state officials have appealed the judgment. Meanwhile, Migliore is still working at the DEM, although the agency has rubbed some salt in the wounds by assigning her to a newly created compliance-assistance office. "I'm still here, but they won't let me do anything of substance," Migliore says. "This is not the career that I hoped for."

Reitsma, who took over Rhode Island's besieged agency last year, has tried to defuse controversies by appointing a department ombudsman to conduct independent, and in some cases confidential, fact-finding investigations when employees file complaints. Migliore says she came up with the ombudsman idea herself, but she doubts it will solve the problem. "If you're somebody like me," she adds, "there's nobody else to go to except PEER."

With the 2000 presidential campaign heating up, PEER, like other environmental groups, is taking aim at Republican Governor George W. Bush's record in Texas. In California, the Sacramento office is now preparing to challenge Democratic Governor Gray Davis for not following up on campaign promises to give environmental concerns high priority. To date, however, PEER has made its most substantive policy impact with the assaults it began four years ago on Florida's pollution agency.

PEER's initial target was Virginia Wetherell, Florida's Department of Environmental Protection secretary under the late Democratic Governor Lawton Chiles. Allegations revealed by PEER's employee surveys inspired a grand jury inquiry into DEP's Pensacola office operations and a state police investigation of pollution-enforcement efforts. No prosecutions resulted; but by the time Wetherell left her post, she'd grown so irritated that she withdrew permission for PEER to conduct lunchtime "brown-bag" discussions at agency offices.

On one issue, however, PEER's persistence in Florida paid off. In 1998, Steven A. Medina, a former Florida DEP attorney who now represents PEER's chapter in that state, petitioned Chiles' cabinet to tighten oversight on how the agency protects the state's submerged coastal and streambed lands against over-development. Internal department audits had suggested that the agency's district officials were approving damaging marina projects, but PEER contended that agency officials weren't alerting the governor to the problems.

When Republican Governor Jeb Bush took

over last year, he named former Massachusetts environmental commissioner David Struhs to head Florida's agency. Struhs met with PEER leaders and quickly agreed to look into the submerged lands program. In addition, Struhs sent a memo to all DEP employees prohibiting managers throughout the agency from retaliating against staff members who question policy decisions. Although Medina says some mid-level Florida officials still try to intimidate dissidents, Struhs credits PEER for focusing attention on problems in the program.

There's nothing wrong with public employees belonging to advocacy groups, and some are long-standing members of industry-led trade associations. But state commissioners worry that PEER's abrasive style is damaging employee morale at a time when the agencies are struggling to transform their traditional culture and implement more cooperative regulatory approaches. "There's a need for whistleblowing here and there, but we better make sure it gets very carefully separated from dissatisfaction among people who have been in government a number of years and are not willing to go through changes," Rhode Island's Reitsma says. "When that distinction gets blurred, that means whistleblowing is stifling innovation."

Nonetheless, it's often difficult to walk that fine line. Keenan acknowledges that before leaving the DEQ in Montana, he allowed his concerns about policy to overlap with personal gripes about his bosses' conduct. "I had a million issues by the time I was done," he says, "but that only makes you look like you're crazy."

Simonich, who took over as DEQ director the year before Keenan made his exit, describes Keenan as "very much a true believer, but he's taken his personal beliefs to an extreme."

Helena's a small-town capital, and Keenan doesn't indulge in the holier-than-thou personal attacks that PEER has launched against other state administrators. Still, it rankles him that Simonich, a former timber-industry executive, has no formal education in the environmental field. Nor did Governor Marc Racicot's two previous DEQ directors come up through the ranks, and Keenan says they've all turned enforcement into a politically driven exercise "that disrupts the system that long-time employees are now attempting to defend." He is convinced that "the vast majority of classically trained experts on the environment share PEER's belief" in traditional regulatory approaches.

In the eyes of Montana reporters and environmentalists, Keenan's exile makes him all the more credible when he contends that Montana's regulators have gotten too cozy with companies they should instead be punishing. That's because he knows the ins and outs of regulating water quality, and he's quick to pick up the rumblings when former colleagues aren't happy with agency decisions.

On average, Keenan gets a half-dozen or so calls a month from unhappy Montana employees. Before taking on somebody's cause, Keenan helps them weed out personality conflicts, then suggests ways to relay what he sees as legitimate concerns to the public. But Racicot administration officials say Keenan is too ready to assume the worst about the agency that once employed him.

For his part, the governor says, "Kevin and I have known each other a long time" and they've traded non-political elbows as opponents in Helena church-league basketball games. But Racicot defends the way Simonich has run DEQ and concludes that PEER hasn't proven the misdeeds that Keenan keeps alleging. Some disenchantment is inevitable in an agency that makes tough policy calls every day, the governor adds. "You could find the same thing within the environmental regulatory agency in any state. There are no easy decisions over there."

# 18. Regaining the Public's Trust*

## G. Edward DeSeve

Recently, I had a conversation with a serious student of government. He was trying to develop a series of ballot initiatives designed to improve government performance. We discussed the relationship between better performance and getting more revenue for government programs. He said that better performance was important because it promoted more trust in government, and he argued that the lack of resources available to government reflected the fact that people didn't trust government to spend their money wisely. He was right.

Trust is essential not just for obtaining resources but also for making government work effectively. Often, we get lost in the techniques of management and forget about the essential bond of trust between the public and their governments. We focus on outsourcing, performance management, cloud computing and other techniques while we ignore the basics. I believe that there are six factors that are paramount in changing the public's perception of government and regaining their trust:

**Honesty**: Ethical behavior is often taken for granted until there is a breach. Ethics training in government is like sex education in middle school: Everyone has to take it but most people don't think they need it. Promoting honesty must go beyond mere ethics training. It has to be built into a culture that won't tolerate even small lies or a little bit of cheating. Schools of public policy and management should make the study of what constitutes ethical behavior mandatory.

**Efficiency**: This is making sure that government delivers "value for money." Producing high-quality public goods and services should be done as inexpensively as possible. All the techniques of private industry should be utilized, and measurement of efficiency should be rigorous and comparative.

**Transparency**: In my younger years, I wouldn't have included this one. However, if you are trying to gain people's trust, they have to be able to see what is going on for themselves. Perception is often reality, so showing the public what is really happening can inspire more-positive perception. New developments in technology—including geospatial mapping and rapid feedback communications—enable government to operate both efficiently and transparently at the same time.

**Accountability**: This is simply telling people what you are going to do and then giving them an accounting of how you did. It works at the level of outputs and at the level of outcomes. Many performance-management

*Originally published as G. Edward DeSeve, "Regaining the Public's Trust," *Governing*, December 21, 2011. Reprinted with permission of the publisher.

systems have been tried and found wanting. Often they are seen as something from the outside that is imposed on managers. That is backwards. Performance management should stretch from "the shop floor to the top floor" and should allow managers at every level to demonstrate how well they are doing their jobs. Pride in doing a good job and performance management should go hand in hand.

**Good policy choices**: These start with good policy-development processes that translate public needs and conditions in the external environment into a coherent set of actionable strategies. Reasonable people will differ on what constitutes good policy, but the electorate knows it when they see it. Again, bringing transparency to policy development and even including the public in developing policies will lead to greater trust.

**Positive outcomes**: Implementation of policy choices honestly, efficiently, transparently and accountably should produce positive outcomes. If it doesn't, managers should rapidly evaluate why the expected outcomes weren't achieved and take corrective action. Program evaluation has fallen out of favor, perhaps because it was seen as something done to managers, not by them.

As with creating an accountability framework, evaluation of outcomes should be in the hands of managers themselves, aided by technical experts if needed.

All of that sounds very simple, doesn't it? If the process were purely linear with no random events, it might be just that easy. However, government is both nonlinear and often random. New York Mayor Rudolph Giuliani was doing just fine managing the city until 9/11 changed everything. It is a great tribute to him and the public workers of New York that panic was avoided and services were quickly restored.

Another element of complexity is that the factors described above have to be executed simultaneously in a dynamic environment. Public servants are sometimes compared to jet mechanics working on the engines while the aircraft is in flight. This may be going a little too far, but feedback from the public can be instantaneous, and change is often the only certainty.

We can't control all of the variables, and the hardest to control is the public's perception of our actions. In 1946, philanthropist Joseph N. Pew, Jr., said, "Tell the truth and trust the people." Today, we have no choice but to go back to basics and try to regain the people's trust.

# 19. New York Corruption Investigation Trends*

## Chelsea A. Binns

New York City investigators have a new way of fighting corruption. They are now leveraging "big data" technology to analyze large, disparate datasets. The result is quicker, more efficient investigations, producing evidence that would not otherwise have been detected.

Corruption is pervasive in New York. The State Integrity Investigation gave New York a "D" grade for corruption risk, finding it to be a "defining characteristic" of the state. New York has recently pushed to improve its methods of corruption investigation. A new data analytics tool, used by the state's Moreland Commission, yielded significant results toward that effort. Notably, the recent arrest of Assembly Speaker Sheldon Silver on corruption charges was precipitated by evidence produced by that commission.

In 2013, New York State, under The Moreland Act, now Section 6 of the Executive Law, established a Special Commission to Investigate Public Corruption. Attorney General Eric Schneiderman deputized them as Deputy Attorneys General, empowering them to subpoena witnesses, administer oaths, hold hearings and summon "any books or papers deemed relevant or mate-

rial." The Commission made significant findings, "yield[ing] more than enough information to warrant sounding the alarm for immediate legislative action."

This tool, originally developed for use in counter-terrorism, integrated vast datasets, including intelligence gathered by investigators. Their dataset included phone records, emails, payroll data, timesheets, reimbursements, legislative office budgets and swipe card access data. Investigators also mined publicly available data about elected officials from social media sites and other databases. In their report, the Commission described their investigative approach. They largely applied traditional investigative techniques, which were augmented with emerging technologies. The traditional approaches included document review, research, interview and undercover work. The emerging technology was a proprietary data analytics tool, which examined large-scale data sets.

The technology proved to be effective. The Commission said the data analytics spotted trends, which were otherwise undetectable. The tool produced intelligence, which "connect[ed] the dots" and enabled investigators to create dossiers on companies, organizations and persons of interest,

---

*Originally published as Chelsea A. Binns, "New York Corruption Investigation Trends," *PA Times*, February 6, 2015. Reprinted with permission of the author and publisher.

and to construct timelines and relationship maps.

As a result, the Commission located suspected fraud and corruption. For example, they found several "pay to play" arrangements; loopholes allowing wealthy donors to side step political contribution limits; use of campaign funds for personal items; double-dipping; conflicts of interest violations; issues with legislatively-directed funding grants and suspected corruption issues in connection with the State Board of Elections. The Commission was also able to identify no-show jobs, instances of nepotism and potentially improper use of public funds.

In one case, the Commission determined that a company was making payoffs to the chairs of the legislative committee that controlled and regulated that company's industry. Because the payments were made via unrelated shell companies, traditional investigative work would have been unlikely to detect this fraud.

The use of technology in investigations is becoming more widespread. In their report, the Commission said numerous government agencies are using similar analytical platforms in a wide variety of complex criminal, civil and intelligence-gathering matters.

Another New York agency employing similar technology is New York City's Department of Investigation (DOI). Formed in the 1870s, DOI is one of the oldest law enforcement agencies in the country. DOI investigates City employees and contractors engaged in fraudulent activities or unethical conduct.

During Commissioner Rose Gill Hearn's administration, from 2002–2013, DOI made 6,000 corruption arrests, resulting from thousands of investigations.

Like the State's Moreland Commission, DOI is also employing the use of data mapping in fraud and corruption investigations. DOI's new Commissioner, Mark Peters, ap-pointed in January 2014, is developing a data-mapping platform to enhance their investigations.

Peters discussed the use of investigative technology in his January 30, 2014, testimony before the City Council Committee on Rules, Privileges and Elections, as reported by Jennifer Baek in CityLand. Peters plans to use technology to cross-compare multiple datasets, and to discern patterns, producing "red flags" which would not otherwise be detected. Per Peters, the technology will "root out vulnerabilities and discourage corruption, fraud and abuse before it happens." In developing the tool, DOI will isolate relevant data from hundreds of repositories and work with developers to design the technology platform to run comparisons against the datasets.

It is interesting to note that DOI has successfully used technology in their investigations in the past. DOI previously used data mapping to uncover pension, unemployment and housing fraud. In their 2013 Fiscal Year Annual Report, DOI reported using technology to analyze city employee pension system data and uncovered fraud targeting the public retirement system.

DOI has also previously leveraged investigative technology to prevent fraud and corruption. Following the pension fraud case, DOI worked to establish a stronger data-matching program that compared pension rolls against national sources on recent deaths, leading to timely identification of fraud.

Despite its value, Peters says the technology won't replace traditional investigative work. Rather, it will allow DOI investigators to work more efficiently.

Overall, evidence demonstrates the use of technology in investigations in New York is yielding important findings. Given its increasing popularity and investigative value, it is likely that such technology will someday be commonplace in the investigative process.

# 20. Lack of Oversight led to Ex-Water Agency Head's Conviction[*]

## Dan Ivers

Newark, New Jersey, officials said they were dismayed by the former head of the Newark Watershed Conservation Development Corporation's guilty plea on corruption-related charges earlier this week—an outcome many felt could have been prevented.

Linda Watkins-Brashear, who presided over the non-profit agency until 2013—just one year before it was dissolved amid widespread allegations of corruption and mismanagement—is facing up to 23 years in prison and $350,000 in fines for conspiracy and filing a false tax return.

She is the second person to plead guilty to charges related to the scandal, though many in the state's largest city consider it a reflection of an agency run amok thanks to the wandering eye of now–U.S. Sen. Cory Booker, who was mayor over the entirety of Watkins' tenure.

"The city … allowed all of these quasi-governmental agencies to run on their own without any oversight," said Central Ward Councilwoman Gayle Chaneyfield Jenkins. "It's just a recipe for disaster."

A spokesman for Booker's office acknowledged a request for comment Monday afternoon but did not provide any statement or additional information.

In filing, Booker denies knowledge of Newark watershed schemes.

The freshman senator said he acted in "good faith" while overseeing the now-bankrupt agency and took immediate action after learning of possible wrongdoing

Questions about the NWCDC began to arise early in Booker's tenure, with investigations by the *Star-Ledger* and citizens groups such as Newark Water Group turning up a series of financial misdeeds.

Those findings were affirmed by the state comptroller's office in 2014, when it issued a report detailing millions in misappropriated funds, doomed stock market ventures, mysterious severance packages and the awarding of dubious contracts to administrators' relatives and friends.

South Ward Councilman John Sharpe James, who was among a group of critics of the NWCDC during Booker's time as mayor, said Watkins-Brashear's guilty plea was bittersweet vindication for those who had long harbored suspicions about the agency's dealings. He heaped much of the blame on the media, who he claimed wrote him and others off as token dissenters rather than fully investigate their allegations.

---

*Originally published as Dan Ivers, "Newark Officials Say Lack of Oversight Led to Ex-Water Agency Head's Conviction," http://www.nj.com/essex/index.ssf/2015/12/newark_officials_say_lack_of_oversight_led_to_ex-w.html, December 23, 2015. Reprinted with permission of the author and publisher.

"It's just another instance where the residents of Newark complained about a situation, were ignored for the most part, and later we come to find out $1 million is missing," he said.

Bill Chappel, a spokesman for the Newark Water Group issued a statement following her plea calling her conduct "as flagrant a violation of the public trust as you could ever find."

"This was an entity that veered out of control years ago in the way it operated and in the way it misspent the public's money when it thought no one was looking," he said.

Mayor Ras Baraka, who had also been a leading opponent of the agency during his time as South Ward Councilman, declined to comment on Watkins-Brashear's admissions.

NJ comptroller alleges rampant corruption at Newark watershed, director pleads fifth.

The comptroller criticized the city for lax oversight of the watershed agency under former Mayor Cory Booker.

Established in the 1970s, the NWCDC was charged with protecting roughly 35,000 acres of forest and reservoirs that provided drinking water for as many as 500,000 across Newark and North Jersey. By 2012, it also controlled the delivery of water to its entire service area.

The NWCDC was officially dissolved in early 2013, though Baraka helped form a new board in December 2014, which quickly voted to file for bankruptcy in an attempt to recover the assets allegedly stolen from the agency.

Earlier this year, court-appointed trustees filed a lawsuit against Booker and 17 others claiming they played a role in the mismanagement, saying the senator had failed to provide proper oversight despite his role as chairman of the organization's board.

Attorneys for Booker have denied those allegations, responding in court filings that he took immediate action once concrete evidence of wrongdoing had been presented.

As part of Watkins-Brashear's guilty plea, she has been ordered to pay $999,000 in restitution to the victims of her crimes. Because the NWCDC no longer exists, however, a federal judge will determine where the money ultimately ends up.

Chaneyfield said she was "saddened" by the fate of a woman she long considered a friend and dedicated city employee. However, she felt the scandal provided a difficult lesson for Newark in respect to its oversight of its various agencies entrusted with public dollars.

"The mere fact that Brick City Development Corp, the Parking Authority, the Newark Watershed and all these other quasi-governmental agencies that did not have the oversight that they should have was a disservice to the residents of the city of Newark," she said.

"Not everyone gets charged when there's a criminal act, but that doesn't mean that they weren't implicit in allowing it to take place."

# 21. How We're Losing the War on Corruption*

## Mark Funkhouser

While the world was watching the General Services Administration scandal, in which a few hundred thousand of the federal government's 3.6 trillion dollars were wasted, little notice was taken of the case in which the comptroller of Dixon, Ill., allegedly stole $30 million from a town with an annual budget of only $8 million to $9 million. The (you'll excuse the expression) money quote from the mayor of Dixon: "The annual audit didn't show anything. Auditors even commented that we were doing fine with our cash controls." Now, of course, the town is in a world of hurt.

The citizens of Dixon hardly are alone in their pain. Recently the *Los Angeles Times* did an article that focused on the enormous legal bills incurred by a number of California cities in which corruption occurred. In Lynwood, the mayor was convicted of funneling about $500,000 in city money into a company he secretly owned. In Bell, the former city administrator and other officials were arrested for allegedly stealing millions of dollars from the city by giving themselves exorbitant salaries and benefits. The Times article points out that in addition to such direct losses, citizens are saddled with enormous legal bills siphoning off money that

could be used for basic services for years to come.

Despite ever-multiplying conflict-of-interest rules, ethics laws and efforts at transparency, theft, fraud and misappropriation of funds continue largely unabated. During the years I taught public finance to public-administration graduate students, I tried to bring to every class an example from the news of the day of a fraud, embezzlement or misappropriation that illustrated the importance of the particular aspect of public finance we were covering that evening. I did this once a week for nearly 20 years, and I rarely had trouble finding my horror story for the night.

So how do we fix this? More rules? More disclosure? In their book *The Pursuit of Absolute Integrity: How Corruption Control Makes Government Ineffective*, Frank Anechiarico and James B. Jacobs argue that "laws, rules, and threats will never result in a public administration to be proud of; to the contrary, the danger is that such an approach will create a self-fulfilling prophecy: having been placed continuously under suspicion, treated like quasi-criminals or probationers, public employees will behave accordingly."

---

*Originally published as Mark Funkhouser, "How We're Losing the War on Corruption," *Governing*, April 30, 2012. Reprinted with permission of the publisher.

We've been adding rules and transparency at a steady pace for decades with little appreciable real effect except that it costs more and more to comply with them all and the situation has become so complex that at any time you can unwittingly fail to comply with one or more of them. We need fewer rules, not more, and we need to embrace two broad policy directions: Stop trivializing ethics and strengthen financial accountability.

On the trivialization front, I've seen a mid-level career employee demoted and transferred to bureaucratic Siberia for allegedly using a government fax machine to send a personal document. I've been in mandatory ethics classes where we were told that it was essentially unethical to take a government-issue pen home from the office or that we were "stealing" time if we showed up for work 10 minutes late.

The real damage is done not by wayward pens or minor tardiness but by officials at the highest level who abuse the public trust in a big way, as in Dixon, Bell and Lynwood. Discussions of ethics usually devolve into sanctimonious diatribes divorced from the real world. If you really want to curb corruption, take Willie Sutton's advice: Go where the money is.

As for financial accountability, we need to recognize that auditing is too important to be left to the auditors alone. In the case of Dixon, I took a look at the financial audit report and, as the mayor said, it indeed gives the town a clean bill of health. But two of the most basic audit procedures clearly were not performed.

First, the review of internal controls should have uncovered the fact that there was no segregation of duties: The comptroller reportedly had a relative pick up the city's mail every day so she could intercept letters from the bank that referenced her secret account. And second, there was no bank reconciliation that included all the city's accounts: The comptroller's alleged thefts were discovered while she was on leave when the person filling in for her asked the bank for all of the accounts—something the auditors should have done routinely.

Citizens depend on auditing as a critical element of their governments' financial accountability. But too many auditors, left to their own devices, are letting the citizens down to the point where today a clean-audit opinion isn't worth a damn. For ordinary folks, like the taxpayers of Dixon, we need to fix that.

# 22. Municipal Employees Retirement System Faces Questions[*]

## Kevin Litten

The Municipal Employee Retirement System of Louisiana could face an ethics inquiry over a Legislative Auditor's finding that the system's executive director and governing board misused funds on expensive dinners and training retreats.

State Treasurer John Kennedy, who is an ex-officio member of the board, said in an interview he wasn't surprised by the findings of the audit, which was released Monday (Dec. 9). But he said that because the Legislative Auditor doesn't make findings on ethical violations, the board should seek the opinion of the Louisiana Ethics Administration to determine whether state ethics law was violated.

A key issue the Legislative Auditor explored was the payments the system solicited from investment firms under contract with MERS. The audit found the system's executive director, Robert Rust, used the money to create an "educational" account used to pay for out-of-state resort stays for training sessions, as well as nearly $13,000 for Christmas party dinners where alcohol was served.

"By incurring and/or authorizing such expenditures that were of little or no benefit to the system or its members, Mr. Rust and the Board may have violated state law and the Code of Governmental Ethics," Legislative Auditor Daryl Purpera found.

Rust resigned from the system in June.

"Clearly, a lot of the things Mr. Rust did were improper," Kennedy said. "The board needs to address that; it needs to address its own involvement in the improper practices. I expect the board to do that in the future."

Asked how the board could address it, Kennedy said, "We need to seek an advisory opinion about the impropriety and do what they tell us to do."

Warren Ponder, the system's general counsel who took over as executive director upon Rust's resignation, said he has provided a copy of the audit to the Ethics Administration but is unsure about whether the Ethics Administration will open an inquiry. He said the board will cooperate if a probe is opened.

Rust's attorney, in a response to the Legislative Auditor's inquiry, disagreed with the finding that the money solicited for the educational fund could be considered public funding—a finding that exposes Rust and the board to ethics charges. He also sought to draw attention to the board's approval of

*Originally published as Kevin Litten, "Municipal Employees Retirement System Faces Questions about Ethics Violations in Spending Scandal," *The Times-Picayune*, December 9, 2015. © 2015 The Times Picayune Publishing Co. All rights reserved. Used with permission of The Times-Picayune.

Rust's planning trips for educational conferences, which the auditor found cost the board more than $14,500.

"The board was fully aware and approved these trips by Mr. Rust and his wife, who helped plan the conference without consideration," Rust's attorney, Jack Dampf wrote in a letter to the auditor. "If the board felt that these trips were improper, they had a duty to not approve them."

Kennedy said he believes the MERS board didn't realize it was improper at the time the educational trips and dinners were booked. But he said once he was alerted to the spending by an investigation by WVUE-TV's Lee Zurick, it became obvious that "this is just a rip off to the taxpayer."

MERS oversees retirement plans for public employees of municipalities across the state and is no stranger to controversy. The board lost $40 million in an investment with Wall Street investment firm Fletcher Asset Management under Rust's leadership, a fact that still roils legislators.

Kennedy said state Sen. Barrow Peacock has approached him about possible legislation that would allow Kennedy and the Commissioner of Administration to vote on MERS actions. Peacock said in an interview that he wants the board to have additional oversight.

In a letter to the system, Kennedy also asked the board to begin divesting what he called "alternative investments" in real estate developments that expose the system to big losses.

Kennedy said in the letter he estimates 40 percent of MERS' investments are "too risky and too illiquid," and pointed out that $145 million—or 18 percent—of the system's funds has been lost in bad alternative investment schemes.

"That is money our current and retired municipal employees will never see again," Kennedy wrote. "Losses of that magnitude demand an immediate restructuring."

Kennedy set a goal of reducing alternative investments to less than 15 percent of all funds invested within two years. In an interview, while he acknowledged MERS isn't considered a public system, it contains contributions to employees' retirement plans from taxpayers.

"If the system gets in trouble, this state will be the first stop asking us to bail them out," Kennedy said. "I'm very worried about the investments."

MERS said in a letter back to Kennedy that it will begin reviewing its alternative investments and shares the treasurer's concerns.

# 23. Responding to an Ethical Crisis*

## Kevin Duggan

For anyone who follows the news to even a modest degree, it is difficult to go a single day without reading or hearing about a report regarding someone caught in an ethical crisis. Invariably, the media will ask anyone even remotely associated with the reported ethical breach three questions. How individuals respond to these questions will often determine how the unfolding ethical problem will affect them.

People are oftentimes seriously challenged in responding to these questions because they can be extremely uncomfortable to answer. With more careful reflection in advance, it is likely that the questions will be much easier to answer.

Keep in mind the questions won't only come from the media. While you should anticipate these questions from the press, also be prepared to respond to the same questions from employers, employees, community members, legal authorities, regulators, neighbors, and others.

The best way to feel confident that you will be able to answer these questions appropriately is to ask yourself the questions first— when you are deciding how to respond to an ethical challenge/dilemma. These questions are:

- What did you know?
- When did you know it?
- What did you do about it?

### What Did You Know?

Whenever an ethical breach is disclosed, the immediate question is, "Who knew about it?" It may be obvious who is/are the central figure(s) in the ethical crisis, but the media and others are going to be interested in who else was involved to any degree.

In particular, organizational members, especially organizational leaders, will be asked about their knowledge of the alleged conduct. Whether fair or not, as soon as you become aware of a real or potential ethical breach, you become part of the issue and certain obligations are created. Organizational leaders, particularly the leaders of public organizations, are expected to act once they become aware of an ethical challenge.

And, even if you can confidently answer that you did not know of the ethical breach, you may then be asked, why didn't you know? In particular, leaders will be scruti-

*Originally published as Kevin Duggan, "Responding to an Ethical Crisis," *PM Magazine,* December 2014. Reprinted with permission of the publisher.

nized by whether it would be reasonable to expect that with "due diligence" they would have known.

## When Did You Know It?

As soon as you are made aware of even the possibility of an ethical breach, the "clock" starts ticking. How quickly you address, and in many cases disclose, the occurrence of the breach or possible breach is critical to how your conduct will be judged.

It is common for persons in authority to be judged as having responded too slowly to an ethical breach. This can be portrayed as the leader minimizing the importance of the issue, being ineffectual in responding, or worst of all, being part of a cover-up.

If the ethical issue becomes public prior to you disclosing your knowledge of the issue to appropriate parties, regardless of your intent to eventually disclose, many will conclude you were never going to address it and take action. This can be an extremely challenging issue since we are appropriately hesitant to accuse someone of an ethical breach prior to having adequate information or confirmation.

In some cases, it is appropriate to disclose the possibility of the breach to a limited audience (e.g., council/governing board, attorneys, appropriate investigative bodies) without making a public disclosure while additional information is being gathered. When and to whom the information is disclosed, however, is a critical factor.

## What Did You Do About It?

And, of course, once you get beyond what you knew and when you knew it, you will be asked what actions you took in response to your knowledge. Did you overreact? Did you minimize the conduct? Did you do anything at all?

Action(s) you take will be viewed as your determination of the seriousness of the conduct. Modest discipline may be viewed as not understanding and appreciating the seriousness of the conduct.

Your own sense of right and wrong can be challenged by judgments regarding the actions that you take. Taking strong action can be viewed by some as appropriate, while others may view your approach as unfair and as an overreaction.

It is critical to carefully reflect on the obligations you have to all your constituencies when considering the appropriate action to take. For those of us doing work in public view, we should not be naive in regard to how our decisions will be judged by a wide array of audiences. We should never take comfort in the belief that our actions will remain sheltered from public view—they seldom will.

Often, otherwise honest and ethical organizational members and leaders become entangled in the unethical conduct of others. This can be the result of not taking the right action at the right time in response to the conduct of others.

There are reasons this occurs, including fear and uncertainty. One way to help avoid becoming the collateral damage of an ethical crisis is to ask yourself the three critical questions before someone else does.

# 24. Ethics: Focus on the Fundamentals[*]

## Martha Perego

At the beginning of this new year, local government leaders may well face significant challenges in delivering ethical, transparent democracy. Limited financial resources at every level of government are likely to force difficult choices about services, commitments, and investments in the future.

Although opportunities and innovation may result as well, it will no doubt be a tough period. Successfully navigating staff, organizations, and communities through challenging times requires leaders to focus on the fundamentals, that is, on ethics. Building a strong ethical foundation is the key to success. During periods of uncertainty, it's prudent for managers to take steps to ensure that the foundation is rock solid.

Is there agreement about the core values that will drive decision making and policies? Do we demonstrate respect for the unique roles and responsibilities of elected officials, staff, and residents? In the push for results and accountability, is it clear to all that how we achieve our goals is as critical as getting there?

Consider these steps to promote an ethical culture:

**Renew your commitment to the profession's values.** Commitment is more than hanging the ICMA Code of Ethics on the wall (although that isn't a bad idea). It is a dedication to the highest standards of honor and integrity in all public and personal matters in order to merit the respect and confidence of those we serve. It is unwavering integrity.

**Engage elected officials.** Use council orientations and goal-setting sessions to encourage elected officials to understand how their conduct and commitment to public service values contribute to ethical government. Take the time to enlighten them about the ICMA Code of Ethics and the values that guide professional local government managers.

**Set organizational values.** If the organization lacks a code of ethics or statement of values, implement a process that engages elected officials, staff, and residents in the definition of core values and acceptable conduct. If you have a code of ethics, is there clarity and agreement on the core values that drive critical decisions? Organizations or teams with shared values produce the best results.

**Ethics training.** It's a myth that good people always make wise choices. Regular train-

[*]Originally published as Martha Perego, "Ethics: Focus on the Fundamentals," *PM Magazine*, January/February 2016. Reprinted with permission of the publisher.

ing builds awareness of common ethical issues, provides tools and strategies for effective problem solving, and, yes, can even inspire someone to do the right thing when faced with a difficult ethical dilemma.

Welcome the dialogue and the dissenter. Make sure that individuals have formal and informal opportunities to raise any ethical concerns they may have about conduct or decisions in the organization. Create a safe environment for those seeking advice or raising a warning.

Transparency, transparency, transparency. Clear and regular communication, complete and accurate disclosure of the facts, taking responsibility for decisions and outcomes, and a focus on transparent processes all work to build trust with those we serve.

As Dave Childs, ICMA liaison, has noted, "We are all experiencing a time of extreme stress in our organizations. A key result is that our employees are justifiably worried about the stability of their jobs, about their personal finances, and ultimately about their own future. In uncertain times, it is imperative that we provide our employees something solid to hold on to.

"And, to that end, what could be more important than having every employee be totally sure of the values and ethics of their workplace and their organization? As the leaders of our organizations, we need to redouble our efforts to bring that sense of stability and grounding to all of the dedicated employees who serve the public each and every day. Building a solid ethical foundation is one of the keys to providing that stability and restoring confidence. And now is the time to begin."

# 25. Ethics, Front and Center[*]

## Troy Brown

When I was in high school in rural Pennsylvania, I vividly remember sitting in history class during the long humid spring and early summer days learning about William M. "Boss" Tweed and his infamous corrupt political reign in New York City during the nineteenth century.

At the time, I had a special interest in learning about Tweed's corruption because I was serving as class president. In particular, I found myself fascinated with the reform that followed his downfall.

Coming from a working-class family and background, I related to the socioeconomic circumstances—prevalent in the country during that time—that Tweed exploited for his personal benefit. It is well documented that immigrants were flooding New York City in waves, chasing the American Dream and seeking opportunities for a better life.

Most had given up everything they had to travel to America for a chance to make something of their lives, and the hopes of our government structure played a huge role in providing those opportunities.

Those aspirations resonated among Americans and to this day, the dreams remain. We rely on our local governments to meet our most basic needs for roads, water, power, sanitation, and public safety. We ask many things, but most of all we don't want local government to get in our way or be a hindrance to our quest for the American Dream.

## A Paradigm Shift

Isaac Newton's law of motion tells us that every action has an equal and opposition reaction that follows. Considering the tension between citizens and government that existed during the 19th century, which was caused by the widespread corruption of organizations much like Tammany Hall, the reform that swept the nation following Boss Tweed's reign changed the role of government service delivery.

It also had a profound impact on ethical expectations of future government administrators.

"In response to this public discontent, progressive reformers fought for and won a series of government reforms that spawned several organization experiments" (O'Neill 2014). The reform that followed set in motion key governance changes and spawned the council-manager form of government.

Under this system, local government managers partner with local elected officials to assist with the development and implementation of public policy. This is done in a collaborative capacity, whereby the professional

---

*Originally published as Troy Brown, "Ethics, Front and Center," *PM Magazine*, September 2014. Reprinted with permission of the publisher.

manager brings such philosophies as civic engagement, transparency, political neutrality, and ethical behavior into the political process.

This paradigm shift is significant because when it's properly administered, it actually elevates the role of elected officials by allowing them to focus on broad policy objectives and setting vision, rather than getting mired in the minutia of day-to-day operations. The significance of this change is most realized when results are achieved and local services are delivered in a fair, equitable manner across all socioeconomic and demographic regions of a community. This is the foundation of why ICMA was incorporated.

In 1924, ICMA amended its constitution integrating the ICMA Code of Ethics into the organization and codifying ethical behavior among its members. This integration impacted the behaviors that managers would display, and also played a key role in advancing governance throughout the world.

Although the Code of Ethics is designed to provide guidelines for managers, at its core it strives to provide citizens the opportunities to self-actualize on a level playing field. When adhered to in a consistent manner, residents, contractors and vendors don't have to be concerned about fairness in political processes, stewardship of public funds among local officials, or corruption within the local government structure.

This is why the Code of Ethics is so critically important—to assist with the promulgation of the democratic process throughout our profession.

## An Evolving Code

The world has evolved dramatically since the adoption of the Code in 1924 and continues to evolve today. To keep pace with the transformation nurtured by ICMA and local managers, the Code has been critiqued

and reviewed a number of times, and subsequently amended in 1938, 1952, 1969, 1972, 1976, 1995, 1998. Guidelines for Tenet 7 were changed in 2013.

The ICMA Executive Board's Committee on Professional Conduct (CPC) plays an important role for professional managers and ICMA members. It serves not only as the investigatory branch for allegations of malfeasance against the Code, but also as a link to our history for reminding us why ethical behavior is important.

CPC members help keep ICMA members accountable to the promises made by those in our past, who fought for fairness and equality along the way so that we and our children can have our own opportunities for self-actualization.

We use the Code as our guide to remind ourselves and members of where we have come from, and which course we must stay on, as we are entrusted with our communities' most valuable asset—quality of life.

Looking forward, we have to remain diligent in keeping up with the Code. We are in the midst of one of our most transformative periods in recent time. The speed and efficiency of technological advances pushes professional managers to be both educators and learners; challenges us to be reformers and to be reformed; and demands that we do this in real time on a daily basis.

To that end, we must ensure that the Code of Ethics remains front and center in our thinking and relevant to the changing times upon us.

That is why each year the CPC takes on the task of reviewing one tenet of the Code of Ethics. During my second year of CPC service, committee members evaluated Tenet 7, which speaks to political neutrality. This year, our efforts were focused on a review of Tenet 12, which provides guidance for endorsements.

Next year, there will be another review of a tenet that CPC members decide to take on. The amendments to the tenets and guidelines are important in keeping pace with the changing environment we all face. Equally important to keeping the Code relevant, however, is the conversation around the Code itself and the dialogue and opinions that we all have a right to share.

This conversation provides a forum so we as managers can debate the guidelines, words, and phrases but also preserve the basic principles behind the Code when it was originated 90 years ago: fairness and equality in public service.

None of us are perfect, and we all have moments that challenge our thinking and perceptions of ourselves and others.

Personally, I have benefitted tremendously by having had the honor to serve on this ICMA committee. I have learned more about myself and the Code of Ethics than I ever could have predicted. For each, single, teachable moment for members that I have encountered during my tenure, I have had two learnable moments for me professionally. The biggest takeaway for me is that it doesn't matter if you're an ICMA member or not, the manner in which local government professionals conduct themselves affects all managers.

Each day I strive to do my part to ensure that residents in the community where I work have the opportunity to chase their dreams and create positive memories about their life so they can share those memories with someone else. It's become part of what defines me as an ICMA member and a professional manager. It has become an intrinsic part of me.

## The Public's Perception

The challenges for managers don't end with their management responsibilities. Whether we like it or not, working in the public sector casts an eye of scrutiny over all of us, regardless of our position or role in an organization.

Not so long ago, as an example, I was perusing my Facebook newsfeed and catching up on the latest births, announcements, pet updates, and food postings of my friends. I saw an article that was posted from someone on the East Coast, which is nearly 3,000 miles away from me, mind you, about a city employee who was being accused of misappropriation of public funds.

My friend commented, "Don't trust government employees, they are all corrupt!" I couldn't leave that hanging out there, so I commented to him that not all government employees are corrupt, and, in fact, a number of communities with millions of Americans are run extremely well. Fortunately, my friend clarified his comments and stated that he wasn't talking about professional managers like me and admitted that he made the posting out of frustration.

This is just one example of the perception some people have of public servants. It didn't even matter that the employee in question was a supervisor in a transit division; his actions had an impact on the general perception of all public employees.

It is not enough to simply be ethical in your personal dealings. We have to promote and emulate ethical behavior in our workplace, support our peers in their ethical behaviors, and dispel misconceptions as we carry out our workplace duties. In short, we have to take care of one another.

Ethics is one of the key pillars for professional management and a tenet for ICMA. This responsibility has been handed down to us by the nineteenth-century reformers who were the catalysts for monumental changes in government. Their dedication in eliminating conditions that fed corruption like a starving animal was the foundation for which future structures would rise and give way to opportunism for all Americans. They left us with a heavy burden in carrying out our duties.

Regardless of the position that one holds in a public agency, a high level of responsibility comes with the role. Public officials are not all cut from the same cloth; we are unique individuals with our own imperfections and varied opinions.

But the one thing we have in common is the responsibility to do our best to be stewards of the public funds and create opportunities for prosperity among all residents. If we don't, then the road that was paved with the actions of the reformers of the past will be the road that we head down into the future as we, ourselves, are reformed.

### Reference

O'Neill, R. J. (2014). "The Legacy of Local Government Professionalism: A 100-Year Perspective." *The Municipal Year Book*, pp. x–xv.

# 26. Local Government Ethics Reform[*]

## *Robert Wechsler*

This is a very good time for local government ethics reform. Large cities, such as Washington, D.C., and Jacksonville, Florida, as well as many smaller cities, counties, and towns across the country, have created or improved their ethics programs over the past year.

And yet most people don't really know what a government ethics program is. It is a program of training, advice, disclosure, and enforcement that helps government officials and employees deal responsibly with conflict-of-interest situations. Conflict situations exist when an official, or someone with whom the official has a special relationship, is in a position to benefit from a matter in which the official is involved. Conflict situations include participating in the provision of a contract to a business associate, taking a gift from a developer, participating in a grant to a client, hiring or promoting a family member (nepotism), and using government equipment or confidential information for personal purposes.

Another problem is that there is very little information about local government ethics reform and few best practices for an ethics program. Every city and county starts from square one. That is why I wrote my new book, *Local Government Ethics Program*. This piece is adapted from a section of this 831-page resource for ethics reform.

Why is government ethics reform so important? The principal goal of government ethics is to increase the public's trust in government and, thereby, increase citizen participation in the organization that manages their community. Also, preventing scandals and the misuse of government resources for personal purposes adds to government performance, to a community's pride, and to the community's attractiveness to businesses.

Ethics reform can happen in many ways. It can happen through the perseverance of good government groups. It can happen through the election of one or more candidates who place ethics reform high on their list of priorities, as happened last year in Chicago. It can happen upon the recommendation of an ethics commission or of a grand jury, an inspector general, an attorney general, or a special task force.

It can also happen as part of the charter revision process or the drafting of a new charter, a change in form of government (as happened in 2011 in Cuyahoga County, Ohio), or a city–county consolidation process (as happened in 1997 in Kansas City/Wyan-

---

[*]Originally published as Robert Wechsler, "Local Government Ethics Reform," *National Civic Review* 101, no. 3 (Fall 2012): 26–30. © 2012 Wiley Periodicals Inc. Reprinted with permission of the publisher.

dotte County, Kansas). And it can happen because the state requires or recommends that local governments pass an ethics code, providing language or minimum requirements.

Ethics reform can take place at the city level, the county level, the regional level, or the state level.

## Scandals

Although there are many ways to create or improve a government ethics program, there is only one principal spark: a scandal involving an official. A scandal is the best way to get ethics reform going, but it is usually the worst way to get an effective, comprehensive ethics program, which is what really matters.

One reason is that the majority of scandals have little or nothing to do with government ethics. They involve everything from a sex scandal to embezzlement. Often they involve crimes such as bribery or kickbacks. Only sometimes do they involve a conflict-of-interest situation, such as giving a contract to a family member or taking a gift from a developer.

There are two major problems with using scandals to create or reform government ethics programs. One is that reformers, inside and outside government, have little or no control over scandals, unless they have special information that they can turn over to the authorities. And even if they have special information, they can't ensure that investigations are made or that, if they are made, they become public. Scandals are a gift to ethics reform, but they cannot be part of a reform strategy. Too often there is no ethics reform movement prepared to accept the gift of a scandal, so it is politicized before reformers can get involved in a meaningful way. This is why it is important to have an ethics reform initiative, even if it takes years before the occasion arises to implement it.

The second problem is that scandals usually lead to two sorts of ethics reform, neither of which is optimal. Sometimes they lead to limited reforms that respond solely to the particular scandal. If it has to do with a family member, a nepotism provision is added or strengthened. If it has to do with a contract, the rules for bidding out contracts are tightened. The fire is put out, and that is all. And since one party or faction is usually involved in the scandal, the ethics reform takes on a highly partisan hue, which does not bode well for its future.

## Origin Stories

A good way to see the wide range of options in attaining effective ethics reform is to look at the origin stories behind some of today's better ethics programs.

Atlanta, Georgia: According to Harvey K. Newman and Jeremy Greenup's *Ethics Case Study* (2009), before the 2001 mayoral election, ten Atlanta officials and contractors (including the chief operating officer and the chief administrative officer) were convicted of corruption-related crimes, and the feds were investigating the then mayor. (He was later convicted of tax evasion relating to the taking of bribes and kick-backs from contractors given no-bid contracts.)

Shirley Franklin was elected mayor with the slogan "I'll make you proud." She promised to appoint an ethics task force to recommend changes to the city's ethics program, and indeed she did this less than a month after winning the election.

The task force worked quickly. It filed a report within three months, recommending the creation of an independent ethics commission with teeth. Four of the commission's five members would be selected by community organizations. (In the end, all members were.) The task force also recommended the hiring of an ethics officer to provide ethics training and assist the commission. It was fortunate that half the council was new and committed to preventing more corruption. There was still much council criticism of the recommendations, but in the end the ethics program actually was stronger than what had originally been proposed.

A principal reason is that, while the council was debating the recommendations, the mayor issued an executive order that applied only to city employees. The executive order jumped the gun by requiring the appointment of an ethics officer (temporarily an assistant city attorney), the establishment of a hotline, and a total gift ban. This upped the ante for the council, effectively daring it to pass weaker provisions to apply to the council and its staff.

When the council later weakened the gift ban by a vote of 11 to 2, the mayor vetoed the amendment, and the veto held by one vote. The prevention of backsliding is nearly as important as passing reforms in the first place.

This origin story has a lot of the most important factors required for true ethics reform: a scandal, committed leadership, and an independent task force that takes its job seriously.

Philadelphia, Pennsylvania: In Philadelphia, the scandal arose from revelations of an ongoing FBI investigation that emerged during the 2003 mayoral election. The city treasurer was convicted on twenty-seven charges of corruption, followed by further prosecutions of friends of and advisors to the mayor.

Philadelphia's ethics reform took place in three parts. The first part, in August 2004, consisted of two mayoral executive orders establishing an ethics commission with staff to oversee training, advice, and financial disclosure. It had no enforcement authority, and it was part of the office of the mayor, who had been reelected in 2003.

The second part, in December 2005, consisted of laws passed by the council. One of the laws, to establish an independent ethics commission, required a charter amendment. This amendment was approved by voters in May 2006.

The third part occurred when Michael Nutter, the council member primarily responsible for the 2005 ethics reforms, became mayor and, in September 2008, created an ethics task force, seven of whose nine members were appointed by community organizations. The purpose of the task force was to recommend further improvements to the city's ethics program. It filed its first comprehensive report in December 2009.

Through all these stages, a local good government organization called the Committee of Seventy put constant pressure, including numerous reports and testimony, on the mayor and council to continue to improve the city's ethics program.

Palm Beach County, Florida: In 2009, three Palm Beach County commissioners and two council members from the county's largest city pled guilty to using their offices to enrich themselves. An article on the scandal in *Time* magazine called the county "the new capital of Florida corruption."

The first response was the creation of a grand jury to make recommendations for changes to provide oversight, transparency, and accountability in the county government. In a May 2009 report, the grand jury made piecemeal but valuable ethics recommendations.

The first response to these recommendations was talk about not being able to afford the ethics reforms, questions about the entities' independence, and stalling from some county commissioners.

A coalition of business groups, including Leadership Palm Beach County (affiliated with the county's chambers of commerce), the Palm Beach County Business Forum, the Palm Beach County Economic Council, and the Voters Coalition, formed the Palm Beach Ethics Initiative to push ethics reform. It wrote an ethics pledge and got dozens of local officials to sign it. A committee was formed to study best practices in ethics, survey opinion leaders, and hold a community-wide forum on ethics in June 2008. (The forum became an annual discussion of ethics reform.) The announced goal of these programs was to change the culture of ethics in the county.

The county commission passed an ethics code in December 2009, creating both an independent ethics commission selected by community organizations and an inspector general, funded by a fee on county contracts.

The biggest complication was having the ethics program apply to independent agencies and the cities and towns in the county. This required a referendum, which passed in November 2010. (It was approved by 72 percent of those voting.) The citizens of every town and city in the county voted to have the ethics program apply to their municipality. A new ethics code applying to all local governments in the county was drafted in 2011, and the county began entering into interlocal agreements with the local governments.

As can be seen in both Philadelphia and Palm Beach County, good government organizations often can provide the necessary leadership for ethics reform when the government itself does not provide it. Task forces, pledges, surveys, forums, reports, testimony—all these are useful means both to attain ethics reform and to keep the process going after the first laws are passed.

It's important to remember that ethics reform does not end with the passage of laws. The laws can be improved and applied to more agencies and local governments; the ethics program's budget needs to be protected and, with additional responsibilities, increased; and backsliding needs to be anticipated and prevented, including such things as budget cuts, the failure to appoint ethics commission members, interference by officials and government attorneys, suits

attacking the ethics commission's jurisdiction, and amendments to the laws. It is the rare ethics commission that does not find itself at war with the local legislative body, at least over application and enforcement of the ethics code and over funding.

## Top Down or Bottom Up?

There are two ways to approach the reform of an ethics program. One is to add a few provisions that currently seem important. This is starting at the bottom and working your way up.

The other approach is to start at the top, with all the possible provisions and aspects of an ethics program that appear, say, in my new book, *Local Government Ethics Programs*. From there, you work your way down: that is, decide which provisions are inappropriate to the particular government, which aspects of an ethics program the government cannot afford, and which provisions are already covered well at the state level or are not permitted by state law.

The start-at-the-top approach might mean more work, but it is the professional way to consider best practices and seek to create the best, most comprehensive ethics program one can afford. (Just as a local government decides to build the best school or waste treatment plant it can afford.) This approach also requires that every aspect of an ethics program be openly discussed, so that there is official explanation and public input on all the basic ethics provisions and all the administrative and enforcement mechanisms, whether they are accepted or rejected.

If a special committee is given the job of recommending ethics reforms, it should take this approach and be required not only to recommend provisions but also to explain to the public and the local legislative body why it chose not to recommend other approaches and aspects of a comprehensive ethics program. Or it can recommend a full range of reforms, carefully prioritize them, and clearly explain that it realizes not all the reforms will be implemented immediately, but at least the others will be there to consider the next time there is interest in improving the ethics program.

In contrast, a bottom-up approach is a lazy, short-sighted way to tackle ethics reform, and a way that lacks transparency. It is also the far more common approach.

The start-at-top-approach also shows how much one aspect of an ethics program depends on another. For example, it is of little value to recommend that an ethics commission be permitted to settle ethics proceedings if the ethics commission does not have the authority to enforce ethics provisions. The reason is that there is little incentive to settle with a body that has no authority.

Here is another example. The goal of depoliticizing the ethics process includes not only the independence of the ethics commission and its staff from anyone under its jurisdiction but also taking council members out of administrative responsibilities, including land use matters, procurement, permits, and licensing, areas fraught with the sort of pay-to-play opportunities that lead to so much ethical misconduct.

A third example is the creation of a hotline, which requires whistleblower protection and can be made more valuable by requiring government officials and employees to report possible ethical misconduct they are aware of.

Another advantage of the start-at-the-top approach is that, after creating a reject pile that includes a lot of good things that the local government would like to do but feels it cannot afford, the local government may come to realize that it can get many of these things by cooperating with neighboring local governments or pooling the resources of all the local governments in the county. A county or regional ethics program saves every town time and money and gives each not only the best and least expensive possible ethics program but also one that is independent of each local government (that is, one that citizens can trust and that officials and employees will use without concerns about politics).

A decision to take the start-at-the-top approach is the most important decision in ethics reform. No government should be allowed to get away without a serious, public consideration of this approach.

## Role of Good Government Groups

As you have seen in the ethics reform scenarios, good government and other community organizations are often the heart and soul of ethics reform. Even when they do not begin an ethics reform initiative, their support, resources, testimony, campaigns, and contacts with officials and other groups make their involvement extremely important. Cities and counties with active good government organizations tend to have better ethics programs. Not only do they help in their creation, but they continue to provide support, seek improvement, and call for more independence and funding (or, in a recession, the maintenance of funding).

A good government organization or coalition can support ethics reform in several ways. It can start the ball rolling by raising the issue. It can sketch out a vision of an improved ethics program or draft an entire ethics code (or amendments). It can explain what government ethics is and why it is important. It can create an ethics pledge and get local officials to sign it (or otherwise endorse serious ethics reform). It can schedule forums for citizens and officials to discuss ethics reform publicly. It can try to get the issue on the local legislative body's agenda, attend meetings, and make public comments. It can write letters to the editor and op-ed pieces, have members appear on local radio shows, set up a special Web site, and give talks and answer questions at community organization meetings. If there is opposition or leg-dragging by the legislative body, it can seek a referendum on ethics reform or petition for a charter revision commission that could insert ethics requirements in the charter.

The most effective good government organizations are generally those that have been around for a while, are seen as nonpartisan, and have deep connections in the community. Some cities are fortunate to have organizations going back to the Progressive Era of the early twentieth century, which pushed through most of the local government reforms we take for granted. But many newer organizations, and specially constituted coalitions of organizations, have been equally effective, especially when there have been local scandals.

A government scandal by itself is not usually enough to ensure effective ethics reform. Without either an organization or coalition of organizations insisting on and drafting or at least outlining serious ethics reforms, all that usually happens are a few minor improvements or, if there was no ethics program, a skeletal program with no guidance, independence, or authority.

Business organizations, including local chambers of commerce, can be of great use in pushing ethics reform. Many local scandals involve local businesses and business owners, and this can be a great embarrassment. Local businesses are also concerned about a community's reputation, because it affects business growth in the area and the desirability of the community to people considering taking a job there. It is hard for a community that is considered corrupt to grow and prosper.

Jack Brown, a corporate executive in San Bernardino County, California, complained in 2010 that the county's reputation for corruption dogged him when he met with businesspeople and officials outside the county. "Who got indicted in your county today?" was a question he was often asked. Officials so often speak about their personal reputations and how they have to protect it. More important to their job is the protection of their government's reputation, for the good of the community.

## References

Florin, H. (2009, January 10). "Palm Beach: The New Capital of Florida Corruption." *Time.*

Newman, H. K., and J. Greenup. (2012). "Ethics Case Study." Atlanta Case Study Project, http://fiscalresearch.gsu.edu/atlanta case study/Ethics%20Case%20Study.pdf.

# 27. Assessing the Ethical Culture of Your Agency*

## JoAnne Speers, Jan Perkins and Arne Croce

Personal ethics are important, but those who manage staff-leaders of agencies, departments, and organizations-are responsible for more than their own personal ethics. If an employee makes an ethical or legal misstep, ultimately it will reflect poorly on the manager. It will also reflect on the public's perception of one's agency.

How then, does a manager promote public confidence in the agency as a whole, as the guidelines to the ICMA Code of Ethics suggest? A key way is to lead one's agency in a way that fosters a culture of ethics.

### Organizational Cultures as a Determinant of Organizational Behaviors

Ethics and public confidence are not just about a manager's faithful adherence to the ICMA Code of Ethics, although clearly that's an important first step. Just as superior organizational performance requires everyone to be pulling in the same direction, so do organizational ethics require that everyone pull together. Members of your staff are likely to engage in behaviors that they believe are valued by management. What signals are you sending about the kinds of behaviors and attitudes you value? What kinds of behaviors are rewarded? Does your organization have a mission or values statement? Are ethical values a part of that statement?

One way to find out what kinds of signals your staff pick up is to assess the staff, either formally or informally. From there, one can determine the agency's strengths and weakness. That in turn can help a manager formulate a strategy to maximize the agency's ethical culture. An assessment can also be a jumping-off point for internal ethics education efforts.

California's Institute for Local Government (ILG) and ICMA have collaborated on a tool to help managers reflect on their organization's culture in terms of ethics. The tool is available online without charge at www.ca-ilg.org/culturechecks. The questionnaire probes such issues as whether employees feel encouraged to:

- Use ethical behaviors in the process of getting results on behalf of the public.
- Comply with the spirit as well as the letter of laws.
- Display civility and respect for their

*Originally published as JoAnne Speers, Jan Perkins, and Arne Croce, "Assessing the Ethical Culture of Your Agency," *PM Magazine*, January/February 2007. Reprinted with permission of the publisher.

colleagues, even when there is disagreement.

The ILG assessment has three parts:

- Employees' perceptions of expectations of the employee.
- Employees' perceptions of management's attitudes and behaviors.
- Employees' perceptions of elected officials' attitudes and behaviors.

The assessment can be used in a number of ways. The first and most modest is for a manager to review the questions and anticipate what kinds of responses the organization's employees are likely to give to the questions. Most managers will have a fairly strong sense of their organization's culture. Thinking about the questions on the assessment can alert a manager to potential ethical blind spots (for example, a get-it-done culture or a whatever-it-takes culture) or problem areas.

The next approach is for a manager to ask leadership teams to complete the assessment. This approach offers a manager the opportunity to receive feedback on the organization's culture and sensitize the management team to the kinds of issues that can either enhance or erode an organization's ethical culture.

Another way the assessment can be used is for all employees to take the assessment. This will give a manager a top-to-bottom assessment of the team's sensitivity to ethics issues and the kinds of prevailing messages in the organization.

## Issues Explored by Ethics Assessment

The Institute for Local Government/ICMA ethics assessment explores the following kinds of issues in an organization:

1. Do employees feel encouraged to come forward and report any unethical practices they see in the course of their duties?

2. Are members of the public treated equally regardless of personal or political connections?

3. What is the prevailing attitude about the acceptance of gifts or favors from those who do business with the agency? Okay? Not Okay?

4. Is an environment of ethics and professionalism actively promoted within the agency?

5. Are employees encouraged to act according to the spirit as well as the letter of the law?

6. Is the public treated with civility and respect?

The assessment asks these questions from three points of view:

- What do respondents do?
- What do respondents perceive management as doing?
- What do respondents perceive elected officials as doing?

Finally, elected and appointed officials can also be included in the assessment process as part of an overall organizational commitment to ethics.

## San Mateo's Experience

The city of San Mateo, California, used a phased approach to assess its organizational culture. The assessment became a focal point for an organization-wide conversation on ethics in the workplace.

The concept was first introduced at an executive team meeting in early 2006. This meeting involved a discussion of general principles of public service ethics and the nature of the assessment process. Top management staff expressed enthusiasm for going forward with the assessment as one step in a process to reinforce and strengthen the city's ethical culture.

The management team agreed to complete the assessment. The manager met with the team to discuss the results of the survey and get the team's thoughts on the city's current environment and how it could be strengthened even further. The team also provided valuable input about how to maximize the effectiveness of the assessment instrument.

The group decided to take the discussion deeper into the organization. The assessment was distributed to line managers (about 50 positions) responsible for major divisions within the city departments. The managers then received the results of their feedback in a workshop that included a review of public service ethics principles and frameworks.

The assessment was then distributed to all members of the city organization. As this article goes to press, the results of the full assessment are still being tabulated. Earlier distributions to management indicated a strong culture of ethics within the organization—a positive sign, of course. Staff also rated the city council's ethics highly, suggesting a strong "tone at the top."

Even though the city already is strongly committed to ethical practices, it is exploring how to reinforce that ethical culture in a number of ways. Department heads are facilitating discussion on the ethical dimensions of issues that their people face. The city is offering training to those departments that request it, and it is also adding ethics as value to the city's statement of core values.

## The Beverly Hills Experiment

City Manager Rod Wood, an early and strong supporter of the ICMA Code of Ethics, decided to engage members of his executive team in discussions about their roles as leaders in building an ethical culture in their organization. Wood used the ICMA Code of Ethics as the framework for these discussions, and he established an ex-

pectation that each member of the executive team would follow the tenets of the code.

The city invited ICMA to conduct training for the executive team on the Code of Ethics, as well as training for the full management staff on practical applications of everyday ethics. The manager and team understood that even though Beverly Hills staff had a strong reputation for professionalism and high standards, ethical challenges can and do arise in a variety of ways for employees, and staff need to be prepared to deal with circumstances as they come up.

In advance of the ethics training workshop for the executive team, members were asked to participate in the online ethics assessment survey. ICMA compiled the results and used them in the workshop to focus discussions with the executive team. The questionnaire helped the leadership team identify where they could best spend their time in fostering an even stronger culture of ethics in the city organization.

Through the assessment tool, executive staff were able to identify where the team believed the organization was doing well and where the team members should focus more attention with staff in helping employees understand how to deal with difficult situations. The city manager and executive team felt the assessment and training were useful, especially in addressing those gray areas in the political arena that we all can face with today's public organizations.

## It's Never Too Early

Asking staff to complete the assessment can be a scary proposition, to be sure. In this situation, what you don't know really can hurt you professionally and personally. Having ethics issues arise within the agency during one manager's watch can damage that manager's reputation; it can also take a significant personal toll in terms of stress and efforts to engage in damage control.

Anticipating how one's staff will respond to the questions can provide food for thought to a manager who has strong personal ethics but may have emphasized other issues in hiring, performance evaluations, and other forms of feedback on what the manager values. For the workforce, simply completing the assessment prompts thinking about ethical issues and behavior. It's never too early to have discussions with staff about your commitment to serving the public both effectively and ethically.

As management expert Peter Drucker observed, "Management is doing things right; leadership is doing the right things." Are you leading your organization to do the right things?

# 28. Building a Strong Local Government Ethics Program[*]

## Michael W. Manske and H. George Frederickson

On April 1, 1997, when the citizens of Wyandotte County and Kansas City, Kansas, voted to merge and consolidate their county and city governments, there were only 31 such consolidations in the United States. The citizens voted not only to reconstruct their local government but also to do away with a long history of political corruption and employee misconduct.

The comprehensive ethics program rests on four pillars:

1. the code of ethics,
2. the ethics education program,
3. the oversight of the ethics commission, and
4. the office of the ethics administrator.

The consolidation referendum called for the establishment of an ethics commission with teeth in it, as well as a jurisdiction-wide ethics program. Mayor Carol Marinovich put it this way: "Elected officials of the newly consolidated city and county governments recognized that the success of any form of government would depend largely upon the trust established between the government and the citizens of the community. They also understood that trust would not evolve without the absolute expectation and en-forcement of high ethical standards of conduct for every elected official, administrative official, and employee."

The newly elected mayor and county commission decided on an ethics program designed to stamp out corruption, bolster public trust in government, and improve public service to the citizens. The foundation of the ethics program was a new ordinance, adopted in May 1998. But a code of ethics would not achieve all the leadership goals that the unified government wanted.

The code was augmented by a multifaceted and comprehensive program that featured a unique method of code administration, as well as a comprehensive education program, complaint hotline, investigation protocol, and independent oversight function. It was believed that this combination of interrelated and supporting functions would work in harmony to promote ethical conduct.

The comprehensive ethics program rests on four pillars: (1) the code of ethics, (2) the ethics education program, (3) the oversight of the ethics commission, and (4) the office of the ethics administrator. Each pillar plays an equal part in the ethics program, and each depends upon the others for reinforce-

*Originally published as Michael W. Manske and H. George Frederickson, "Building a Strong Local Government Ethics Program," *PM Magazine* 86, no. 5 (June 2004). Reprinted with permission of the publisher.

ment and support. An ethics education program, for example, supports the code by giving each elected official and employee the needed instruction in the code of ethics, as well as in the policy rationale behind the rules. Even the finest code of ethics would be rendered ineffective if government officials did not understand its provisions or why those provisions were there and what their importance was.

An independent ethics commission continually monitors the activities of government, recommending amendments to the code when appropriate and advising on policy matters, as well as ruling on ethics complaints. And finally, the ethics administrator supports the ethics commission as its executive agent and is responsible for comprehensive ethics education and for engaging in ethics investigations and preparing advisory opinions.

Implementation of the Unified Government Code of Ethics and management of the jurisdiction's comprehensive ethics program are contracted out. This contract calls for the appointment of a part-time ethics administrator, an extensive ethics education program for all jurisdiction officials and employees, an ethics complaint hotline, and staff support for the ethics commission. Subcontractual work is directed by a team from the University of Kansas.

Over the past five years, this interdependent combination of functions has proven worthwhile. County Administrator Dennis Hays says: "There has been a huge impact on the unified government organization since the consolidation of governments in 1997. Prior to consolidation, there was great discontent among the citizens with the ethics of political leadership and with jurisdiction employees regarding propriety.

The presence of an authoritative body of citizens who can exercise independent oversight is essential to promoting public integrity in government.

"Through the establishment of the ethics administrator and ethics commission, and with the development of the code of ethics, there is a much greater sense of trust and confidence in the government and within the organization. This confidence and trust is further regarded as a high standard by the public, as there has been no public outcry regarding a public official."

## Code of Ethics

The code of ethics was adopted by the unified government as an ordinance, which set clear rules of ethical conduct in government and the mechanisms for enforcing these rules. The code includes many rules of conduct common to governmental ethics, such as prohibitions against conflicts of interest, gratuities and kickbacks, nepotism, and objectionable outside employment. It sets clearly defined rules for the acceptance of gifts, handling of confidential information, and appropriate exercise of official duties.

These standard provisions are joined by a comprehensive statement of both permitted and prohibited political activities. The code includes a whistle-blower protection provision and provides for confidential communication of ethics complaints through several "hotline" vehicles. It both prohibits retaliation against officials and governmental employees who make complaints and provides redress. Constant review and refinement have kept the code relevant and timely through a series of amendments recommended by the ethics commission.

## Ethics Commission

The presence of an authoritative body of citizens who can exercise independent oversight is essential to promoting public integrity in government. In the unified government, this function is the responsibility of the commission and established by ordinance.

The five-citizen panel is charged with monitoring governmental activities, recommending code amendments, and issuing advisory opinions.

The commission is responsible for important policy debates that affect the overall ethical environment of the government. It also reviews and recommends discipline on ethics complaint cases and responds to inquiries from officials and administrators on the ethical review of proposed policies and activities.

Ethics commissioners are not appointed by the mayor or by the county commission but by three "politically insulated" and independent officers in the government: the chief judge of the district court, the district attorney, and the legislative auditor. The important point is that neither the mayor nor the commission of the unified government appoints the members of the ethics commission. The ethics commission, which is therefore independent of jurisdictional politics, is able to advise the mayor and commission objectively on matters of ethics and, should it be necessary, even to oversee investigations of elected officials.

Ethics commissioners are chosen by region, serving voluntarily and without compensation in staggered four-year terms. With a previously published agenda, commissioners meet once a month in regular sessions open to the public. A typical meeting agenda includes a review of contemporary ethics issues, complaints suitable for investigation and disposition, and inquiries from the government that have been resolved through advisory opinions.

In the past three years, the commission has advised the board of commissioners or the county administrator to adopt a whistle-blower protection amendment to the code of ethics. The commission also has led the following six initiatives: (1) to standardize appointment procedures for appointed boards and commissions; (2) to make vendor lists more generally available to the public; (3) to allow employees of the unified government to run for elected office without the requirement of prior resignation or termination; (4) to set policies and procedures for the receipt, acceptance, and distribution of complimentary tickets to Kansas Speedway races; (5) to supervise more closely the electronic mail of individuals using unified-government computers; and (6) to monitor the pressure put on employees concerning the amount and character of their charitable giving.

These initiatives illustrate the capacity of the commission to keep the code current and to keep ethics matters part of the public dialogue. By virtue of its leadership and autonomy, it has been instrumental in bolstering public trust in the ethics program.

## Ethics Administrator

The office of the ethics administrator was established in the code of ethics ordinance. Like commission members, the administrator is an outsider independent of jurisdictional politics and, also like the ethics commission, the administrator is selected by the same three-person committee. This is done to ensure the highest credentials and independence. Ethics administrator is a part-time position, provided under a contract overseen by the legislative auditor.

The administrator serves as the executive agent of the commission, preparing meeting agendas and minutes and support materials for commission meetings. He or she operates the ethics hotline, conducts ethics training, investigates allegations of misconduct, and recommends disciplinary measures, should they be called for.

## Ethics Education

After the code of ethics became effective on January 1, 1999, the office of the ethics administrator began an aggressive ethics education program designed to train every official, administrator, and employee of the unified government. These introductory training sessions began with the newly elected mayor and the members of the board of commissioners.

Ethics commissioners are not appointed by the mayor or by the county commission but by three "politically insulated" and independent officers in the government: the chief judge of the district court, the district attorney, and the legislative auditor. The important point is that neither the mayor nor the commission of the unified government appoints the members of the ethics commission.

Ethics training then branched out to include more than 2,200 senior administrators, supervisors, and employees of the departments and agencies within the government. Each introductory session consists of a two-hour block of instruction in which the provisions and policies of the code are presented, together with spirited discussions of ethics dilemmas wherein the rules of conduct are tested, validated, and given practical meaning and effect.

Training sessions also include an overview of the components of the ethics program and their respective functions, as well as a thorough review of the complaint and investigation processes. At the end of each introductory session, trainees are asked to take an ethics pledge as their commitment to ethical conduct; then they receive certificates of completion, to be annotated in their personnel files.

The education component of the ethics program proceeds along a two-pronged track. Not only does it include introductory sessions for existing officials, administrators, and employees but also it requires sessions for each newly elected official or recently hired employee (within his or her first 90 days of service).

After successfully completing the introductory session, each official, administrator, and employee receives a "training anniversary date." Three years after their introductory training, all elected officials and employees participate in a continuing education session to review and refresh their commitment to ethical conduct.

Continuing education sessions consist of a one-hour block of instruction in which trainees again work through a series of ethical dilemmas. But unlike the introductory sessions, the ethical-dilemma cases in the continuing education sessions involve the most frequent ethical challenges encountered in the unified government during the past three years. Completion of a continuing education session is noted in the personnel file, and the employee's training anniversary date is reset for another three years.

The curriculum for the ethics education program has been carefully constructed to facilitate meaningful instruction in ethical conduct. The formal language of the code of ethics has been restated in an easy-to-understand format, and ethical-dilemma cases have been developed to present clear— yet challenging—vehicles through which practical application may be enhanced.

Two sets of scenarios have been written: a set of general principles to be used in the introductory sessions, and a focused and timely set to be used in the continuing education session. Employees do not simply relearn the previous lessons; they benefit from topical treatment of current issues. In almost all training sessions, there is a lively discussion and an in-depth analysis of ethical issues faced by employees.

## Hotline and Investigations

The ethics hotline is actually one of five confidential mediums continually monitored to ensure responsiveness both to complaints and to inquiries: the telephone hotline itself, e-mail messages, United States Mail service, telefax letter transmission, and a verbal complaint process. The hotline telephone number, e-mail address, and fax numbers are prominent parts of all ethics training and are posted widely in jurisdiction buildings and offices.

The first and most important purpose of the ethics hotline is to provide unified government officials and employees with a reliable source of advice on ethical dilemmas. The second purpose is to report allegations of ethical misconduct.

All hotline complaints are guaranteed confidential handling so that citizens, elected officials, and employees can make an ethics complaint without fear of reprisal. If there is substance to an ethics complaint or allegation, the administrator works with and through the administration to determine appropriate discipline. Cases involving serious breaches of the code, other ordinances of the unified government, or the laws of the state of Kansas are turned over to the district attorney.

Complaints and allegations involving possible code violations by elected officials are handled directly by the ethics administrator. Should the course of action recommended by the administrator, based on the facts of the allegation, not be agreed to by an elected official, the administrator can take the matter to the ethics commission, and the commission, in open meeting with the media present, can recommend a course of action.

The telephone hotline is the most popular communication method through which contacts are made.

The telephone hotline is the most popular communication method through which contacts are made. The hotline is a confidential answering machine remotely accessed every 48 hours (necessary because the office is not otherwise staffed, nor is telephone reception available outside normal working hours). The answering-machine message advises callers about the confidentiality of their calls and provides the assis-

tant director's home telephone number, in case the call is not returned within 48 hours.

A response is made to all contacts received, and in the case of requests for advisory opinions or other information, 100 percent of contacts receive favorable resolution. A little more than half (almost 54 percent) of the contacts alleging an ethics violation have concerned, in fact, not violations of the code of ethics but important complaints all the same.

Resolved through an appropriate referral are: reports such as complaints by employees against their supervisors (purely personnel issues properly handled by management), complaints for which only a private remedy exists (subject to private litigation), complaints of a political nature (campaign conduct and the like), and general complaints about government (problems with services or benefits provided by local, state, or federal government). All other contacts result in either informal or formal resolution.

## *Making Progress*

In the five years since unification and the adoption of the ethics program, the Unified Government of Wyandotte County and Kansas City, Kansas, has made considerable progress. Property values have increased sharply, population decline has stopped, new housing developments are springing up, and large commercial development with hotels, theaters, a NASCAR track, and large regional "destination" stores like Cabela's and Nebraska Furniture Mart have been built.

The ethical climate of the unified government is now high, and there have been no political scandals. Mayor Marinovich describes progress in this way: "Since the city and county governments were consolidated and the ethics program was established, a significantly positive change has occurred in the growth, economy, and political atmosphere of Wyandotte County. Property values are increasing, delivery of services has improved at lower cost, neighborhoods have started working together to increase quality of life, and major reinvestment is being made in the community. The county is experiencing new life and new hope for the future.

"Of course, the ethics program is not [alone] responsible for the resurgence of governmental effectiveness, but it did play a part. Through the establishment of the ethics program and the priority placed on public integrity, trust in honest and effective governance is being reestablished in our community. Public integrity breeds trust, trust breeds partnerships, partnerships breed action, and action breeds progress. One cannot be done without the other."

"In my opinion," says County Administrator Dennis Hays, "since the consolidation of governments in 1997, the public's trust and confidence in the government have increased dramatically. I am proud that there has been no public wrongdoing; however, should something arise, with the proactive avoidance through the ethics program, a swift and unbiased judgment will be made."

District Attorney Nick Tomasic is of the opinion that "the extensive ethics training sessions for all elected officials and employees of the unified government have produced visible changes in the conduct of local government employees. The continuing training teaches new public servants a keen awareness of ethical behavior and the rules they are expected to follow, as well as reinforcing these expectations in veteran employees."

"The ethics program has been instrumental in promoting good government and reassuring public trust. While there have been isolated incidents of misconduct, they have been quickly identified and dealt with swiftly and openly. The ethics commission meets regularly in open sessions and allows citizens and employees the opportunity to report misconduct. This transparency and accessibility in the process has built trust among members of the public, who too often are skeptical and mistrustful of government."

Finally, former Kansas Lieutenant Governor Gary Sherrer says: "Throughout my public life and private life, I have never been part of such a dramatic political, social, and economical change as what has occurred in Wyandotte County. While ethics alone would not have produced all that has been achieved, all that has been achieved would not have been accomplished without the strong emphasis on ethical behavior."

Building a successful local government ethics program is not unlike most other aspects of good management and leadership. Here are some lessons learned from the ethics program experience:

1. A successful ethics program cannot be just a code of ethics or just an ethics-training program or the work of an ethics administrator or a citizens' ethics board. All are necessary, and all must be carefully integrated.

2. Independence and autonomy are essential. An ethics administrator or a citizens' ethics board appointed by elected officials will be reluctant to look at ethical issues associated with these officials.

3. Confidentiality in the treatment of allegations and investigations is vital. Persons with credible claims of misconduct must know that their identity will be protected.

4. Trust is critical. Citizens, elected officials, employees, and employee unions must trust the administrators of the ethics program to be approachable, fair, just, and reasonable.

5. While it is important to find misconduct when it is occurring and to fix it, it is equally important that this discovery not be made with an attitude of "gotcha." The purpose of an ethics program is to promote good and honest local government. It is essential that administrators of the programs understand that their work is part of the general administration of the jurisdiction.

# 29. Ethics: Alive and Well[*]

## Elizabeth Keller and Jan Perkins

Ethics has been at the core of the city and county management profession since ICMA was founded in 1914. And ethics can never be taken for granted.

As Clinton Gridley, city administrator, Woodbury, Minnesota, puts it: "Our organization's ethical underpinnings need constant tending, just like a garden. The organization may have a good reputation, but if there are momentary lapses, all of the good work and reputation we have built can be blown away."

Woodbury enjoys a strong reputation, consistently ranking in the top three local governments in a biennial citizen survey of some 50 communities in Minnesota. And yet, even Woodbury is not immune to an occasional ethical lapse. Gridley recounted that not long ago the city found that some city employees had misused the Internet to view pornographic sites from their city computers.

Although the employees' actions were not illegal, they were contrary to the organization's values. Gridley and the department directors were stunned to find anyone in the organization would have shown such poor judgment. The city put more restrictive Internet firewalls in place to make sure there would be no recurrence. The city's action caused inconvenience to some staff, but it was a small price to pay to restore confidence.

But Gridley wanted to do more than apply a corrective action to a particular problem. He turned to ICMA for local government ethics training to reinforce Woodbury's values. Gridley explains it this way: "As Stephen Covey would say, it's important to sharpen the saw. Ethical judgment is like the blade of the saw. It can get dull without training. ICMA's case examples stimulate active discussion and make people think."

Woodbury has a strong culture that builds on a "We HELP" values statement that was adopted some years ago:

- Help
- Effective
- Look ahead
- Professional

Employees are recognized when they exhibit what Woodbury calls "HELPish" values, sometimes with a written thank you, an intranet "pat on the back," or an employee award. After their ICMA ethics training, Gridley has encouraged top management to engage in ethical conversations. They now are sharing stories about particular ethical problems they have faced and are learning from each other. "What happens in one de-

[*]Originally published as Elizabeth Kellar and Jan Perkins, "Ethics: Alive and Well," *PM Magazine* 89, no. 1 (January/February 2007). Reprinted with permission of the publisher.

partment can easily be repeated in another part of the organization," Gridley says.

Inspired by Patrick Lencioni's book, *The Five Dysfunctions of a Team: A Leadership Fable*, Gridley is challenging Woodbury's leadership to develop more skill and comfort in being honest and open with each other. In a "nice" culture like Woodbury has, Gridley recognizes it is not easy to learn how to criticize politely and appropriately. "But this is important to our goal of building and keeping the public's trust," he adds.

Terry Stewart, city manager, Cape Coral, Florida, and John Maltbie, county manager, San Mateo County, California, agree that it takes conscious effort and sound management practices to build an ethical culture. San Mateo County leaders have long worked to ensure there is a clear vision, mission, and expectations for people in the organization. Leaders must act consistently with the values they want to see in others.

Maltbie speaks at the new-employee orientation each month to share his vision of public service. He emphasizes that, as a county employee, each person must be accountable to the public, act in a transparent and open way, respect the people who are being served, and collaborate with others in the county and outside the organization to accomplish public service goals.

Cape Coral reinforces ethics in its personnel system. Ethical behavior is integrated into the organization's management style, which is open, encourages employees to speak their minds, and rewards ethical conduct. Stewart recalls the Cape Coral code enforcement officer who investigated a complaint about housing conditions.

Cape Coral had offered housing to a number of evacuees from Hurricanes Charlie and Katrina. When the code enforcement officer found appalling conditions in one home where a young family of evacuees lived, he took action that exceeded his responsibility of writing up code violations. He found a better city-owned home for the family and secured plugs for the electrical outlets so that the young children would be safe. Cape Coral made that code enforcement officer "employee of the year" for going beyond the call of duty and demonstrating ethical leadership.

A measure of an individual's ethical courage or an organization's ethical culture is how that person deals with problems when something goes wrong. When Jim Keene, now executive director of the California State Association of Counties, was city manager in Tucson, Arizona, he had to deal with a sticky accountability issue involving an elected official's staff.

Each member of the Tucson city council has six staff members who support them. One city councilmember had asked his staff to collect water bill payments. These employees had not been screened to do that kind of work, and no controls were in place to ensure that payments were processed appropriately. Keene told the councilmember that this practice could not continue, and he proposed that the city set up a satellite office to provide this service if there was a customer service issue that needed to be addressed.

The councilmember did not agree and took his case to the media, arguing that residents would be upset with any change. Keene continued to press for change. "This is a bad business practice and the city will have problems if we don't change," he said.

One month later, the city councilmember went to the city attorney to disclose that "a lot of money was missing" and asked the attorney what to do. The city attorney immediately brought Keene into the communication loop, and Keene launched a police investigation.

Because the recordkeeping was poor, the police said that it would be difficult to prosecute anyone for wrongdoing. The money collected for bills had been commingled with petty cash that staff used for a variety of needs, and cursory notes about various amounts of money had been left in the till. Keene handled the problem discreetly by sending a memo directly to the councilmember to require that the councilmember stop collecting payments for water bills in his office.

It was an election year, and Keene did not copy the entire city council on the memo. The councilmember himself, however, went public with the problem and accused one of his staff of misusing the funds. A reporter filed a freedom of information request and got a copy of Keene's memo. This reporter wrote a story about the problem three days before city council elections. The councilmember accused Keene of leaking the memo to the media. The city settled with the individual who had been accused by the councilmember. The councilmember narrowly won his bid for reelection.

One lesson that Keene draws from this experience and other ethical challenges he has faced is that a crisis can be a time to press for positive changes. "When things seem the darkest and the loneliest, the best strategy is to dive directly into it," he says. "It can be an opportunity for a shift in thinking and to recognize that many in the public are with you."

In Cape Coral, Stewart recalls the time when one of his subordinates demonstrated courage. Two years ago, the finance director became concerned that Stewart, the city manager, might have been trying to circumvent the city's system after he saw a memo that Stewart had written requesting that an individual be paid for his work. He came directly to Stewart to ask about it. Stewart thanked the finance director for raising the concern with him, saying, "I am glad you are paying attention to these issues. It was not my intent to go around the system. I just wanted to be sure we did all we could."

Stewart says that many organizations have problems because employees may fear speaking up. ICMA's ethics training reinforces the importance of ethical leadership and responsibility. Stewart adds that employees also need to understand that no "monkey visits" are allowed: "Employees cannot bring me a monkey and expect me to carry it on my back. If someone brings a problem to my attention, I am going to act. That is my responsibility, especially if it deals with a serious matter like sexual harassment."

County Manager John Maltbie has a similar perspective. He believes ethics is about two issues: discernment and discipline. Discernment is the ability to determine right and wrong. Discipline is the ability to act on the knowledge of what the right thing is to do, even when it is difficult or painful. The county counsel's office regularly helps the management team deal with difficult ethical issues so that staff know they have a place to go for advice that goes beyond the legal issues.

"We're engaged in the business of public service," says Maltbie, "which means our decisions and actions must promote the integrity and good intentions of government." He sees the profession of city and county management as one of the most ethical in the world. Maltbie says local government managers are held to a higher standard, and he believes they should be. He draws his leadership philosophy from his belief in the value of public service and the imperative to act consistently for the benefit of the public.

Although an individual's personal leadership is important in supporting an ethical culture, it is equally important to embed ethical values and expectations in the organization's systems, behaviors, and actions. Local government leaders are stewards of the public trust. Building and supporting an ethical culture is a legacy that may not be as visible as a beautiful downtown, but it pays dividends to the community for years to come.

# 30. Ethics in Public Management Education*

## Alicia Schatteman

The State of Illinois, like many states around the country, is home to its share of corruption in public service. We tend to only hear about the big cases like the $54 million fraud case in Dixon, Illinois or how former Governor of Illinois, Rod Blagojevich, was convicted of trying to sell then Senator Barack Obama's senate seat. These cases, which are played out in newspapers, websites and television, help to further chip away at the public's trust of government.

According to Pew Research, trust in the federal government remains at an historic low of 24 percent, a steady downward trend since Pew starting tracking trust in government in 1954 when it was 73 percent. What's happened since then? Is there more temptation to choose unethical behavior, less sanctions for ethical behavior, higher expectations for ethical behavior or a combination of all three? What can public management programs do to support ethical behavior of public servants?

As a state university, Northern Illinois University is now subject to the 2009 Illinois Governmental Ethics Act and State Officials and Employees Ethics Act. Part of this law requires all state employees to take an ethics test every fall. This is one way to draw attention to possible conflicts and ethical challenges by state workers and elected officials. However, we need to train our future public service leaders on the importance of ethics and transparency to support transparency and build public trust in government.

At Northern Illinois University, our MPA program has undergone many curriculum changes to address ethics and other competencies as outlined by the Network of Schools of Public Policy, Affairs and Administration (NASPAA). NASPAA "is the membership organization of graduate education programs in public policy, public affairs, public administration and public & nonprofit management," according to its website. NASPAA's 2009 accreditation standards moved toward an outcome-based approach, focusing on student learning specific competencies as they relate to public management. They specifically outlined five universal competencies that graduates of all accredited programs should demonstrate the ability to:

- Lead and manage in public governance.
- Participate in and contribute to the policy process.

*Originally published as Alicia Schatteman, "Ethics in Public Management Education," *PA Times,* January 27, 2015. Reprinted with permission of the publisher.

- Analyze, synthesize, think critically, solve problems and make decisions.
- Articulate and apply a public service perspective.
- Communicate and interact productively with a diverse and changing workforce and citizenry.

Each program will then further define learning outcomes for each competency. Other schools have adapted their programs similarly such as James Madison University, a case written in the *Journal of Public Affairs Education.*

The faculty of the MPA program at Northern Illinois University created 14 specific learning outcomes from these five universal competencies. Specifically, competency #10 says that upon completion of the MPA degree, students should be able to incorporate professional codes of ethics in public service decision-making to enhance integrity of public services." To ensure that our students are meeting these learning outcomes we created a multi-prong approach to measure this competency:

- Self-assessment of incoming MPA students where they rank themselves on a scale from not at all, foundation, application or integration based on the Bloom's Taxonomy and Dee Fink's Designing Courses for Significant Learning.
- In the survey course, we reinforce the program competencies by creating an assignment based on the selection of an ethics framework, and one of the final exam questions asks students to write about their own ethical framework. In this course, students also begin to build their e-portfolio with

specific examples of how they have demonstrated the learning competencies in coursework and their internship.

- Graduating students also complete the same self-assessment ranking themselves on the same scale (noted above). This same survey is sent to graduates one year and three years after their graduation to further track their learning over time.

As public servants, there a number of ethical frameworks that students can use in their progressions. These include but are not limited to:

- International City/County Management Association (ICMA) Code of Ethics.
- Government Finance Officers Association of the U.S. & Canada (GFOA) Code of Professional Ethics.
- American Society for Public Administration (ASPA) Code of Ethics.
- Association of Fundraising Professionals (AFP) Code of Ethical Principles and Standards.

In our introductory course, students research these codes of ethics and then make a commitment to follow one of them for their professional career. So as faculty of future public servants, is this enough? Can we in effect instill ethics and values in our students so they make ethical decisions?

We are about a year into the process but preliminary results are hopeful. We hope that through a very open and deliberative process our students think of ethics as a guide for the way their work at all times.

# 31. Key Elements to Building Transparent Communities*

## International City/County Management Association

Corruption in government systems lowers the quality of governance and services and erodes public trust. The impact of corruption is especially insidious at the local level, where citizens are closest to the government. By eroding public confidence, corruption inhibits citizens' willingness to collaborate with government. It also lowers investor confidence and limits economic growth opportunities.

Transparency in local government, on the other hand, is fundamental for effective and efficient services, increased trust and confidence on the part of citizens, healthy economic development, and improved governance. Generally speaking, the relationship between transparency and corruption is direct and inverse: more transparency leads to less corruption.

While transparency and accountability are important characteristics of a community, the ultimate goal is to improve the lives of citizens by providing quality services and promoting local economic development in an open, competitive, and fair manner.

## A Vision of a Transparent Community

While local governments play a critical role in facilitating transparency and accountability, the term community is used to acknowledge that all stakeholders—civil society and the private sector, as well as the government itself—must be held to standards of transparency and accountability. All three must be actively engaged in identifying solutions and promoting transparency in their own organizations. All three have a responsibility to communicate openly and work together to facilitate change.

This article identifies five "critical success elements" for creating transparency and accountability. While it is widely recognized that corruption in government has an adverse affection the quality of service delivery and on economic growth, it is also true that complacency by civil society and the private sector has the same effect. Thus, rather than targeting individuals, these critical elements focus primarily on actively engaging stakeholders in reforming institutions and systems.

There are many ways to address these "suc-

*Originally published as ICMA, "Five Key Elements to Building Transparent Communities," http://icma. org/en/international/resources/insights/Article/101970/Five_Key_Elements_to_Building_Transparent_ Communities," September 10, 2009. Reprinted with permission of the publisher.

cess elements," and while the model outlined here is broadly applicable, the specific approaches and tools used must take into account a myriad of factors unique to each community, including the nature of corruption within it; its local, state, and national legislative frameworks; and its resource base.

## Initiating Reforms at the Local Level

An environment lacking in transparency, professionalism, and accountability allows corruption to thrive. Before initiating reforms, however, it is important to understand the challenges facing local governments and their communities. With decentralization, local governments often have the mandate, but not the resources, to deliver quality services to citizens. Operating within national and subregional legal and policy frameworks, local governments may also lack the autonomy and ability to undertake reforms. Clearly, any transparency initiatives at the local level have the greatest chance of succeeding when they are undertaken as part of broader, nationwide anticorruption efforts.

There are many benefits to working at the local level to promote national reforms. Local-level efforts often result in rapid, tangible improvements that may take decades to emerge at the national level. And local institutions are much more accessible and visible to most citizens, facilitating a clearer understanding of the direct link between increased transparency and improved service delivery. As part of a broader, integrated national-level reform program, local-level initiatives can be used as best practice models to inform both local and national decision making. Finally, local-level reforms tend to be more institutionally focused than those at the national level, which may involve broader legal, parliamentary, or constitutional issues.

## Critical Success Elements

To foster the active engagement of participants and ensure long-term sustainability, it is essential to establish a vision of the transparent community that is common to all stakeholders. This vision may include improved service delivery and/or local economic development. Solid local government systems should:

- Reflect agreed-upon community priorities and service provision needs
- Productively and positively involve all stakeholders with a focus on sustainable institutional and systemic reform
- Promote public awareness and open dissemination of information.

The five critical success elements are:

- Political will
- Integrity in local government systems
- Information sharing and continuous learning
- Monitoring and evaluation
- An ethic of public service.

All must be combined with active communication among and engagement of local government, civil society, and the private sector.

## Political Will

Political will is characterized by community leaders prepared to be held accountable to citizens for their public decision making and willing to impose consequences on those who undertake inappropriate behavior. These leaders should operate on the basis of clearly articulated, applied, and enforced rules and standards of ethical conduct, not just legal status.

Windows of opportunity exist in which to foster political will. A change in administration in a local government or a community organization may facilitate reform, particularly in the wake of a corruption scandal. Elections provide another incentive for leaders to embrace improved public service, especially if elected officials are eligible to serve more than one term.

## Integrity in Local Government Systems

For a local government to deliver quality services and promote economic development, administrative processes and procedures must be simplified and standardized across all systems and departments so as to minimize opportunities for individual discretion and corruption. Three key systems that must function in a transparent and accountable manner are human resource (HR) management, procurement, and financial management.

Human resource management: Transparency in HR management systems provides internal controls and reduces incentives and opportunities for corruption. These systems include a well-structured pay schedule that guarantees a living wage for public employees and removes the need for seeking wages outside, clear definition of roles and responsibilities, and corresponding performance measures providing a basis for evaluation. Standards of integrity and commitment must be reinforced through merit-based hiring and promotion practices.

Procurement: Procurement processes should be open and accessible to all eligible suppliers, including businesses that are small, disadvantaged, or owned by women or minorities. Procurement procedures should involve the preparation of standardized bid documents that include nondiscriminatory specifications and clear and transparent evaluation criteria. Local governments must promote competitive bidding, publish all tenders, and document the award and the decision-making process.

Because procurement systems are also open to exploitation by the private sector, local governments may consider establishing prequalification mechanisms for public bidding, with those organizations known to have offered bribes or engaged in collusive activities being barred from participation in the open process. This also opens a channel for collaboration with organizations representing the private sector. Chambers of commerce or industry may participate in efforts to educate their members about public procurement processes and establish codes of ethics for companies competing for public tenders.

Financial management: A transparent and integrated financial management system is inextricably linked to the community participatory planning process, as it formalizes citizen input into resource allocation and decision making and provides citizens with the tools to hold local governments accountable.

Financial management should include an accounting system based on internationally accepted standards, an open budgeting process, and the reporting of financial and performance-based results or progress to the community. Performance budgeting is a powerful performance management tool; it links allocated resources to measurable outcomes in order to assess progress toward meeting agreed-upon community priorities.

In addition to performance budgeting, other means of ensuring that the budgeting process is open and transparent include:

- Multiyear capital needs budgeting
- Budget education workshops for citizens
- Open workshops with councils to discuss the inextricable ties between the budget and such issues as growth management, land use, transportation, and economic development planning
- An annual "report card" issued at the

end of the budget year highlighting key sections of the budget, including what was spent and not spent and why, and includes a discussion of the process for starting new fiscal-year budget planning.

Local governments also must develop internal controls and undergo regular independent audits. The information from an integrated financial management system will enable them to produce transparent, credible financial statements that can be objectively audited. This, in turn, will allow them to be assessed for creditworthiness, an important step for stimulating economic growth by attracting investment.

## Information Sharing

In order for all stakeholders to engage in building a transparent community, they must have free access to accurate and complete information in an accessible format. This may include local government budget reports, detailed posting of local government services and any associated fees, and publication of public tenders. In order to use this information effectively, stakeholders also must know how the public sector functions and understand the constraints that apply to budgets, procurement, and human resources, as well as the legal framework within which local government operates.

In addition to providing information, local governments must create opportunities for constructive dialogue and stakeholder input into local government decision making and resource allocation. This reinforces to residents that they have a role to play in local government and the management of their community. And all stakeholders should undertake a coordinated public awareness campaign to educate and mobilize their constituents around the issue of building transparent communities.

## Monitoring and Evaluation

At the onset of any transparent community initiative, an initial evaluation should be conducted to provide baseline data and identify critical issues. This evaluation may include a corruption vulnerability assessment of the local government, citizen surveys reflecting perceptions of corruption, and/or transparency assessments undertaken by civil society organizations.

As initiatives evolve, effective monitoring and evaluation on the part of all stakeholders can be used to benchmark progress, foster healthy competition among communities to encourage higher performance, and advance accountability and sustainable transparency efforts.

Monitoring and evaluation processes can be institutionalized (e.g., an independent body or an ombudsman), or they can be undertaken informally by different stakeholders using customized tools and methodologies. Any such institution must be able to handle complaints from both inside and outside the local government and must be free to act and report as an independent entity. Any actions it takes will provide the community with rapid and visible proof that corruption is not acceptable. Individuals identifying incidents of corruption must be free from direct or indirect retaliation or retribution.

## An Ethic of Public Service

While the importance of effective controls, such as legislation, cannot be overlooked, promoting transparency and accountability should become ingrained in the institutional culture of all stakeholders.

Promoting and demonstrating compliance with existing laws, such as freedom of information acts, campaign finance disclosure acts, and laws mandating asset disclosure by public officials, may help reinforce the local government's commitment to the vision of a transparent community. So, too, may passage of additional legislation, such as local ordinances that formalize budget hearings and performance reporting.

To create sustainable institutions dedicated to the ideals of transparency and accountability, all stakeholders must play an active role in promoting integrity in public service. In local government, codes of ethics and of conduct are valuable tools for establishing shared ethical parameters and providing guidance for employees. Local governments should also provide employees with resources, including continuous education and informal discussions where they can address questions and concerns about what constitutes ethical behavior. Civil society and the private sector should have access to training resources as well to help them educate their constituents and mobilize citizens in support of transparent and accountable local governments.

## Conclusion

This model of a transparency requires the engagement of all stakeholders—local government, civil society, and the private sector—in efforts to ensure sustainable institutional reforms. Using the five elements described here, stakeholders can work toward the common objectives of improved service delivery and economic growth.

Initiatives at the local level often yield rapid successes, particularly when compared with similar initiatives at the national level. This inspires stakeholder confidence, builds momentum, and increases commitment to institutional reform efforts. And these successes, in turn, can be used to inform policy dialogue at the national level and be replicated in other communities to achieve the ultimate objective: an improved quality of life for everyone.

# 32.  A Dose of Transparency*

## Penelope Lemov

If you suffer from heart disease and live in Florida, you can click on a state Web site and figure out which hospital in your county—or anywhere in the state for that matter—has the best record for cardiac care. FloridaCompareCare.gov will tell you each hospital's survival rates for, say, coronary artery bypass surgery—plus how well the hospital does with surgical infection prevention. And that's not all. The site lets you know how much each hospital charges for the procedure and its accompanying hospital stay—and how that compares to other hospitals in the state.

The idea behind the site, which lists information for a dozen health problems, is, says Alan Levine, who headed Florida's Agency for Health Care Administration when the site was being developed, to "improve care and reduce costs" by giving citizens "the tools to compare outcomes and prices between health care providers and medical services."

It's a consumer-driven world out there. Health care costs and provider performance are becoming the business of patients. That's because patients are increasingly bearing the brunt of a shift in who pays the health care bill. A significant number of employers, for example, are asking employees to pay not only a greater share of the insurance premium but also larger co-payments for doctor visits and various procedures. In addition, consumer-driven health plans, such as Health Savings Accounts, are edging into the mainstream of insurance coverage. HSA plans, for instance, put money in an account that employees use to pay for their day-to-day health care. If they use it all up, they can end up paying a significant portion of their health bills out of their own pockets.

With these new responsibilities, patients need more information about the cost and quality of care. Along with Florida, a handful of states—Maryland, New York and Texas, among them—are or will shortly be feeding that need with state-backed Web sites offering comparative information about hospitals and, in some cases, individual physicians.

But consumer service is only a piece of the picture. There is an even loftier goal: reducing overall costs within the health care system. That is, in the best of all possible worlds, patients would choose the highest quality facility—the hospital with, say, the lowest mortality rates and the best score on

---

*Originally published as Penelope Lemov, "A Dose of Transparency," *Governing*, September 2006. Reprinted with permission of the publisher.

infection rates. Over time, the hospitals that perform poorly—those with, say, high infection rates that add unnecessary costs to the system—would be driven out of business. The information on price could push physicians at the high end of the spectrum to voluntarily lower their fees.

In the real world of day-to-day practices and habits, however, questions abound about whether consumers are in a position to benefit from the information available to them. Despite the increasing pressures on them to compare quality and price, they may actually be drowning in data and finding it difficult to make use of the information. That raises the issue of whether state efforts to create Web sites that offer quality and cost comparison shopping are worth the political hassle it takes to get them up and running.

## Changing Behavior

It would seem prudent for a patient who is ill—facing, for example, heart surgery or a hip replacement—to check out the bona fides of possible service providers. But many factors run counter to that instinct. Patients may, in fact, have little choice. "If you're desperately ill," says Elizabeth Teisberg, co-author with Michael E. Porter, of *Redefining Health Care: Creating Value-Based Competition on Results*, "you are in your doctor's hands and not likely to argue with him about which hospital he's going to send you to for an operation—or to change physicians to use a doctor who operates at a high-rated facility."

The record on consumer reaction to Web site information echoes Teisberg's observation. Take a recent assessment of New York's public report card on deaths from coronary bypass surgery. For 15 years, the state has been keeping tabs on hospitals and doctors who perform the surgery, and researchers have found that heart patients who pick a

top-performing hospital or surgeon from that report card are half as likely to die as those who pick a poor-scoring provider. However, according to the recent analysis of patient behavior, patients and their cardiologists are not flocking to the top-rated providers. "Patients can dramatically cut their chances of dying by selecting a top performer," says Ashish Jha, lead author of the study and a professor at Harvard University's School of Public Health. "But there's no real evidence that patients use the information to pick a better hospital, even though it's free and easy to access."

Jha's findings are confirmed by a study of another program. Mathematica Policy Research analyzed Hospital Compare, a federal program that gives patients a means of comparing hospitals in terms of quality measures and thereby choosing the best one for the type of care they need. To provide potential patients and their families with information to make such judgments, Hospital Compare asks the institutions—4,200 acute-care and critical-access hospitals nationwide participate—to submit data on quality measures for treating heart attacks, heart failure and pneumonia, and for preventing surgical infection. Hospitals are asked, for instance, how often they prescribe a beta-blocker drug when heart attack patients are discharged and whether they check to see if pneumonia patients have received an influenza or pneumococcal vaccine. These are accepted as "best practices" or appropriate performance measures for hospitals, and now that information is available for patients and their families to use.

As in Jha's study, however, Mathematica researchers found that patients aren't benefiting all that much from Hospital Compare. There is, Mathematica senior health researcher Mary Laschober notes, "little empirical evidence that consumers have altered their behavior in response to publicly reported quality measures."

Laschober's next point, however, keys in on what may be the ultimate importance of a Web site that provides comparative data. "Hospitals," she writes, "respond in positive ways to public reporting." Many of those in the Hospital Compare database immediately began improving their scores from one reporting period to the next. Eight in 10 reported significant improvement on one or more scores while only 5 percent reported a decline in one measure or more.

Similarly, when the state of Maryland began putting a hospital reporting system in place a few years ago, hospitals were given several years to prepare for the public disclosure and even practiced the data review process for six months before the data went online. During the tune-up phase, the hospitals were able to spot their failings, and most of them changed policies to meet the standards.

Teisberg points out that, unlike patients, providers—doctors, hospitals, clinics—are competing and "they don't want to show up in the bottom 25 percent." Teisberg, who is an associate professor at the University of Virginia's Darden Graduate School of Business, adds that "the importance of reporting results is to enable not just patients to get information but physicians to improve."

## Pressure from the Feds

While many hospitals do act to improve, plenty of them don't. The Mathematica study asked hospital administrators what they saw as the barriers to boosting their scores. Several fobbed off the low scores by saying their poor showing was simply a failure of physicians and other staff members to document that appropriate care was given. But other hospitals reported that they were unable to get physicians involved in quality-improvement efforts or that they did not have the financial resources to devote to improvement strategies.

It's also true that some hospitals—and many hospital associations—are less than enamored with the whole exercise in transparency, in part because prices for any one procedure are likely to vary widely even within a single hospital, with different tabs for various insurers and others for the uninsured. For years, hospital and insurance associations have been successful in lobbying to keep lawmakers from mandating Web sites that would provide comparative quality and pricing data on hospitals. But change is in the air. One reason is a countervailing pressure from the federal government. Hospitals that treat Medicare patients are rewarded financially for reporting their performance data.

But pressure is being felt in the states, as well. Comparative sites are seen as a way to get a handle on quality and price and, thereby, force down the cost of health care. The new mood was palpable in Ohio this year when the legislature considered a bill to have the health department set up a site so consumers could measure hospital mortality rates on certain procedures and compare various charges, such as private and semi-private rooms and common services available through emergency, operating and delivery rooms. The road to passage was far from easy. "It took about two years to work through and pass," says state Representative Jim Raussen, who sponsored the measure. Legislators had to work closely with health insurance companies and the hospital association to craft a bill everyone could live with.

## Price Points

Most state Web sites have a price list of sorts: what hospitals charge for a limited number of services. Unlike Web sites sponsored by health insurance companies, which carry the fees the insurance company has negotiated with the provider (and whose sites are available only to those insured by the company), the state sites are open to everyone and carry a range of charges or average prices. The New York State Health Accountability Foundation, a public-private partnership, maintains a Web site that offers, county by county, the average length of stay in the hospital for 14 different procedures and the average charge. At Albany Medical Center, for instance, surgery for a hip replacement currently means three to four days in the hospital (3.7 is the hospital's average) at an average cost of $21,425, while over at St. Peter's Hospital, hospitalization is closer to four days (3.98 days on average) but the charges are slightly lower at $20,905.

For a patient with a consumer-driven health plan or insurance that requires significant co-pays or deductibles, price is an important factor. But the charges listed are not necessarily what the patient will end up paying. Complications can arise; additional therapies may be needed. And the listed price does not factor in what a particular insurance plan allows or will pay for. "The idea of posting prices poses difficulties," says Robert Doherty, a physician who is also senior vice president of public policy for the American College of Physicians. "There is not a single retail price."

Moreover, Doherty points out, most of the health care dollar is spent in the last few months of life where "people aren't going to pay much attention to price. They just want to get the care they need. So I'm pretty skeptical that posting prices will be a huge boon to lowering health care costs."

Even for those willing to shop for the best price, the information is often difficult to digest. If the prices are presented on a piece-by-piece basis—a site might show that a hospital charges $1,000 for a surgical procedure, $1,200 for the operating room, $500 per day for the hospital bed, $30 for two aspirin—they won't be able to make much sense of it. Moreover, prices for every procedure are not available. Usually, a site will list up to 30 of the most common procedures. But that doesn't mean the surgery or therapy the patient faces is on the list.

Gerard Anderson, a professor of health policy at Johns Hopkins University, sees a possible solution to comparison-shopping in having providers list what percentage of the Medicaid charge they pay. A hospital might report that it charges 125 percent or 200 percent more than the Medicaid base. "That would give people one number to compare," he says. "It would be one number that people could understand."

What health economists such as Teisberg note is that the point of the quality and price reports is not necessarily to put consumers in charge but to drive quality and efficiency simultaneously. "In most industries, that's what happens," she says. "But it requires competition at the right levels. And that is not currently the case in the health care industry."

To the extent that public and easily accessible information puts pressure on hospitals to perform up to a gold standard, the Web sites may be worth state efforts. They could be a force for driving down costs—if they bring about pressure for the widespread use of evidence-based medicine and a beefing up of quality and performance measurements. Otherwise, they are nothing more than another trend-of- the-day solution. "It's just this year's model," Anderson says, "unless we get the methodology right, and we're many years away from getting it right."

# 33. Introducing the Cycle of Transparency[*]

## Paul Blumenthal

Government transparency is that rarest of political phenomena—a great idea with support across the political spectrum and popularity among the public. Yet, here we are in the 21st century with every tool we would need to make government more transparent and accountable, and still we are operating with a government that often behaves as it did in the 19th century.

So, transparent government is a good thing, but we do not yet have one. Now what?

It's clear that there is a breakdown between conceptual support for the idea of government transparency and enacting the changes necessary to make it so. There is fear and resistance to change inside government that requires cultural, political, and attitude adjustments. And there's a large gap between the good intentions of citizens and watchdog groups and think tanks and reporters, and translating those good intentions into effective results. Many people want to act, but they rarely know how or where to begin.

For many, the concept of transparency still simply feels too vague to get behind in a meaningful way. People strongly support transparency in theory, but don't know what they would need to do, or how they would

need to think, to create the "open, transparent government" we talk about.

We've grappled with these challenges at Sunlight since our founding four years ago, and have been thinking about it with increased urgency over the last year in particular. How do we connect all the necessary parties and resources, and how do we put them together and act on them in the right way to actually make government more open and transparent?

Perhaps even more challenging: How do we explain it to people in a way that helps them know where they fit?

Now, the pieces are falling into place.

We know that at the heart of the open, transparent government we seek is 'open' government data that is available online and in real-time.

Government information should be as accessible to us as information about the weather, sports scores or knowing what's going on in the stock market—and we need it to be this way so we can both hold government accountable and create new enterprise with what is made available to us.

In order to reach our vision of an open government—or an online, real-time government—we also know there are a number

---

[*]Originally published as Paul Blumenthal, "Introducing the Cycle of Transparency," *Governing*, May 6, 2010. Reprinted with permission of the publisher.

of "things" that must occur—and not just occur once, but continue to happen over time and continuously reinforce each other along the way.

This "Cycle of Transparency" demonstrates the specific actions and the variety of actors that need to work together to create the open, transparent government we seek. We hope the Cycle can be a useful tool in thinking about how to make city, state, federal, and even international governments more transparent.

Each type of actor and action complements the others in the Cycle to make every other element easier, or even possible at all. Of great importance is that just about anyone—from hardcore Internet developers to academics to government staff to reporters to activists—has a place in it.

One of the first places we often start in talking about transparency is in the crafting of policies that require the release of data from government. While no one piece of this Cycle is "first" or more important than others, the legislative component is a useful starting point. (Mostly because it's the first one we wrote down.)

Lawmakers, lobbyists and think tanks (as well as citizens) all play a role in articulating new transparency policies and pushing them through the twists and turns of government processes. Those policies must adhere to core principles of openness, such as making sure government data is "raw," that it is complete, or that it is searchable (in total, there are nine of these openness principles that government data should adhere to).

These principles aren't things that government is accustomed to just yet, so the advocacy process is pretty difficult, and the subsequent "gap" between writing new legislation and actually getting legislation passed is more like a "chasm."

One of the beautiful aspects of open government, however, is that while laws are written (and should be passed) to require the release of government data, Congress, federal agencies, states and cities can—in most cases—become more open and transparent without new laws.

Sidenote: A great example of "enacting without law" is that no law has been passed requiring all federal legislation to be available online for 72 hours before it is debated by Congress. Yet in 2009, Congress showed again and again that it could post bills online for three days before debate without the law requiring that action. Similarly, the "Open Government Directive," released in a memo by the White House, has made all kinds of new government data available without laws to require it. (Though, it would be ideal if Congress codified the Directive into law to give it a lasting impact.)

Once data is released, government agencies (such as the Department of Energy or Transportation) and web developers anywhere can build the necessary technology to organize the data and make it usable. Federal repositories like Data.gov or Sunlight's National Data Catalog are great examples of this type of public/private foundation building.

In the way of analogy, one way to think about this entire process is that it turns government into a type of public data wholesaler through which the public can build retail outlets.

With data being made easily accessible, journalists and bloggers can begin to dig into it, mix it up, identify relevant information and give the data context. As that critical context is provided, citizens absorb it and spread the information to others—both online and face-to-face—and make the data actionable.

Ultimately, informed citizen action creates greater public awareness; citizens become more effective, responsible advocates; holding government accountable becomes informed by data rather than inside-the-Beltway pundits, and better decisions can be made for our democracy.

As each element of the Cycle of Transparency moves forward concurrently, bringing about the changes we need to create a more transparent government, we also identify new needs. At the end of the day, the process that the Cycle of Transparency describes is about creating a government more deserving of our trust, and ultimately, a government that allows its citizens to fully participate and hold government accountable as our Founders intended.

# 34. Council-Manager or Strong Mayor?*

## *International City/County Management Association and California City Management Foundation*

Everyone wants strong political leadership—neighborhoods, civic leaders, and the business community included. And today's complex communities cannot succeed without the guidance of effective mayors who provide a sense of direction and contribute to the smooth functioning of a local government.

But communities also need thoughtful, dedicated council members, who work with the mayor to establish appropriate policy, and competent, professional managers to carry out those policies. None of the three are mutually exclusive; they can and do work together today in many of the country's successful council-manager communities.

Today council-manager government is the fastest growing form of government in the United States; it frees up the elected body to establish policy, which is carried out by an appointed manager and an administrative staff. The manager is accountable to the entire council for the satisfactory implementation of council policy and the day-to-day administration of municipal affairs.

There are compelling reasons why many

of the nation's most successful cities and towns have adopted council-manager government rather than the "strong-mayor" form. Council-manager government encourages neighborhood input into the political process, diffuses the power of special interests, and eliminates partisan politics from municipal hiring, firing, and contracting decisions.

People who take time to learn the facts about council-manager government are likely to join the ranks of those who favor this popular form. Consider the following when deciding which form of government is best for your community:

### Neighborhoods Strengthen Their Voice

The council-manager form encourages open communication between citizens and their government. Under this form, each member of the governing body has an equal voice in policy development and administrative oversight. This gives neighborhoods

*Originally published as ICMA and California City Management Foundation, "Council Manager or Strong Mayor? The Choice is Clear," http://icma.org/en/icma/knowledge_network/documents/kn/Document/302618/CouncilManager_or_Strong_Mayor_The_Choice_is_Clear, 2009. Reprinted with permission of the publisher.

and diverse groups a greater opportunity to influence policy.

Under the "strong mayor" form, political power is concentrated in the mayor, which means that other members of the elected body relinquish at least some of their policy-making power and influence. This loss of decision-making power among council members can have a chilling effect on the voices of neighborhoods and city residents.

## *The Power of Special Interests Is Diffused*

Under the council-manager form of government, involvement of the entire elected body ensures a more balanced approach to community decision making, so that all interests can be expressed and heard—not just those that are well funded. Under the "strong mayor" form, however, it's easier for special interests to use money and political power to influence a single elected official, rather than having to secure a majority of the city council's support for their agenda.

## *Merit-Based Decision Making Vs. Partisan Politics*

Under council-manager government, qualifications and performance—and not skillful navigation of the political election process—are the criteria the elected body uses to select a professional manager. The professional manager, in turn, uses his or her education, experience, and training to select department heads and other key managers to oversee the efficient delivery of services. In this way, council-manager government maintains critical checks and balances to ensure accountability at city hall.

Functioning much like a business organization's chief executive officer, the appointed professional manager administers the daily operations of the community. Through a professional staff, the manager ensures the effective provision of services and enforces the policies adopted by the elected body. He or she, in turn, uses merit as the leading criterion for making all hiring and personnel decisions.

Appointed local government managers have no guaranteed term of office or tenure. They can be dismissed by the council at any time, for any reason. As a result, they constantly must respond to citizens and be dedicated to the highest ideals of honesty, integrity, and excellence in the management and delivery of public services.

Under the "strong mayor" form of government, the day-to-day management of community operations shifts to the mayor, who often lacks the appropriate training, education, and experience in municipal administration and finance to oversee the delivery of essential community services. Also, under the "strong mayor" form, the temptation is strong to make decisions regarding the hiring and firing of key department head positions—such as the police chief, public works director, and finance director—based on the applicant's political support rather than his or her professional qualifications.

## *Many Successful Cities Use Council-Manager Government*

Council-manager government works! It balances diverse interests, responds quickly to challenges, and brings the community together to resolve even the toughest issues.

Currently, more than 92 million Americans live in council-manager communities, and the system continues to flourish. This form of government is used by thousands of small, medium, and large jurisdictions, including Charlotte, N.C.; Dallas, El Paso, Fort Worth, and San Antonio, Texas; Las Vegas, Nev.; Oklahoma City, Okla.; Phoenix and Tucson, Ariz.; Sacramento, San Jose, and

Anaheim, Calif.; Wichita, Kans.; and Colorado Springs, Colo. Consider these examples:

## History Argues for the Council-Manager Form of Government

Nearly 100 years old, the council-manager form of government has proven its adaptability; today it is the most popular choice of structure among U.S. communities with populations of 2,500 or greater.

Council-manager government, however, was not always an option. In the late 19th and early 20th centuries, there was widespread corruption, graft, and nepotism among U.S. cities. The stories of New York City's Tammany Hall and Kansas City's Pendergrast machine are only two examples of the misuse of local government power during this time.

By the early 20th century, reformers were looking for ways to return control of municipal government to citizens. Those reformers advocated the council-manager structure of government to eliminate the corruption found in many cities. With its emphasis on professional training and accountability, the council-manager form of government was first formally adopted in 1912 (following appointment of the first manager in 1908), and was subsequently adopted by a number of cities in the 1920s and 1930s.

It took years to diffuse the power entrenched in turn-of-the-century city political machines and special interests. Today, however, citizens throughout the U.S. have resumed control by adopting or retaining council-manager government in their community and enjoying representative democracy at its best.

# 35. A Cost-Effective Way to Bust (and Prevent) Contractor Fraud*

## Jim Sullivan

Fraud by government contractors and vendors is all too common, and attempts, particularly by local governments, to spot or prevent it often fall short due to limited funds and staff with too much work and not enough time.

Governments seeking an alternative to a too-often-underfunded inspector general's office, an overburdened contract-compliance unit or an audit staff focused only on internal operations may want to consider an independent monitor. A monitor can keep a watchful eye on contractors and slam the door on potentially unscrupulous vendors before they have an opportunity to engage in fraud.

In the past, independent monitors have been reserved for corporate deferred-prosecution agreements, allowing a business to avoid prosecution after law enforcement has exposed fraud or serious compliance violations. But why wait for the fraud to occur? For governments, it's far better to take a proactive approach and avoid reputation-damaging news about wasted tax revenue.

In considering the independent-monitor approach, it's important for governments to analyze their history. What problems have occurred in the past? Do staff members feel ill-equipped to effectively and efficiently respond to complaints? Would an audit by a funding source reveal agency wrongdoing? If so, a monitor may be the answer to these concerns.

But how can a government with limited funds and a host of programs to service afford to fund an independent-monitor program? The answer is that they can pass the cost on to the contractors themselves. They can build a provision into their requests for proposals and inform potential vendors that they will bear the cost of the monitoring, and vendors can then build the cost into their bids.

So instead of increasing long-term budget allocations to properly fund oversight offices, expenditures will increase incrementally and only on matters that warrant further inspection. Once in place, the monitor reports to appropriate staff inside the government agency who can review any significant findings, report to management if necessary and determine the proper course of action.

To start, though, governments should follow a couple of straightforward guidelines for developing a successful independent-monitoring program:

---

*Originally published as Jim Sullivan, "A Cost-Effective Way to Bust (and Prevent) Contractor Fraud," *Governing*, February 19, 2015. Reprinted with permission of the publisher.

- When issuing requests for qualifications for independent monitors, governments should evaluate respondents based on their neutrality, objectivity and professionalism. Then evaluators can create a pool of qualified service providers—preferably numerous vendors in each service area. A few red flags to watch out for include respondents that would likely have conflicts with the engagements needing monitoring, inexperienced respondents and vendors that have other business with the governmental agency.

Governments also should provide the contractor with a list of approved and available professional service firms and let them select one, subject to the government's approval. After a conflicts check to ensure that there are no hidden relationships, the monitor can begin the engagement with a scope of work written by the government.

So what's the return on investment for governments? An effective independent monitoring program can investigate bribery and kickback allegations, ethics policy violations, compliance with minority and women-owned business participation requirements, over-billing, false claims and a myriad of other potential schemes. For example, an independent monitor could require a contractor in an industry known for wining and dining public officials to allow the monitor to review all relevant employee expense reports. This drastically decreases the potential for fraud in this area.

As governments increasingly face tighter budgets and increasing pressure to protect taxpayer dollars, it's crucial that they identify ways to put fraud checks in place across all levels of their organizations. Employing independent monitors is a cost-effective way to help ensure that governments focus on their primary mission: better serving their constituents.

# 36. City-State Oversight of Funds Given to Nonprofits Lacking*

## Zach Patton

When investigators examined the operations of a sprawling New York social service organization, what they uncovered was deeply troubling. Board members of the Ridgewood Bushwick Senior Citizens Council had almost no experience in nonprofit management. Several couldn't name any of the group's programs. Two of them could not identify the executive director, who in turn told investigators she was unaware of a fraudulent scheme carried out under her watch: Employees had squandered or stolen most of an $80,000 city grant.

As a result of that July 2010 report by New York City's Department of Investigation, both the city and state quickly pulled the plug, suspending the organization's grants, which provide practically all of its funding. But just as quick, the Brooklyn-based group won back its government support on the condition that it enact corrective measures, and today, the council has active grants from the city and the state totaling more than $50 million. Maybe that's because the organization provides critical services, such as senior care and affordable housing, as a city spokeswoman said when funding was restored. But the council may also be thriving because its founder, Vito Lopez, was for years one of New York's most powerful politi-

cians—a state legislator who spent much of his career channeling that power through Ridgewood Bushwick.

Lopez personally directed at least $505,000 in state grants to the organization from 2007 through 2010, the only years for which data are available, and has reportedly had a hand in millions more. He helped elevate the group's employees to political office. Other candidates, elected with Lopez's help, have directed even more public money to Ridgewood Bushwick in return. The council's former executive director, forced out in disgrace, was Lopez's campaign treasurer; she later pleaded guilty to lying about a raise that hiked her salary to $782,000 for the fiscal year ending in June 2010. And Ridgewood Bushwick's housing director is Lopez's girlfriend.

This may look bad. It's not unusual. Vito Lopez is but one example of a surprisingly common phenomenon afflicting state legislatures. Since 2010, at least eight New York lawmakers or their related charities have been investigated, charged or convicted of pillaging public funds. Earlier this year, former state Sen. Shirley Huntley pleaded guilty in two separate cases, one in which she sent state grants to a nonprofit she had founded before pocketing the money, the other in which she helped her niece and a

*Originally published as Zach Patton, "State Oversight of Funds Given to Nonprofits Lacking," *Governing*, June 12, 2013. Reprinted with permission of the publisher.

former aide steal funds she directed to another group that, yes, Huntley herself created.

New York's legislators outshine their peers in this department, but they're not alone. Two former Florida state senators repeatedly directed state funds to a struggling group on whose board they sat, apparently not a violation of state law. A Pennsylvania charity had its state funding frozen after a state audit found it allegedly gave no-show jobs worth hundreds of thousands of dollars to a pastor and his aide at the direction of a state lawmaker. Illinois, Ohio and South Carolina all have seen similarly close ties between certain legislators and charities they helped fund.

While several examples led to criminal charges of theft and fraud, others appear to be perfectly legal: public officials are simply tipping the scales in favor of groups they are associated with or have a family member working for.

"The issue to me is what's legal, and the fact that there's a tremendous amount that's legal," said John Kaehny, executive director of Reinvent Albany, a group advocating government transparency. Kaehny said public officials in New York have used charities to conduct "widespread looting" of taxpayer funds with little repercussion.

As for Lopez, he's gotten into plenty of trouble in recent weeks—but not for anything related to Ridgewood Bushwick, despite reports of federal investigations back in 2010. Instead, in May, the New York Assembly forced Lopez to resign after the state's ethics commission released a report exposing lurid details of several sexual harassment complaints against him.

Lopez and his attorney did not return calls seeking comment. James Cameron, who became CEO of Ridgewood Bushwick in 2011 after the city ordered the group to overhaul its leadership, said the organization is fully independent of Lopez. Any ties exist simply because it operates in the neighborhoods he has represented for decades.

"He does not control, influence or dictate anything that happens in the organization," Cameron said. "But it's a large organization. If he's talking to staff out there in the field I would have no way of knowing." The former executive director, interviewed by city investigators three years ago, likewise distanced herself from her subordinates' actions, saying she had no "crystal ball" to know if employees were dishonest. Ridgewood Bushwick and affiliates employ 2,100 people.

Lopez is now running for a seat on the New York City Council and has received campaign contributions from at least 10 employees of the organization.

Rick Cohen, who has written extensively on the links between politicians and charities for *Nonprofit Quarterly*, said that in state capitols across the country, lawmakers direct taxpayer money to their pet groups irrespective of whether they need or deserve scarce public dollars. "I've seen very little evidence in … states that do this," he said, "that there's an accountability regimen or the oversight that's needed."

## A Lack of Scrutiny

Over the past few decades, state governments have increasingly outsourced many functions to community-based nonprofits in an attempt to provide more effective, flexible social services. But the result, some say, has been the creation of what is essentially another arm of government.

"The function may be outsourced, but a lot of the funding is coming from government," said Susan Lerner, executive director of Common Cause New York, a good government group. Ridgewood Bushwick, for instance, derived $13.4 million of its $15.5 million in outside funding in the fiscal year ending in June 2012 from government grants (affiliated groups pulled in some $42 million more, mostly in government health care contracts). When independent nonprofits spend that cash, rather than a government agency, Lerner said, public money does not receive the same level of oversight. "It has a tendency to fall into nepotism and favoritism and cronyism."

Separating favoritism from efficient use of funds has proven to be a daunting task for state governments. Some ethics experts say states should draw a clear line: that lawmakers cannot be involved in sending funds to any group with which they have a direct link, even as an unpaid board member.

"Where there's a real personal connection, financial or otherwise, I think it makes sense for the law to say that you can't be involved in that," said Peter Sturges, who served as executive director of the Massachusetts State Ethics Commission from 2000 to 2007. "You can't be making decisions objectively."

But few states draw such a line. Most laws consider a situation a conflict only if an official derives a direct financial benefit; sending money to your pet project, regardless of merit, is fine as long as you don't get a cut. In many states, lawmakers do not have to disclose if they hold an unpaid board position with a nonprofit in their community, or if family members or political staffers do (New York is among the few that do require this disclosure, though it does not extend to staff members of the lawmaker or grown children).

Ethics oversight bodies have weighed in on the topic in several states, and in most cases, they have allowed the lawmakers to help fund nonprofits with which they are associated.

In Texas, one lawmaker who worked for a nonprofit wanted to solicit contributions for the group (Texas, like most states, has a part-time legislature). The Ethics Commission said that solicitations "could be viewed as improper under certain circumstances" and advised the legislator to use "extreme caution," but in January the body gave its approval.

Two 2006 advisory opinions from Colorado's Ethics Board allowed lawmakers to vote on or sponsor legislation that benefited nonprofits they were associated with, one as a paid director, the other as an unpaid board member.

The general counsel for Florida's House of Representatives has issued four relevant opinions since 2007, each time determining that soliciting funds or voting on a bill that could benefit the nonprofit did not raise a conflict of interest. In one case, the lawmaker was a paid employee of a nonprofit, while the other three had volunteered for the group, co-hosted events, or were otherwise associated with an organization or its founders.

In one of these cases, a legislator wanted to solicit funds for a group the lawmaker volunteered for and sometimes partnered with on "joint community projects." The general counsel said the lawmaker was free to solicit the funds, but highlighted state laws against using an official position for personal gain or to grant special privilege, saying, "it would be prudent to keep these in mind." The opinion adds that while "the law grants latitude to members," because they serve part-time, "what may be a legally tolerated conflict of interest may be viewed as inappropriate or corrupt" by the public.

The counsel was sounding a common theme: the gulf between what is legally permissible but seemingly inappropriate.

"I'm certainly aware of a growing trend nationally of public officials having ties with nonprofits and those nonprofits perhaps, not always, benefiting from the public official's position of power," said Carol Carson, executive director of Connecticut's Office of State Ethics. She said state employees, including executive branch officials, often come to her office to ask whether they can be involved in awarding a grant to a group they are associated with. As long as the grant doesn't directly benefit them financially, she tells them yes. "That might not pass muster with the court of public opinion," she said, "but under the Code of Ethics, that would be allowable."

## Trouble in Gotham

"It's become a routine headline in New York: Politician pinched in charity scandal," said a September 2012 article by Andrew J. Hawkins in *Crain's New York Business*. "The story changes little from case to case: An elected official funds a nonprofit and staffs it with cronies. Sometimes the group works on his campaigns—or does no work at all."

Assemblyman William Boyland, Jr., accounts for several of these tales just by himself. Boyland Jr., comes from a line of Brooklyn legislators: he gained his post through a special election in 2003 after his father resigned; his uncle held the seat previously. The district is covered with the family name—a street, a school, a housing project and more are all named for the elder Boylands.

Boyland Jr.'s activities first came to light in March 2011, when federal prosecutors charged him with taking bribes, in the guise of consulting fees, from the executive of a nonprofit that operates hospitals in exchange for helping the organization, MediSys, secure millions in state funds. Boyland Jr., had worked for MediSys before taking office, and continued earning a salary after his election without reporting it as required, prosecutors said. The MediSys executive was eventually convicted of offering bribes to Boyland Jr., and two other lawmakers, but a jury acquitted Boyland Jr., in November 2011. One juror told *The New York Times*, "We could not say that because he got the money, he advocated for MediSys.... We couldn't do that beyond a reasonable doubt."

Within a month, however, prosecutors charged Boyland Jr., in another, unrelated bribery case. The allegations include the solicitation in an Atlantic City hotel suite of more than $250,000 in bribes from undercover FBI agents posing as real estate investors. According to the indictment, in exchange for the cash, Boyland Jr., was to help with development deals in his district and secure state financing for the purchase and resale of a hospital building. Prosecutors had just filed the first set of charges against him, so Boyland Jr., needed cash to pay his lawyers, he allegedly told one of the agents.

In May, prosecutors updated the new charges to include allegations that Boyland Jr., from 2007 through 2010, sent public funds to a nonprofit group while directing some of the money to be spent on political events and expenses for the lawmaker, including the printing of T-shirts that said "Team Boyland." (The family reportedly had handed out these shirts for years.) Boyland Jr., is facing 21 criminal counts and has pleaded not guilty. The trial has yet to start.

Boyland Jr., has ties to another, upstate New York charity, the Altamont Program, which also has operations in Brooklyn. The FBI and state authorities raided the upstate offices in December. *The Albany Times Union* said agents were looking into Boyland Jr.'s direction of $1.2 million in state grants to Altamont and a related group from 2004 to 2009, using a controversial legislative vehicle called "member items" that put state funds at the discretion of individual lawmakers. Boyland Jr.'s father went to work for the organization as a consultant after he resigned as a legislator in 2003. Boyland Jr.'s sister also reportedly worked for the group.

Boyland Sr., says he worked for the group from 2008 to 2010. He was reportedly fired after the organization discovered that he had used a company credit card for personal expenses. In an interview, the elder Boyland did not deny using the card for the purchases, but said that in consulting work, it's impossible to distinguish between business and personal expenses.

A spokeswoman for Boyland Jr., referred questions to his lawyer, Nancy Ennis. She did not return phone calls and emails requesting comment.

Many a similar scandal in New York, including Huntley's and Lopez's, has been fueled by those "member items"—part of a gentlemen's agreement between legislative leaders and the governor that for years disbursed hundreds of millions of dollars to groups of lawmakers' choosing with no oversight or trail of who got what. In 2007, Gov. Eliot Spitzer pushed a bill that required the legislature to disclose each member item. The same year, the Attorney General's office reached an agreement with the legislature that required recipients to certify the funds were being used appropriately. But even with this level of oversight, watchdogs and some legislators ridiculed the practice as corrupt and wasteful.

"It's a system which invites abuse," said Lerner, of Common Cause.

In 2010, Gov. David Paterson vetoed thousands of member items in the budget, citing fiscal austerity, and Gov. Cuomo has continued to veto the requests, effectively ending the practice for now. But there are still funds from multi-year grants that have not yet been spent. And political insiders in New York say new tricks have taken the place of the "member item" abuses.

"There are lots of ways to direct money," said state Sen. Liz Krueger, who has co-sponsored a bill that would ban legislators from giving member items to groups that employ family members or staff and would apportion them equally to each district. Traditionally, the majority party controlled most of the funds and disbursed them as it pleased.

## Machine Politics in Illinois

Lawmakers in other states have their own ways to send money to charities, particularly in states with hefty budgets. In Illinois, legislators can direct funds without having to disclose they were the source, much as in New York. In 2009, for example, a paragraph tucked into an appropriations bill included a $98 million grant to the United Neighborhood Organization, a Latino community group that builds and operates charter schools in Chicago.

Over the past several years, the group built close ties to the state's most powerful politicians, pushing the boundaries of appropriate activity by tax-exempt charities, which are barred by federal law from working on political campaigns. After the organization's CEO, Juan Rangel, co-chaired Rahm Emanuel's successful campaign for Chicago mayor, Emanuel jokingly referred to the fact that the charity is not supposed to be directly involved in politics. The organization's staff and lobbyists include former city officials, and some of them have left to enter politics. Rangel regularly endorses candidates. Contractors hired by UNO (often with public money) have contributed to those candidates. Rangel hosted a fundraiser for state House Speaker Michael Madigan in October, with the organization's contractors giving more than $24,000 to Madigan, according to a *Chicago Sun-Times* report.

The close relationships paid off with that 2009 grant of $98 million. But in February, a report by the *Sun-Times* revealed that UNO had spent millions from the grant on insider contracts with relatives of the organization's staff and political allies. Within days, Rangel said the organization had launched an internal review and had suspended some of the suspect contracts. He also said, however, that all of the contractors were qualified and that the work had been fulfilled. The organization's vice president, whose brothers had won a contract, resigned. The state determined that the practices constituted apparent violations of the grant, and in March suspended what remained of the grant. In response, the group hired a full time compliance officer and Rangel stepped down from the board of directors (though he stayed on as CEO). In June, the state restored the flow of funding.

Officials at UNO did not respond to requests for comment.

Steve Brown, a spokesman for Madigan, who sponsored the spending bill that included the grant to UNO, said the speaker is a supporter of the organization, but that the grant had nothing to do with the contributions from the Rangel fundraiser, which he described as modest in relation to Madigan's overall fundraising.

Rey López-Calderón, executive director of Common Cause Illinois, said some nonprofits have become modern-day political machines in Illinois, citing UNO as the prime example. Groups receive state grants with the help of politicians and in return, he said, their members contribute money and even time to the officials' campaigns. "That kind of activity is rampant in Illinois."

Other nonprofits or their employees in Illinois have been questioned about the extent of their ties to legislative patrons. In 2010, for example, a federal grand jury subpoenaed records related to dozens of state grants for nonprofits linked to at least one lawmaker. Thomas Homer, the state's legislative inspector general, said there are no requirements that lawmakers disclose their ties to nonprofits unless they receive a salary from the group, and that there are no ethics rules that apply to the situation beyond general laws prohibiting bribery and kickbacks. He said his office refers complaints of schemes involving nonprofit groups to the FBI, and that there are several open cases, though their nature and number remain confidential.

## Behested Payments

In addition to state grants, lawmakers have found another source of funds they can direct to nonprofits: corporate contributions. It's become common practice in many states and in Congress for corporate donors and lobbyists to contribute money to specific charities at the request of lawmakers, in what's often called a behested

payment. A few states have formal systems to regulate this, but in many cases it's an uncharted field.

The payments present a "win-win situation all around," said Nola Werren, a client specialist at State and Federal Communications, which provides corporate clients with information about state lobbying laws. "The lawmaker gets this benevolent image for his constituents and shows that he cares," while the corporation gets its name on the donation and the nonprofit gets the money. But the arrangement can also serve as a route around restrictions on gifts to lawmakers or campaign contributions, allowing corporations to curry favor with politicians, frequently without disclosure.

California is one of the few states that does require disclosure, but that hasn't discouraged the practice, said Phillip Ung, a spokesman for California Common Cause. Last year, 57 lawmakers reported such contributions, totaling $2.3 million.

Ung pointed to state Sen. Roderick Wright, who has directed $166,500 in corporate contributions to the National Family Life and Education Center from 2010 through 2012. In the fiscal year ending in June 2011, the last year records for the organization are available, the payments comprised more than half of the group's outside income. Wright has co-hosted several events where the group handed out prizes, school supplies and provided health screenings to families in his district.

In an email, Ung praised the fact that the funds are helping the community but added, "there is the ethical question of why are these corporate interests giving at the behest of Mr. Wright and what do these behested payments earn them in political influence."

Among the contributors are AT&T, Time Warner Cable, Edison International and the Morongo Band of Mission Indians. Wright is the chairman of the Governmental Organization Committee, which oversees gambling by Indian tribes in the state, and sits on the

Energy, Utilities and Communications Committee.

Cine Ivery, Wright's chief of staff, said the nonprofit helps mentor youths in the senator's district, and that it couldn't do the work without the corporate donations. The companies get nothing in return, she said. The organization did not return phone calls or emails.

The practice is on the rise across the country, Werren said. Her company has gotten so many requests from clients about the rules covering such payments that it decided to canvass state laws. According to State and Federal Communications, only 14 states require lobbyists to disclose such gifts. California is the only state Werren knows of that requires lawmakers to disclose them, and only New York and Maryland prohibit behested payments.

## Changes Slow to Come

Even as experts say the questionable ties between nonprofits and politicians are on the rise, many states have been slow to enact reforms that might prevent them. One step would be to ban, or restrict, discretionary spending directed by a single lawmaker.

But there are many reasons why even advocates for reform say this could be a bad idea. "Legislators, if they're good, know what their district needs. They know the good organizations," said Sturges, the former Massachusetts regulator. "Why should they not be able to direct funds to the best organizations in their districts?"

There's no doubt that many charities provide critical services in poor communities as a result of grants shepherded by their representatives. Sen. Krueger of New York pointed out that some small community groups do not fit the pre-packaged conditions required by many state grant programs, but are worthy recipients nonetheless. And, both Krueger and Sturges said,

there's no indication that leaving such decisions to governors or other executive branch officials produces markedly better results.

In lieu of prohibitions, many good-government groups are pushing for increased disclosure of all budgetary spending. They say that whatever discretionary funds do exist should have strict requirements tied to them that would dictate what types of projects can be funded and prevent staff, relatives or associates of public officials from being associated with any recipients of the funding.

Kaehny, of Reinvent Albany, has called for more disclosure from the nonprofit world as well. In New York, for example, he said that an independent body should regulate charities, rather than the politically charged Attorney General's office, and that all the data that is already public from tax forms and other documents should be added into a searchable database.

Lawmakers have introduced bills that would require their colleagues to disclose positions with nonprofit organizations in Arizona and Florida, but neither bill has passed. In response to a series of scandals, Pennsylvania's House and Senate adopted rules in 2007 and 2013 restricting members' ability to form and fund nonprofits. But two bills that would have gone further, including one that would have ended "legislative initiative grants," the state's own version of member items, failed to pass the legislature. The bill that Sen. Krueger cosponsored in New York to reform member items has also failed to pass. As have repeated efforts to require disclosure of Illinois' own version of the funding, called "member initiatives."

Cohen, of *Nonprofit Quarterly*, said that any changes face an uphill battle because most of those with the ability to enact them, from lawmakers to charities, benefit from the status quo. "There are a lot of players that have a stake in this," he said, "and want to see it continue."

# 37. Vigilance Required for New York Government Employees[*]

## Chelsea A. Binns

New York government employees are under siege in the 21st century. From the scourge of public corruption, to the threat of agency data breaches, these public servants face constant reputational risk and security challenges. While the recent proliferation of data breaches is especially concerning, experts are recommending that employees remain vigilant, which may serve to reduce the likelihood of these events.

The recent federal employee data breach, disclosed by the Office of Personnel Management (OPM), exemplifies today's unique risk to government employees. This breach may have affected "all federal workers," which could mean as many as 14 million past and present public servants, including federal employees in New York. The personal information of these victims was compromised, for presumably nefarious reasons, which are speculated to include punishment, blackmail or spy recruitment.

This case has raised a dialogue about the opportunities for government employees to increase their level of vigilance. Recommendations have included increasing individual user awareness and cyber security proficiency.

It is possible that employees may unwittingly contribute to data breaches by mishandling agency data. For instance, it was reported the stolen federal data might not have been encrypted. This fact has started a debate among experts. While some argue that the failure to encrypt the subject data was an "abysmal failure on the part of the agency," others say encryption would not "guarantee protection." Nevertheless, the OPM is reportedly increasing their use of encryption, following this breach.

Similarly, a review of past government data breaches, reported by the Privacy Rights Clearinghouse, suggests that workers have often unknowingly contributed to data thefts. In fact, in many of the reported breaches affecting New York City government, workers leaked sensitive information by "accident" via email, "discarded" it in plain view or had it "lost" or "stolen" from them. In one case, the Social Security numbers of 8,400 homeless persons were accidentally emailed to several parties. In another case, files containing Social Security numbers and birth dates of public housing residents were inexplicably found discarded in the street. The agency said these discarded files should have been shredded.

To address the problem of corruption in

---

[*]Originally published as Chelsea A. Binns, "Vigilance Required for New York Government Employees," *PA Times*, June 26, 2015. Reprinted with permission of the author and publisher.

New York, employees and citizens alike are actively seeking opportunities to increase their vigilance. In a Civic Conversation earlier this year, featuring Attorney General (AG) Eric T. Schneiderman, New Yorkers gathered to discuss the issue of corruption in New York and potential reform. In his speech, AG Schneiderman discussed the infamous history of corruption in New York, with Albany as "the nation's most consistent epicenter of public corruption, since the days of Alexander Hamilton and Aaron Burr, through Roosevelt and right up until today."

Nevertheless, the answer to the question of the evening, "Can New Yorkers Fix Albany's Corruption Problem?" was "yes." While corruption will never be completely eradicated, it was clear that improvement is possible. Panelists Richard Briffault, Hon. Richard Brodsky and Jennifer Rodgers, espoused the potential for New York citizens and employees to combat corruption by increasing "awareness," becoming more "efficient and effective" and serving as "watchdogs."

Recently, DOI Commissioner Mark G. Peters also addressed the importance of vigilance in reducing corruption. In a talk he gave at New York Law School, Commissioner Peters said "Successfully tackling corruption means that it must be talked about, it must be confronted, consistently and openly. This is especially so because corruption, fraud and waste have a profound affect beyond criminality and they sap the efficiency and effectiveness of New York City government and how it serves its people."

As such, Peters' answer to rooting out systemic corruption is "constant vigilance." To illustrate his point, Peters cited a recent case which demonstrated the critical nature of the lack of employee vigilance. As part of an undercover investigation announced by DOI in November 2014, a DOI investigator successfully smuggled contraband including illegal drugs, alcohol and a weapon through staff entrance security checkpoints into Rikers Island Correctional Facility.

Although the problem of corruption in New York may seem discouraging, government investigators are winning the battle as discussed in my previous article titled "New York Corruption Investigation Trends." They are employing dynamic investigative methods, such as DOI's undercover operation, in order to understand the root of the problem.

While it is true that New York government employees today are under siege, it is clear that the potential exists for them to increase their vigilance and institute positive changes. AG Schneiderman confirmed the "surge in headlines" can be beneficial, because it means government corruption will remain a focus of public attention thus increasing the likelihood of a solution.

# 38. Lessons of Bell, California[*]

## Michael McGrath

In 2010, while covering a story in a nearby community, reporters for the *Los Angeles Times* happened across a sensational public corruption case in Bell, California, a city of about 35,000 people in southeast Los Angeles County. Officials in that small city had manipulated the local charter and subverted the electoral process to award themselves absurdly generous salaries and other forms of payments.

Since that time, the very name "Bell" has become almost a synonym for official corruption, at least in the State of California and among those who closely follow trends in local government and public management. One report on the ABC national news Web site referred to Bell as possibly the "worst corruption scandal in California history." This suggestion would probably surprise most students of California history (worse than San Francisco during the 1890s), and I myself can think of equally egregious cases in recent years.

The story was significant, however, for a variety of reasons, most notably for two: First, because it was not an isolated incident. A partial list of nearby communities that have experienced public corruption investigations between 2003 and 2010 would include South Gate, Lynwood, Bell Gardens, Cudahy, Maywood, and Vernon. Second, Bell was significant because the main figure accused and later convicted of wrongdoing, Robert Rizzo, was the appointed city manager. What's more, the corrupt officials were cleverly using provisions of their home rule charter to enrich themselves without the knowledge of local residents. This was a subversion of the original purpose of home rule charters and professional managers, to discourage corruption.

Some who have looked into the situation in Bell in other southeast Los Angeles County cities have compared this outbreak of corruption to failed states in third world countries. Others have noted that many of the residents in this region are immigrants from Latin America where corruption is often thought to be more endemic than in North American suburbs, but one need look no further than the history of American cities to find parallels to the corruption cases in southeast Los Angeles County.

What leaders in some of these communities were attempting to create was an old-fashioned clientelist regime, a patronage system reminiscent of the crooked bosses and party machines of the late nineteenth century. It might be useful at this point to remember that patronage played a critical role in the development of democratic institutions in the United States. In the late

*Originally published as Michael McGrath, "Lessons of Bell, California," *National Civic Review* 102, no. 1 (Spring 2013): 51–54. © 2013 Wiley Periodicals Inc. Reprinted with permission of the author and publisher.

nineteenth century, patronage was a form of social welfare in poor, immigrant neighborhoods before there were government forms of welfare, such as unemployment insurance of social security. For supporters of the Tammany Hall organization in New York City, patronage came in the form of jobs, bail, and even funeral costs. For businesses, party machines acted as brokers for permits, licenses, and franchises. Patronage was a powerful means of political organizing and voter mobilization. Job seekers were particularly avid political volunteers, working at the ward or precinct level to motivate supporters of their particular party or faction. In the earliest days of the emerging republic, patronage wasn't even considered a bad or corrupt practice; quite the contrary. In fact, when Andrew Jackson first implemented his system of "rotation," the wholesale replacement of federal job holders with party loyalists, the British reformer Jeremy Bentham wrote an approving letter. Jackson himself viewed patronage as a means of uprooting an entrenched professional bureaucracy of elites in Washington, D.C. Unfortunately, from the beginning, the dark side of patronage, corruption and self-dealing, was all too evident. Though Jackson complained about the very real corruption that existed in the Monroe administration, the dealings of his appointee to the New York City Customs House were even more flagrant than those of the corrupt officials who came before him.

Even before Jackson's first term, mini versions of the spoils system were already taking root at the state and local levels. Martin Van Buren, head of the Bucktail faction of the Democratic-Republican Party in Albany, New York, was a particularly enthusiastic practitioner of political patronage. Historian Edward Pessen wrote in his study of politics and culture during the age of Jackson that the Bucktails' "cardinal rule was that office and influence were to be granted only to those who accepted without question the authority of the leadership. Those who would challenge regency control were removed from appointed office and barred from patronage" (p. 240). The opportunities for patronage began to grow in the late nineteenth century as the population of the United States swelled and the country made the transition from a rural to an urban society. The unwieldy, decentralized municipal government systems of the times gave ample opportunities for all kinds of patronage and corruption. It is estimated that the Tammany machine in New York controlled as many as 60,000 jobs at one time. In Cincinnati, lower-rank city officials paid a percentage of their salaries to the local party machine. Candidates for office and local contractors made generous donations in the hopes of winning support.

Reformers began to push for civil service standards in the 1870s, but it wasn't until the assassination of President James Garfield by a deranged would-be spoils seeker that the civil service reform movement began make inroads. Congress passed the Pendleton Civil Service Act shortly after the assassination, and New York State passed a bill requiring written examinations for employees in municipal government the next year. Many other states and localities followed suit in subsequent years. The reforms didn't end with civil services regulations, however. A wave of municipal reformism changed the very nature of local government in the early to mid-twentieth century. By professionalizing municipal management and enacting (in many localities) nonpartisan elections, the reformers disrupted the connection between employment and political participation. Patronage didn't disappear. It simply became less obvious, acceptable, and disruptive.

In their book *Pinstripe Patronage*, Martin Tolchin and Susan J. Tolchin have argued that political patronage is "alive and well" in contemporary America (p. 2). Examples of these favors would be no-bid federal contracts, congressional earmarks, and appointments to gubernatorial and presidential staffs, to name a few. In the meantime, old-fashioned examples of patronage and corruption are revealed at the state and local levels from time to time (and not just in southeast Los Angeles County). The authors identify examples in all parts of the country and at all levels of government, including school boards, country commissions, cities, state governments, and judicial appointments.

In the meantime, the question of what to make of the plethora of corruption cases in and around Bell and South Gate, California, is a complicated and delicate one. Is the fact that so many of the residents are recent immigrants or second-generation immigrants relevant (shades of late nineteenth-century American cities)? Is it significant that voter turnout rates in those communities tend to be lower than the statewide average? Are those two factors related? What about the lack of media coverage in recent years? Many of these communities used to have their own weeklies that closely covered local government affairs. These factors are worth looking into as long as we don't fall into easy assumptions or racial and cultural stereotyping, which was a not-uncommon vice among municipal reformers in the late nineteenth and early twentieth centuries.

Yet I certainly don't agree with the suggestions of some observers that the form of government in Bell, the city council/city manager form, is to blame for what happened there. It may be true that professional managers have been responsible for some of the corruption in southeast Los Angeles County—and in at least one case they used the charter as a means of corruption. The same could be said of the other forms of government at the local level, and I know of no data to suggest that the council/manager form is prone to abuse. What may be true is that certain aspects of the municipal reform agenda of the early twentieth century, notably at-large, nonpartisan, off-season

elections, may have discouraged voter participation. It should be remembered, however, that breaking the link between public management and party loyalty improved the overall quality of city government. The challenge for "good government" advocates of the twenty-first century, it seems to me, is to combine the higher standards of professionalism sought by the reformers with the spirit of participation of Jacksonian democracy.

Some simple lessons that I think can be drawn from these and other examples of corruption are that when the public is disengaged, when government decisions are made without public participation and support, bad things can happen, and often do. The story of South Gate, which journalist Sam Quinones captured in his book, *Antonio's Gun and Delfino's Dream*, offers a potentially hopeful story of how a community with a large immigrant population and low voter turnout rates can rally to fight corruption and restore higher norms and standards for local government. Quinones argues that the community organizations developed to engage the public in efforts to address crime issues and improve schools served as models for political education and democratic organizing and assisted opponents of a corrupt regime in building support for a recall movement. These organizations made it possible for the newer residents to interact with local institutions and older residents in an effort to oust the corrupt officials who were bankrupting and embarrassing their community.

As many social commentators have observed, notably Harvard political scientist Robert Putnam, declining memberships of traditional service and fraternal organizations have diminished the social capital that communities need to address difficult issues. The South Gate example suggests that new organizations can arise and take the place of the older membership organization to serve as networking agencies and repositories of social capital. "South Gate hadn't entirely lost its anonymity," writes Quinones. "But people now knew more of their neighbors. South Gate had become an unashamedly teary-eyed, heartwarming Norman Rockwell painting, updated to the twenty-first century. Young shaved-headed Latinos and blue-haired ladies stood shoulder to shoulder during the campaigns [to oust the corrupt leaders] and ate from the same box of donuts" (p. 111).

In South Gate, residents banded together to replace the corrupt council majority with a more civic-minded group. Once in office, the new council majority sought assistance from the League of California Cities to create a new management structure. Even Bell, despite its notoriety as a poster child for public corruption, is experiencing something of a civic resurgence. Last year the city's interim city manager brought in Pete Peterson of the Davenport Institute at Pepperdine University to advise on the 2012–2013 budget process. The institute helped the city set up a series of public forums to get residents more engaged in thinking about budget challenges.

These examples suggest a new purpose for advocates and practitioners of pubic engagement/democratic governance movement: to help struggling cities come to grips with corruption and mismanagement. As editor of a journal that originated during the Progressive Era and served for many years as the primary forum for ideas on municipal governance, I find these stories intriguing and hopeful. During the Progressive Era, local reformers changed the face of municipal government, mostly for the better. The most glaring exception to this story of successful reform, as I have argued in past articles, is the declining rates of participation, notably the lower voter turnouts that followed the reforms. The causes of this decline in participation are varied and complex, but many have argued that the reforms themselves contributed to the decline. The possibility that professional norms and safeguards can have negative effects, however, does not obviate the need to guard against corruption and mismanagement, as these examples in southeast Los Angeles County attest, but the search for solutions to both problems, disengagement and bad government, point us in the same direction: to community building, boosting social capital and civic infrastructure, and increasing levels of public engagement.

## References

Fremd, M. Von, and J. M. Metz. (2011). "Bell, California: Former City Manager Snoozes at Pay Scandal Court Hearing." ABC World News Tonight website, March 1, 2011.

Pessen, E. (1969). *Jacksonian America: Society, Personality and Politics*. Homewood, IL: Dorsey.

Quinones, S. 2007. *Antonio's Dream and Delfino's Dream: True Tales of Mexican Migration*. Albuquerque: University of New Mexico Press.

Tolchin, M., and S. J. Tolchin. (2011). *Pinstripe Patronage: Political Favoritism from the Clubhouse to the White House and Beyond*. Boulder, CO: Paradigm.

# 39. Where Our Profession Is Making a Difference[*]

## Kevin Duggan

On Friday, July 15, 2011, the recruitment deadline closed for an interim city manager in Bell, California (35,500 population). Applications were counted up. They totaled zero. The Bell brand was definitely in trouble.

A little more than 18 months ago the local government management profession was rocked by the compensation scandal in Bell. Although there will always be isolated examples of members of the profession not meeting the demands of the ICMA Code of Ethics and the expectations of their communities, the extreme conduct in Bell, along with the intense media attention it generated, created challenges for the profession both in California and across the country.

While ICMA was already focused on efforts to better explain the role and value of professional management through its upcoming "Life, Well Run" campaign, one of the worst possible examples of our profession became the best-known city manager in the nation. The greatest impact of this scandal, however, was on the residents of Bell. It became their challenge to reclaim their local government.

## Painful Impacts

Among the impacts of the Bell scandal was an intense interest in public sector compensation in both national and local media. The response of the profession, including ICMA, was to focus on communicating the reality of compensation in the public sector and to identify best practices. Increased efforts were undertaken in California and other parts of the nation to develop compensation guidelines.

While these efforts were under way, Bell's citizens began the hard work of reclaiming their community. The city manager and other high-level staff members were removed from their positions, and some had criminal charges filed against them. By early 2011, the previous council had been recalled and a new council was in place. The new councilmembers faced daunting challenges.

The scandal revealed not only outrageous issues regarding compensation but also significant management and leadership deficiencies and major financial problems. Compounding the problems was that the new council found itself with a much-depleted leadership team and one not of its choosing.

[*]Originally published as Kevin Duggan, "Bell, California: Where Our Profession Is Making a Difference," *PM Magazine* 94, no. 2 (March 2012). Reprinted with permission of the publisher.

Councilmembers were also continuing to deal with significant community distrust and an overwhelming number of serious and challenging issues. There also was a lack of experienced leadership on both elected and appointed levels. An additional challenge was that all this was played out in the glare of intense media scrutiny.

As the new councilmembers struggled to try to move the community forward, their aspirations were further impacted by the impression that government professionals were unwilling to become involved in such a negative, difficult, and demanding circumstance. By the summer of 2011, the news media were beginning to conclude that no one was willing to help the city.

Although there were a number of reasons for the challenges faced in obtaining professional assistance, clearly one was the stigma associated with the previous city leadership and its impacts. When it came to ICMA's attention that Bell was having difficulty obtaining the professional assistance needed to reestablish effective governance and services, it was clear that action was necessary.

As painful an experience as Bell continued to be, it was time for our profession to offer help. The mayor and council immediately responded with enthusiasm to ICMA's offer to assist them in finding professional interim leadership. Also responding quickly and positively to partner with ICMA and its California affiliate, Cal-ICMA, were the League of California Cities (LCC) and its City Manager's Department and California City Management Foundation (CCMF).

The initial assistance consisted of contacting the membership of these organizations to request help. The challenge quickly became urgent when members of the new council determined they did not wish to extend the contract of the temporary chief administrative officer they had inherited from the previous governing body.

In lieu of the contract being extended, the mayor became the interim CAO, a circumstance that neither he nor his council colleagues wanted to continue any longer than absolutely necessary. ICMA, LCC, and CCMF needed to move quickly to identify professional interim leadership.

## Bell Honor Roll

The number and diversity of professionals and professional organizations that came together to assist in restoring Bell and to demonstrate the difference that professional management can make in a community is impressive. These groups and individuals deserve our thanks and appreciation for their efforts.

## Individuals

Ken Hampian, Retired City Manager, San Luis Obispo

Pam Easter, ICMA Senior Adviser, Rancho Cucamonga

Arne Croce (ICMA-CM), ICMA Life Member, San Mateo

Al Venegas, Deputy Police Chief, Santa Monica

Kevin O'Rourke, ICMA-CM, Cal-ICMA Committee on the Profession. Fairfield

Dave Mora (ICMA-CM), ICMA Senior Adviser/Range Rider, Salinas

Linda Barton, ICMA-CM, Past President, City Manager's Department, League of California Cities, Sacramento

Chris McKenzie, Executive Director, League of California Cities, Sacramento

Wade McKinney, ICMA-CM, President, California City Management Foundation, San Diego

Bill Garrett, Executive Director, California City Management Foundation, San Diego

Bill Statler, Retired Finance Director, San Luis Obispo

Mike Multari, Retired Community Development Director, San Luis Obispo

Bill Smith, Retired City Manager, Westminster

Susan Loftus, City Manager, San Mateo

Norma Gauge, City Clerk, San Mateo

Wandzia Rose, City of San Mateo

Marvin Rose, Retired Public Works Director, Sunnyvale

Dave Hill, Retired HR Director, Anaheim

Linda Spady, HR Director, San Mateo

Sheila Canzian, Parks and Recreation Director, San Mateo

Dave Bass, Retired Finance Director, Bell Gardens

Vern Ficklin, Retired Manager, Public Works Department, San Mateo

David Schirmer, IT Director, Beverly Hills

Melissa Lindley, Housing Department, Santa Monica

Rod Gould, City Manager, Santa Monica

Jeff Kolin, City Manager, Beverly Hills

Steve Belcher, Interim Police Chief, Bell

Debra Kurita, Interim Community Services Director, Bell

Kristine Guerrero, League of California Cities, Sacramento

Julie Hernandez, International Hispanic Network, San Jose

Nancy Fong, Interim Community Development Director, Bell

JoAnne Speers, Institute for Local Government, Sacramento

## Organizations

International Personnel Management Association

Alliance for Innovation

## Ken Hampian's Story

After some direct outreach by professional colleagues, Ken Hampian, ICMA member and the retired city manager of San Luis Obispo, California, offered his services for a 30-day period. This provided time for the recruitment of a longer-term interim manager.

Not only was Ken willing to change a number of personal plans for those first 30 days, but he also insisted that he serve without compensation. He did not want any questions raised regarding his motivation to assist.

Since retiring from city management in January 2010, Ken had not been interested in pursuing interim manager positions. He was enjoying other kinds of work and service and believed the city hall portion of his life was over. But, as Ken describes it, to his surprise he had a great urge to "answer the Bell."

He viewed the opportunity as a mission and not a job and an opportunity for our profession to demonstrate what professional service and management are really about. He was also motivated by a strong desire to change the impression created by those who preceded him and claimed to be public servants.

Within five days of the vacancy occurring, Ken interviewed with the Bell council. Within 30 minutes of meeting Ken, councilmembers appointed him interim CAO, and he immediately found himself sitting in the CAO's chair for a jam-packed council meeting. He provided advice and suggestions at the meeting that lasted until 2 a.m.

As Ken quickly found out, the challenge was much greater than helping the organization and community recover from the compensation scandal. He found an organization in shambles. Policies, processes, hierarchy, equipment, training—the normal accouterments of organizational life—were nonexistent or severely withered.

There were no department heads or citizen advisory bodies. Ken found the remaining staff dedicated but skeletal and shouldering an overwhelming workload. He also found Bell entangled in a net of bad debts, bond levies, lawsuits, and grant violations.

Ken was immediately immersed in an almost overwhelming number of issues ranging from those having great significance to the mundane. Compounding the challenge was the absence of staff support in key areas and the complete lack of organizational infrastructure to address even the most routine of inquiries.

He also quickly discovered that, although this working-class community had accomplished through the recall process the initial recapture of their community, they were severely handicapped by a lack of governing experience and civic involvement. The community's dignity and self-respect had also taken a serious hit, and trust was greatly lacking.

Although a dedicated, committed, and intelligent mayor and council had been elected, they were not experienced in local government and its services. It became apparent immediately that the challenges were so great that Ken needed some direct assistance. Within days, additional local government professionals offered their help.

Of particular note was the assistance of the city of Santa Monica (City Manager Rod Gould), which immediately freed up Deputy Police Chief Al Venegas to serve as a chief of staff to Ken and assist with addressing the overwhelming number of pending issues. Deputy Chief Venegas used two weeks of his personal vacation time to help out during this critical initial period.

While immediately prioritizing a wide array of serious issues and problems and providing stability to the provision of essential daily services, the management professionals realized that a major challenge was to find a highly qualified professional to replace Ken after his 30-day emergency assignment. Again, ICMA, CCMF, and the LCC joined together to advertise and review applicants for recommendation to the council.

A committee, under the leadership of retired city manager and Cal-ICMA member Kevin O'Rourke, ICMA-CM, sprang into action. The response to an extended deadline and additional professional outreach was gratifying. A strong group of candidates was identified, with three ultimately recommended to the council for interview.

Ken and other dedicated volunteers made great strides toward stabilizing the Bell organization and to help the council move the community forward during this initial period. Trust and confidence in professional management was already significantly restored after Ken's time in Bell.

His service was greatly appreciated, and when he completed his 30 days of service the community graciously expressed its gratitude, not only to Ken but also to ICMA/Cal-ICMA, LCC, and CCMF.

## Eight Lessons of Bell

Bell, California, represents both the worst and the best of our management profession. In reflecting on the story of Bell up to this point, these lessons are suggested:

1. Significant authority is part of being a local government manager. Managers can make a great impact on a community by the way in which they undertake their professional responsibilities. This authority must be exercised in a professional and ethical manner.

2. Successful communities need to have effective professional management, effective and public-spirited elected officials, an interested and involved community, and a vigilant media.

3. Personal interests can never impact professional decision making.

4. Openness and transparency are essential ingredients for effective local governance.

5. Professional management can have a

significant positive impact on local communities.

6. Our profession is often more valued and appreciated by residents and elected officials than we fully realize.

7. Members of our profession believe in good government and the value of professional management and are willing to sacrifice to demonstrate their belief.

8. Without adequate checks and balances and the willingness to confront inappropriate conduct, all organizations are at risk.

## Arne Croce's Story

Arne Croce, ICMA-CM, ICMA Life Member, and the retired city manager of San Mateo, California, has had a number of professional adventures since leaving full-time city management in 2008. In addition to providing consultant assistance to several California public agencies, he also promoted professional local governance through service in Iraq and Kosovo.

Shortly after returning from Kosovo, he was encouraged by fellow local government professionals to consider the challenge of the long-term interim CAO assignment in Bell. He was one of the several highly qualified applicants solicited to apply and was one of three final candidates recommended to the council. He was subsequently interviewed and selected to replace Ken. The joint recruitment and selection process by ICMA, CCMF, and LCC was, amazingly, completed in less than three weeks.

Arne knew that this task would require him to be away from his home in northern California for at least nine months while working for less than would normally be expected for this type of interim assignment. He was drawn to this challenge by his desire to assist the community after it had been ravaged by an individual who claimed to be a member of the management profession. He also was drawn to the opportunity to work with elected officials who were committed to making things right again.

Although a great number of problems had been initially addressed by Ken and his team of volunteer professionals, the vast majority of problems still faced Arne. Among these were helping to establish effective community dialogues, including at council meetings, addressing the daunting financial and budget challenges, and hiring a team of department heads.

At the same time, Arne felt warmly welcomed to the Bell organization and community. He found the community positive and supportive. There was obvious appreciation for his willingness to join them in their efforts to restore the community. He also sensed their relief in having professional management that they could trust and that would provide good advice and day-to-day management to their organization. He found the employees receptive to new ideas and open to change.

Among Arne's immediate priorities was to further expand the cadre of professional volunteers to help on a wide variety of projects and assignments. These included the development of an RFP process for a refuse collection contract, the need to create basic HR policies and procedures, and the necessity to address poorly maintained mobile home parks that he had discovered were owned by the city.

A major step forward was Arne's ability to assemble a small but highly skilled and professional group of full-time interim department heads. Although they are compensated, they have been willing to serve for payment that's below what they could otherwise earn; they have accepted their temporary jobs because of their belief in the important work being done. He has seen tremendous progress through the efforts of these dedicated professionals.

Arne has also greatly expanded the number of volunteer part-time professionals who provide valuable help on a wide variety of topics. Also, a number of professional associations including ICMA, the Alliance for Innovation, the Institute for Local Government, and the International Personnel Management Association have offered assistance in a variety of ways. Other cities, including San Mateo, California (City Manager Susan Loftus) and Beverly Hills, California (City Manager Jeff Kolin, ICMA-CM), have provided specific assistance in such areas as upgrading the technology infrastructure in city facilities.

Arne sees the organization moving in a positive direction, with the greatest achievements so far being the establishment of professional interim leadership in departments, triage of critical problems and issues, initiation of an effective budget process, and creation of an expectation for openness and transparency relating to all municipal business.

His overarching goals for his time in Bell include stabilizing the organization, establishing permanent professional staff, creating needed internal organizational infrastructure, and stabilizing the city's financial condition. The bottom line for Arne is to have his time and the time of his fellow professionals demonstrate what can be expected from honest, open, and professional local government management.

## Pam Easter's Story

Pam Easter, a retired city manager, assistant city manager, and ICMA Senior Adviser, is one person in an extraordinary group of dedicated volunteer professionals who stepped in to support Ken and subsequently Arne and who is continuing to provide assistance to the Bell community. As she watched the compensation scandal unfold, she fully appreciated the negative impact it had on the Bell community and on our profession.

Immediately upon hearing of the challenges encountered by Ken Hampian, Pam volunteered to serve and subsequently undertook a long daily commute in order to help stabilize the organization. Like Ken and Arne, she wanted to be part of the effort to help Bell recover as well as demonstrate the positive impact that professional and ethical local government management can have on a community.

Pam found that the councilmembers and staff were dedicated to the difficult work of reforming and rebuilding the organization. Although greatly impacted by the actions of a few Bell leaders, the staff was committed to creating an organization and community of which they could be proud. Pam was encouraged to find that the new council understood the importance of professional and ethical management.

What had initially been an offer to assist Ken for the first few challenging days of his service turned into a much longer commitment. Pam provided critical support during Ken's month as interim city administrator and then continued her service after Arne arrived. Pam has served in a variety of capacities ranging from interviewing employees to helping assess the organization, undertaking administrative analysis, and serving as acting interim city administrator and interim finance director.

She found a group of employees who were still committed to providing public services but who had suffered from the absence of professional and ethical leadership. Employees had also been severely impacted by the barrage of negative publicity and the constant negativity regarding all things related to Bell.

They also were operating in an atmosphere of great uncertainty on almost all levels, ranging from finances to organizational leadership. Pam was impressed to find that, after looking deeper than the now stereotypical view of what to expect in a "Bell employee," she found a committed and concerned group of staff members doing their best to provide services under difficult circumstances.

Pam was able to help employees stay focused on their obligation to provide important and often vital public services. She also got great satisfaction from being able to serve as an example to the staff of how professional managers conducted themselves.

Working with Ken and Arne, she was able to demonstrate that organizational leaders can serve as role models and can work positively and constructively in a team environment with their fellow employees while providing support and encouragement.

Pam's commitment and the commitment of many other volunteers to the management profession and all that it stands for is being demonstrated every day in Bell.

### Rebirth of Bell: Online Article Available

An important commitment for professional local government managers is to advocate professionalism in communities outside their own. As you will read in the article "Rebirth of Bell," ICMA, Cal-ICMA, and the California City Management Foundation worked together to help Bell, California, overcome a year of intense public scrutiny to make significant strides toward restoring the public trust.

Bell came so far that it celebrated its "rebirth" at a special press conference on August 24, 2011, during which ICMA, the League of California Cities, and the California City Management Foundation (CCMF) were praised for their contributions to the city's success.

### Conclusion to Date Is Positive

Ultimately, as is the case in all of the communities in which managers serve, the success of Bell and the Bell community is in the hands of its residents and council. Even with the great progress that has already been made, it could take years for the community to recover from the poor leadership and governance of the past.

Though the challenge is long term, the current budget development process is a clear example of progress. A community-involved budget process (totally lacking previously) is underway and will lead to clear city goals and priorities. The budget format is being revamped to include basic workload and performance measures. Progress against goals, priorities, and performance will be regularly monitored and reported. While these steps may appear basic for most communities, these are major steps forward for Bell.

With the help of professionals dedicated to the public interest, the elected officials in Bell and the community as a whole are working to reform and restore their community. Although the experience of Bell has been difficult for the local government management community, the story is changing and it is hoped that Bell can one day serve as a positive example for the profession.

The response to the call to assist by so many organizations and individual professionals has been a clear demonstration of what our profession and the individuals who compose it represent. Only a small fraction of the many offers of help could actually be accepted. All of us who are committed to good governance and effective and honest local government management owe all of these organizations and individuals our gratitude and appreciation.

While the negative example of the previous Bell leadership will be difficult to overcome, we can be grateful to the new community leaders and dedicated professionals who are striving every day to create a positive example of how effective local governments can function.

Professional local government management makes a significant difference in our communities. This is now being proven every day in the city of Bell.

# 40. Prudent Options for Balancing Public Budgets[*]

## Roger L. Kemp

Public officials in communities across the nation have to balance their respective budgets, keep tax increases to a minimum, and make every effort to maintain existing public services. Particular fiscal problems can be state specific, but at this difficult time in our nation's history, all local officials must cope with these difficult issues.

Local government officials can make good use of lessons learned from the past. There is no need to reinvent the wheel when it comes to balancing public budgets in hard times.

The national pressure for cutback management began in the state of California a generation ago. At the time, I was both working for the city of Oakland, California, and preparing my doctoral dissertation. For my dissertation I chose the subject of coping with Proposition 13 because I had been assisting in developing the city's budget in response to the revenue reduction imposed by this citizens' mandate. The practices I learned from this experience, plus my other budget reduction experience that has been gained from serving in communities on both coasts of the United States since then, are reflected in this chapter.

Over the years, numerous budget development processes have projected, enhanced, and protected revenues; guided department managers and elected officials; and worked to ensure that public services were reduced only marginally, with the goal of balancing the annual budget in the most positive way possible.

Strategies, measures, tactics, and programs useful for today's public officials—both elected and appointed—are noted below. The purpose of presenting these options is to ensure that budget reduction practices and adoption processes are prudent yet optimize the use of existing revenue sources and make every effort to minimize the reduction of public services to citizens being served.

**No new public services.** During difficult financial times, there must be a policy of no new public services. No additional services should be added to the budget unless they are cost covering from a revenue standpoint. This means that, if user fees and charges cover the cost of providing the service, then it can be approved. If not, consideration of the service must be postponed until subsequent fiscal years. This is a fact of life when revenues are limited.

**Implement a hiring freeze.** One of the

---

[*]Originally published as Roger L. Kemp, "Managing Government in Hard Times: Prudent Options for Balancing Public Budgets," *PM Magazine* 91, no. 4 (May 2009). Reprinted with permission of the publisher.

most obvious ways to save money is to impose an organization-wide hiring freeze. During these difficult financial times, elected officials early in the budgetary process should officially approve a hiring freeze. This creates immediate savings in salaries, fringe benefits, and other budget line items used in the provision of public services. Everyone should know that the elected officials are taking such action to avoid or at least minimize layoffs of employees and reductions of services later in the budget development process.

**Form a union-management cost-savings committee.** To balance public budgets, it is a positive measure to involve major stakeholders such as public unions in the process. The local government manager should meet with union representatives as appropriate (usually one member from each union) and ask for their cooperation in reviewing expenses and operations and in jointly recommending ways to save funds and avoid employee layoffs if at all possible. Asking elected officials for approval to form such a committee should have a positive effect because a message is being sent to citizens that both management and unions are involved in reducing the budget.

**Update user fees and charges.** Reevaluating the user-fee structure seems self-evident, but few cities and counties routinely update their user fees and charges for public services. Although the private sector updates prices annually because of increased costs, governments seldom perform this task with any regularity. User fees and charges should be updated to reflect the actual cost of providing the services rendered to the public. It is also appropriate to provide discounts or free-use periods to selected citizens subject to the approval of their elected representatives.

**Check existing enterprise funds.** The national trend is to create enterprise funds in which the user fees and charges generated by the service make it cost covering.

These funds are appropriate when only the users of a specific service benefit from its provision (sewer, water, arenas, stadiums, museums, golf courses, parking, and the list goes on). As budgets increase for such services, the user fees and charges should increase also, to ensure that the revenues cover the entire cost of providing the service. If discounts are approved for certain groups, user fees and charges must be increased for other citizens who use the service in order to offset this revenue loss.

**Create other enterprise funds.** After you check your existing enterprise funds, also review your government's public services to see whether other services should be set up in this manner. Sewer and water services have long been cost covering from a revenue standpoint, but other public services must be considered for enterprise fund status when they do not benefit the entire community. If a public service benefits only certain citizens, then those users should pay for the cost of the service. Funding for golf courses, arenas, stadiums, zoos, and museums is headed in this direction.

**Use one-time revenues wisely.** It is not usually fiscally prudent to use one-time revenues or budgetary savings to fund future operating expenses. The only sound financial practice is to use one-time revenues or budget savings to fund one-time expenses, both operating and capital, as appropriate and subject to the approval of elected officials. Using one-time revenues and budget savings to finance operating expenses merely exacerbates an organization's fiscal problems in the future.

**Always seek available operational grants.** Make sure that the staff is informed and knowledgeable about all existing grants from other levels and types of governments as well as appropriate nonprofit foundations. Every public agency should attempt to take advantage of all external funding sources for which it may qualify, including grants made available from nonprofit foundations. Most public libraries have reference books that list both regional and national nonprofit organizations and the programs for which they provide funding.

**Optimize the use of available infrastructure grants.** The federal government has made these grants available in the past under different administrations. When city and county managers know these funds are available, they should have their elected officials approve a projects list and start preparing plans and specifications to fast-track major projects that qualify for this funding. It is common for a local government to spend money up front to obtain engineering services in order to have important projects shovel ready when the grant funds become available. These project-related costs are often reimbursed subsequently by such grant programs.

**Take measures to accommodate the truly needy.** Elected officials and their staffs should not forget that, when public services are reduced and user fees and charges are increased, special consideration should be given to truly needy citizens. Special provisions, as defined and approved by elected officials, should be made for these residents. Modest user fees and charges, along with discounted charges that can include free use during low-utilization periods, are entirely appropriate during difficult financial times.

**Consider employee work furloughs.** The use of employee layoffs to balance a public budget should be a last resort. Efforts should be made to work with employee unions to avoid layoffs. One of the options available to save public funds and balance budgets is to have an employee work furlough. This requires selected employees to take time off for a number of days, up to a few weeks, typically staggered throughout the fiscal year, to reduce costs and minimize disruptions to public services. Elected officials usually favor this option because public services are not reduced substantially.

**Avoid employee layoffs.** Several options are available to save money, balance budgets, and avoid employee layoffs. Management and union representatives can agree to open labor negotiations to discuss various cost reduction and expense deferral options. Because governments basically deliver services, most of which are provided by people, public budgets are driven by salaries and fringe-benefit costs. All of these expenses can be reduced or deferred to avoid employee layoffs and severe service reductions. This is an appropriate option for major budget reductions.

**Follow prudent bonding practices.** The staff should recommend, and elected officials should approve, fiscally responsible bonding practices for all bond-funded public projects. Revenue bonds can be used to finance those projects with a solid revenue stream. General obligation bonds are typically used to finance public improvements and land acquisitions when no, or minimal, revenues are generated by these projects.

General obligation bonds are backed by the full faith and credit of the issuing government and have lower interest rates than revenue bonds. Public officials should also have established cost-limit policies for capital projects, land acquisitions, and major equipment purchases to qualify for bond financing. Also, some states provide bonding services to their local governments, which serves to aggregate purchases and thus provide lower interest rates for a bond issue.

**Provide timely budget information to everyone.** When reducing a public budget, make it a point to pursue all financial options to reduce operating costs and generate additional revenues. This means that all available operational and fiscal options should be listed and presented to elected officials for their review and consideration. It is entirely appropriate to start such budget review practices early during the fiscal year. This means that city and county managers should have their staffs prepare revenue projections early to allow time to work with department managers and employee unions to explore all service reduction, revenue enhancement, cost reduction, and expense deferral options.

**Direct department heads to look for accrued savings.** Early in a difficult fiscal year, a directive should be sent to all department managers asking them to review their approved budgets with the goal of holding down expenses, including employee-related expenses such as overtime as well as those operating expenses that can be reduced immediately without negatively impacting public services. Everyone should be told that this effort is being made to increase budgetary savings to offset the projected deficit for the coming fiscal year and to minimize possible future service reductions and employee layoffs.

**Consider early retirement programs.** Everyone agrees that senior employees cost more than entry-level employees. To the extent that an early-retirement program, such as a small pension incentive, can be offered to encourage senior employees to retire, it will save any public agency considerable funds in the future. New employees for most jobs start at the entry level, saving salary and fringe-benefit expenses. The hiring of new employees can also be deferred, if necessary. Early-retirement programs are considered a favorable expense reduction option by public unions and their employees.

**Implement prudent financial policies.** More public agencies should be approving prudent financial and budgetary policies, especially during these difficult economic times. This is a public and official way to give direction to all employees. Many local governments wait until there is a budgetary or financial problem before adopting financial policies.

Because of this, such policies sometimes tend to be problem-specific. Now is the time to proactively adopt sound fiscal policies. By doing this, public officials will give permanent direction to their staffs and mitigate the impact of future financial difficulties during the coming years. When such policies are established by elected officials, and approved publicly, they stay in place until they are changed by majority vote at a future public meeting.

**Review existing funds for appropriateness.** Periodically, when the annual audit takes place, the auditor and top management and financial staff should be requested to review all of the organization's funds, and their balances, for appropriateness. Some funds may have been established for a purpose that has been changed by subsequent circumstances or legislation.

The size of all existing funds should also be reviewed to ensure that the funds do not exceed the level desired when they were established. Any changes to existing funds, or their levels of funding, should be reviewed with elected officials and must be changed at a public meeting as a part of the budgetary process. Any excess fund balances, or funds no longer needed, can be transferred to the general fund to offset a potential financial deficit.

**Rank public service levels.** One of the greatest problems in reducing any budget is the highly political question of the relative value of various public services. Public services may be categorized into four service levels:

Level 1 comprises essential public services, which should not be reduced under any circumstances. Basic minimal levels of police, fire, health, and public works services fall into this category.

Level 2 comprises those programs that are highly desirable, but not absolutely essential.

Level 3 comprises the nice-but-not-necessary services that have significant value but do not provide essential or necessary services to the public.

Level 4 services can be described as the first-to-go programs because they are not essential and serve only a small portion of the community.

The criteria used to rank public services should be determined by elected officials as they consider budget reduction options.

Evaluate the impact of service-level reductions. To properly assess proposed service reductions, their relative impact on prevailing services must be determined. Many program reductions, because of existing personnel vacancies, may have no substantial impact on services; however, other service reductions may have a measurable impact. Four stages of service reductions can be used for this purpose:

Stage 1 reductions would reduce a substantial portion of a program or eliminate the program entirely.

Stage 2 reductions would reduce a sizable portion of a program but would not affect basic services.

Stage 3 reductions would reduce only a small portion of a program and not affect essential public services.

Stage 4 reductions would have little or no impact on prevailing public services.

Management can recommend such criteria, but elected officials determine the final rankings.

**Prepare public service impact statements.** Last but not least, before final decisions are made on reducing a government's budget, citizens should be informed of the impact that a monetary decrease has on the services selected for possible reduction. Each budget reduction proposed should come with a public service impact statement. This information should be provided with the list of proposed budget reductions given to elected officials.

The statement should also be made available to citizens at the public hearings and meetings held on budget reductions. If time permits, signs should be prepared and placed at those public facilities where services might be reduced. Public officials have an ethical obligation to properly inform the public of the operational impact of their financial and budgetary decisions.

There is no doubt that these are difficult financial times for local public officials who represent the citizens and manage their organizations. All of these financial, budgetary, and operational choices are difficult to make, but they are a sign of the times. The sorting and prioritizing of public programs, and the rational reduction of government spending, form the most pressing challenge facing public officials today. Analyzing the political and administrative choices implemented by other local governments over the years will facilitate the use of orderly and sound options by today's public officials as they balance their communities' budgets.

These suggested guidelines are offered with the intention of providing insight and clarity to this arduous process. Budget reduction and revenue enhancement strategies that reflect responsibility, not only to the beneficiaries of public services but also to those who must foot the bill, must ultimately prevail.

Welcome to the difficult world of sorting out the relative value of public services and making sound financial and budgetary decisions so that public budgets are balanced to meet available revenues!

# 41. The Seven Deadly Sins of Public Finance[*]

## Liz Farmer

The temptation of the quick fiscal fix has seduced just about every lawmaker at one time or another. Scraping pennies together to balance the budget? Perhaps skipping a contribution to the public employee pension plan is the best way to get through the year. Can't afford to pay for building maintenance? Push some of it off into the following year's liabilities. Governments have been using these and other money-shuffling tricks since balanced budgets and municipal financing were invented. But in the aftermath of the Great Recession, short-sighted gimmicks like these became more common as governments looked for any solution to combat dwindling revenues. Revenue is back up now in most places, but some of the fiscal trickery has hardened into common practice.

"If it happens for a year or two in a down economy, that's understandable," says Tom Kozlik, an analyst with the finance firm Janney Montgomery Scott. "In 2009 and 2010, you didn't want that to be the time you raise taxes. But, as an analyst, if I'm looking at a situation where the same things are happening pre- and post-recession, then it's a significant problem."

What follows is *Governing*'s list of the most tempting financial schemes that can severely weaken a government's fiscal future when practiced as a matter of course. Although the consequences aren't necessarily lethal, those that make heavy use of these 7 Sins of Public Finance find that they only succeed in digging deeper financial holes.

### Balancing the Budget with One-Time Fixes

States and many cities have a legal obligation to balance their budgets each year. But there are all sorts of tricky maneuvers that can place a government in technical compliance with that rule. Shifting payments into the next fiscal year, for example, can instantly take the problem off the current books. But it serves only to make the following year's budgeting that much more difficult. Borrowing money for operating costs, another common tactic, may be even more dangerous. It adds to the public's long-term debt without creating any related future public benefit.

Bad Choice: One of the most perilous quick fixes is the practice of taking costs out of one fund and transferring them to an-

*Originally published as Liz Farmer, "The 7 Deadly Sins of Public Finance," *Governing*, June 2014. Reprinted with permission of the publisher.

other. New York did that in 1992, when it balanced its general fund budget by taking the state's historic canal system and moving it to the Thruway Authority. The canal system, which includes the Erie Canal, has traditionally been a financial albatross—it costs up to $90 million to run each year but generates only a few million dollars in revenue. The deficiencies are highlighted every time the Thruway raises its tolls, particularly during a stretch in the 2000s when it raised tolls four out of five years to cover the canal system. The problem is that New York never solved the real issue—the canals are simply draining a different fund. "You're creating the illusion that things are in balance but you haven't actually changed any of the financial facts," says Peter Hutchinson, a state and local government consultant for Accenture. "In the case of the Thruway Authority, the issues with the Erie Canal didn't go away."

Better Choice: DeKalb County, Ga., was downgraded by rating agencies in 2012 after years of transferring money from one fund to bail out another in an effort to meet operating costs. The result was an overall deficit that never seemed to go away. Finally officials in DeKalb took a painful but responsible step. They raised taxes, cut expenses (including a reduction in staff) and added to cash reserves. The county also imposed new controls on fund transfers. By the 2014 fiscal year, DeKalb had stopped cash-flow borrowing and its credit outlook was raised to positive.

### *Ignoring the Long-Term Consequences of a Deal*

Few governments have a long-term financial plan and even fewer have multiyear budgets. Many don't even require a fiscal analysis of proposed legislation. That's made it possible for some, facing immediate demands for wage increases, to buy off public employee constituencies by increasing re-

tirement benefits at an unsustainable long-term cost. Other governments have been wooed by the prospect of privatizing assets as a way to get quick cash, a move that some have called the governmental version of an unwise payday loan.

Bad Choice: In 2008, Chicago accepted a one-time fee of a little more than $1 billion in exchange for giving up control of its 36,000 parking meters for 75 years. The public outcry started almost immediately as the new private owners pushed through a substantial increase in parking rates. A report by an inspector general brought in to assess the consequences estimated that the process used to award the deal cost the city $974 million, and that the amount charged to the private purchaser should have been much higher.

Better Choice: Chicago learned a lesson. Five years later, Mayor Rahm Emanuel, elected in 2011, halted a possible deal to privatize Chicago's Midway International Airport. Citing the problems with the city's parking deal, he insisted that an airport privatization arrangement share revenue with the city and demanded a Travelers' Bill of Rights to cap parking costs and food prices. The demands were enough to scare off the potential investors, almost certainly a benefit to the city in the long run.

### *Taking on Too Much*

One of the reasons privatizing assets has become alluring to governments is because many of them have been burned by taking on more public investments than they could handle. This frequently involves development projects funded by municipal bonds. If a project's tax revenues don't deliver, governments have to pay the difference to bondholders out of their general fund budgets—a promise that becomes an embarrassing burden for some that can ill afford the actual risk. "It's a question of scale," says Julie

Beglin, vice president of Moody's Investors Service local government team. "Is the scale affordable for the government if the project doesn't go well?"

Bad Choice: In 1996, Hamilton County, Ohio, got voters to approve a sales tax increase to help pay for two new Cincinnati sports stadiums by offering them a property tax break. But the stadiums, which cost more than $1 billion, never generated the downtown business that local officials had hoped to see. As the county found the stadium debt financing eating up an increasing share of its budget, it repealed the property tax break, then raised taxes. It sold off a hospital and refinanced the stadium debt. But the annual stadium costs—$30 million in 2008—keep rising. In 2014, the county is projected to put as much as $50 million toward its two stadiums.

Better Choice: By contrast, the development of a downtown sports arena in Washington, D.C., in the mid–1990s has been heralded as the starting point of a hugely successful revitalization of the center of that city. The arena was privately developed; the city provided the land and infrastructure in what was then a barren and oft-times dangerous part of town. Now the area is home to retail, restaurants and hotels that churn out millions in annual tax revenue. The city is attempting to apply the same concept today with a major league soccer stadium after local officials refused to take on the main responsibility for developing the project.

## Misapplying a Temporary Windfall

This is the sin that many governments commit when it seems like the good times will never end. Every economic boom is followed by a bust, but elected officials are often tempted to spend money as if that weren't true, using one-time surpluses in especially good years to cover recurring expenses that they will have to meet in the bad years. When the downturn comes, the money to meet these expenses isn't there. "State and local officials get into this over and over again," says Steve Dahl, a consultant for Deloitte. "They make very generous decisions at the top of a bull market run instead of recognizing where they are in the economic cycle."

Bad Choice: In the early 2000s, California reacted to its booming economy by granting pay raises and increased benefits to public employees, including some benefits that were awarded retroactively. Thanks to that decision and to the stock market crash later in the decade, the state and its localities have seen their entitlement bills multiply. In the first 10 years of this century, the state's pension contribution mushroomed from $611 million to $3.5 billion. Had pensions been left alone, today's bills would not be nearly as high.

Better Choice: Meanwhile, in Southern California's Riverside County, the Eastern Municipal Water District was using its skyrocketing revenues from connection fees during the boom to pay only for one-time expenses. It expanded wastewater treatment plants and water storage facilities, and improved its recycled water program. "So, when everything went bust, their expenses were very affordable as they hadn't incurred debt," notes Suzanne Finnegan, chief credit officer of Build America Mutual. "It's ironic sometimes that when you really need the discipline is when things are going well."

## Shortchanging Pension Obligations

The most serious threat to some government pension plans has been a chronic unwillingness by lawmakers to contribute what is necessary to keep the plans fully funded. To be sure, many governments skipped or pared down payments into pension plans during the recession. But some places did that for years prior to the downturn and continue to do it today. The longer they delay, the larger the long-term liability becomes.

Bad Choice: Over the last decade, New Jersey's public employee pension system has gone from a fully funded enterprise to a roughly $56 billion unfunded liability. The financial crisis certainly played a part. But the situation in New Jersey is worse than in most other places mainly because the state wasn't making its full pension payments even before the crisis began. In 2011, lawmakers passed a new pension law that legally spared the state a portion of its annual payments into the fund. It also gave New Jersey seven years before it had to start making its full contributions. "In other words," says Howard Cure, director of bond credit research at Evercore Wealth Management, "rather than continue to fully fund the pension, they used it as an excuse. Now they're back to the same hole." This year, in response to that hole, Gov. Chris Christie retroactively changed the pension funding formula to allow the state to contribute $94 million less in order to help balance the 2014 budget. Now, thanks to the formula change, the state is slated to put a total of $900 million less into the fund by the time it's required to start making its full payments. The likely outcome is that the unfunded liability will continue to grow.

Better Choice: Lexington, Ky., had a similar problem with habitually shortchanging its pension plan. But in 2012, it put together a pension task force made up of city officials and public employee union representatives, guided by an outside financial consulting firm. The result was a new agreement that guarantees Lexington will increase its annual contribution to the pension fund to $20 million from $11 million. In return, employees agreed to an older retirement age and increased paycheck deductions.

## Making Unrealistic Projections About Rate of Return

Every budget or financial planning document has to start with some assumptions about the rate of interest that will be earned on an invested portfolio. It's tempting—too tempting sometimes—to stretch those assumptions beyond what sensible economics can justify. Some pension funds still base their total liabilities owed on an expected annual investment return of more than 8 percent, a figure that affects the formula used in figuring out how much governments should contribute each year. "That means they're targeting a pension funding level that's lower than what most people might consider prudent," says Donald Fuerst, a senior pension fellow at the American Academy of Actuaries. Similarly, a budget that expects too much from a volatile revenue stream like the sales tax can be burned in any given year if the economy hits the skids.

Bad Choice: In 2012, Rockland County, N.Y., faced a $40 million budget deficit and was hit with a credit rating downgrade to one step above junk status. In its downgrade action, Standard & Poor's cited the county's "vulnerable" management practices based on overly optimistic budgeting. The following year, the county based one-fifth of its revenue returns on sales tax receipts—and expected a 4 percent increase in those returns when consumer spending growth had been far slower. The financial practices prompted the state to step in, demanding that county officials scale back their estimates and develop a realistic financial plan to escape Rockland's deficit woes, which had mounted to $125 million by 2014.

Better Choice: Many states that assumed at least an 8 percent return on investment from their pension funds have since reduced their expectations. New York state's public pension funds, for example, lowered their target return rate to 7.5 percent from 8 percent in 2010 (in addition to other changes in actuarial assumptions concerning career duration, salaries and life expectancy). This had the effect of increasing the unfunded liability (and thus, the state's required contribution) but it was more in line with the fund's financial realities. Starting this year, pension funds throughout the country will have to follow new accounting rules that include a lower assumed rate of return on their unfunded liabilities.

## Ignoring Financial Checks and Balances

Don't lose track of the money you have. It seems like the most obvious advice in the world. But in government finance and fund accounting, where there are many different ways to count the same revenue, weak financial controls can lead to serious dollar losses. Governments can lose track of how much money they actually owe one of their special funds. Or lax internal monitoring can result in poor financial choices not getting flagged until it's far too late.

Bad Choice: Earlier this year, a legislative audit criticized Idaho Treasurer Ron Crane for acting on investments without the guidance of others. At issue were $31 million worth of mortgage-backed securities that Crane transferred from the Local Government Investment Pool to the state's Idle Pool in order to protect the credit rating of the

local pool. (Both pools are vehicles for storing government cash that isn't needed immediately.) Later, Crane took $31 million in cash from the Idle Pool and put it back in the local one. The problem cited by the audit was that while the securities had a face value of $31 million, their market value was only $19 million as the move was made during the depths of the recession. The audit concluded that the treasurer's office overrode internal controls meant to contain financial risks, resulting in inappropriate transfers that cost at least $10 million in "a disproportionate share of investment losses."

Better Choice: A number of organizations have published best practice guides that help governments limit their vulnerability to financial reporting problems. The Government Finance Officers Association recommends that reporting systems incorporate an antifraud program and that financial managers periodically evaluate internal control procedures to ensure they are still working as envisioned. The Association of Local Government Auditors recommends that, at a minimum, governments have an ethics policy, established performance measures and an audit committee. State governments also cite best practices for their local governments to follow. Vermont, for example, has fact sheets available to localities offering advice on financial management of fixed assets, cash receipts and accounts receivable.

# 42. Body-Worn Cameras: Using the Wealth of Data Effectively[*]

## Paul Figueroa

It seems like every time one looks at the news these days, there are disturbing videos of community-police interactions. On every channel, pundits weigh in on the legality of these interactions and the impact they have on society. Although police departments have been recording video for decades via in-car video cameras, the explosion of community member–recorded interactions has changed the discussion about law enforcement in recent years. The proliferation of body-worn cameras is adding even more video to the field, and video undoubtedly plays a key role in U.S. policing initiatives. Generally, the video has been viewed as an important accountability measure, but the footage can also be used to proactively identify good policing practices or de-escalation strategies. It is vital to provide timely feedback for performance improvement and reinforcement of positive practices.

At a recent White House Police Data Initiative (PDI) meeting, the use of body-worn camera technology was a central topic. The PDI was created to further the goals of the President's Task Force on 21st Century Policing. The PDI was formed as a partnership of cities and private organizations across the United States to focus on two commit-

ment areas: (1) using open data to build transparency and increase community trust and (2) increasing internal accountability and effective data analysis. Body-worn cameras are germane to both areas of focus (Austin and Smith 2015). The discussion provided here began in a break-out session during the PDI meeting, and it is hoped that it will spur further thoughts about ways to make the best use of body-worn camera technology.

## Current Level—Accountability

Today, body-worn camera video is generally used for accountability purposes, such as:

- documenting circumstances of how and when force is used;
- documenting everyday interactions between the police and community;
- proving or disproving allegations of misconduct against officers;
- documenting evidence; and
- recording witness or suspect statements in the field.

It is commonly accepted that the use of body-worn cameras can increase account-

[*]Originally published as Paul Figueroa, "Body-Worn Cameras: Using the Wealth of Data Effectively," *Police Chief* 83, no. 1 (January 2016). Reprinted with permission of the publisher.

ability by documenting officers' actions, thus contributing to greater transparency in policing. It can also be argued that the use of cameras during police interactions makes police staff and members of the public who are being recorded more accountable for their behavior. In essence, most people who know they are being recorded will behave more appropriately. The full effect of all participants' knowledge of body-worn cameras on the scene deserves further analysis.

Like many other agencies, the Oakland, California, Police Department (OPD) attributes a significant portion of a reduction in use-of-force incidents and complaints against police personnel to the use of body-worn cameras. The OPD began deploying body-worn cameras in 2010. Initially, the department deployed slightly fewer than 200 body-worn cameras; currently, 611 body-worn cameras are in use for a total sworn staff of 722 officers. Six years of data show a correlation between an increase in the number of body-worn cameras and a 72 percent decline in police use-of-force incidents and a 54 percent decline in complaints against the police. Although more research across more agencies is required, this effect is consistent with other research conducted to date (White 2015).

Over the past 10 years, body-worn cameras have become smaller, cheaper, and better. According to a 2013 U.S. Department of Justice, Bureau of Justice Statistics, survey of camera use in local police agencies of all sizes, about 68 percent of agencies surveyed used in-car video; 32 percent used body-worn cameras; and approximately 6 percent used weapon-attached cameras (Reaves 2013). The survey indicated that 76 percent of departments used "in-car, body-worn, or weapon-attached cameras" (Reaves 2013). Because federal, state, and local effect of all participants' knowledge of body-worn cameras on the scene deserves further analysis governments have made funding body-worn cameras a priority, the number of body-worn cameras deployed across the United States is growing and will continue to grow rapidly.

## Three Levels of Analysis and Review

With the introduction of body-worn cameras, a wealth of information has become available. Those with access to the videos now have the ability to examine elements like facial expressions, body language, and word patterns. The richness of these data has created opportunities for deeper analysis of police-community interactions and has the potential to improve policing by identifying best practices and then using the knowledge gained to train current and future officers.

Although approaches to analysis are still being developed by many agencies, three levels of review are likely to be used by law enforcement agencies in the near future.

- First level: Straightforward analysis performed by agency supervisors, commanders, and internal affairs or auditing personnel.
- Second level: A more in-depth review conducted through formal engagement with an external academic institution or evaluation group.
- Third level: Computer-assisted analysis of large amounts of video data.

## First Level: Basic Analysis or Supervisory Review

The first level of analysis occurs when supervisors or other assigned personnel review footage for a specific purpose, such as to establish the facts and circumstances of an event under review because a complaint was made or force was used or to observe on-camera interviews taken at the scene of a crime. In addition, as a proactive risk management strategy, videos may be randomly chosen for review to identify exemplary performance, areas for improvement, and compliance with policy or practice. While basic analysis uses videos in a proactive way, it can be time-consuming. The person most likely to review the videos, a supervisor with eight or more assigned officers and multiple responsibilities, is already stressed for time.

## Second Level: Deep Analysis

The second level of analysis requires formal engagement with an external assessment or evaluation group with the capability to conduct a more rigorous review of the video. An example of this kind of engagement is found in the partnership between the Oakland Police Department and Stanford University Professor Jennifer Eberhardt, a 2014 MacArthur fellow. Dr. Eberhardt investigates the consequences of the psychological association between race and crime.

Initially, the partnership focused on analysis of existing data related to vehicle and pedestrian stops. In the past, formal analysis of these kinds of stops was limited to written documentation of the interaction in a police report or on the specific forms officers were required to complete for each stop they made. However, as the work on analysis of enforcement and stop data continued, it quickly became apparent that the large reservoir of rich body-worn camera footage now being taken at discretionary enforcement stops could also provide invaluable data about police-community interactions. In addition to a formal analysis of stop data, Dr. Eberhardt and her team are now focusing on using these data to increase everyday positive interactions between the police and community by identifying potential disparities in treatment among various racial groups and providing recommendations to mitigate identified disparities.

Because it is completed by a third party, second-level analysis provides the agency with an independent review by experts, which can mean that findings will be perceived as significantly more credible by the public. Second-level analysis can also include larger amounts of video data than first-level analysis. However, as with the first-level reviews, in-depth reviews are time-consuming. Therefore, the scope of review will most likely be a sampling limited to a specific time period. The downside to this is that video not sampled may contain valuable information that will not be included in the analysis.

## Third Level: Full Analysis

The partnership between OPD and Stanford raised the possibility of a third type of analysis. What if it were possible to have a basic review of all footage captured? The Stanford team is working to create automated technology that can rapidly analyze large amounts of body-worn camera data. The goal of the project is to provide officers and supervisors with timely, high-quality feedback regarding their interactions with community members. This information could potentially also be used in early warning systems to track officer behavior, both positive and negative, alerting supervisors to positive behavior as well as potentially problematic conduct.

While an artificial intelligence system may someday be used to flag behavior on a video based on select indicators, the flagged video still requires human review. An automated system of analysis could help focus a supervisor's or manager's attention on the most relevant video involving their subordinates, which may be more effective than hoping to catch key indicators through an audit of a small portion of the video. Rather than replace the need for supervisory (first-level) review, this third type of analysis would enhance a supervisor's ability to analyze relevant videos.

## *Using the Three Types of Review to Improve Training*

The ability to evaluate and improve training through judicious use of all three types of reviews is of major importance.

For example, video can provide invaluable information about the impact of training on communication techniques. Significant knowledge is available about verbal and non-verbal communication, and effective communication training on a regular basis is required for California law enforcement officers. In the basic academy, trainees learn communication techniques such as paraphrasing, expressing empathy, and other techniques to diffuse tense situations. Officers are trained in escalating and de-escalating force depending on changing circumstances. More recent training has also emphasized the importance of incorporating the tenets of procedural justice (voice, neutrality, respect, and trustworthiness) in all police interactions.

Why not evaluate significant amounts of police enforcement actions to determine if the training is having a positive impact? Reviewing pre- and post-footage would go a long way toward providing a much richer analysis of training efforts and ultimately positively affect everyday enforcement interactions between police and the community. Video of real-life positive policing could be used to help trainees see the value of such interactions.

## *White House Police Data Initiative*

As stated earlier, the PDI has two goals: (1) using open data to build transparency and increase community trust and (2) in-

creasing internal accountability and effective data analysis. The partnership, which includes the International Association of Chiefs of Police, is also working towards greater transparency by opening up significant segments of police data to the public so that "communities [can] gain visibility into key information on policing/citizen encounters" (Austin and Smith 2015). Although there are some limitations, body-worn cameras can often provide the best documentation of police encounters.

The implications of releasing body-worn camera videos are still being debated across the United States. Automated systems that can analyze footage have the potential to produce performance and accountability reports, which would provide the community with a summary of key performance indicators. A summary of the information could provide the community with the information they desire while respecting privacy rights by not releasing all raw footage.

## *Conclusion*

As body-worn camera programs continue to grow across the United States, many issues remain to be addressed, including storage, use requirements, technological limitations, appropriate level of viewing by officers prior to report completion, privacy rights of those recorded, and policy implications. Each of those identified topics is worthy of study and discussion, which will continue to take place within law enforcement organizations, legislative bodies, and communities across the United States. Of particular note, the continued inclusion of labor representation in policy formulation is critical to ensure all perspectives are heard during the policy formulation and implementation. To assist agencies with the rapidly evolving field, the U.S. Department of Justice, Bureau of Justice Assistance, has created a website to provide a central location as a resource for agencies to use as a toolkit for effective implementation (www.bja.gov/bwc).

Recent conversations about body-worn cameras have focused on their use for accountability, and rightfully so. However, the opportunity to identify and reward good policing practices should not be overlooked. Reviews must begin to shift from focusing on correction and accountability to a greater emphasis on identifying good policing practices. This simple change will go a long way toward maximizing the use of this technology by all in law enforcement.

Many chapters of the body-worn camera story remain to be written. The massive amount of video that is being collected represents a rich source of data never before available in the field. In the new reality of heavy scrutiny of police, it is vital that law enforcement leaders use this wealth of information to proactively improve safety and provide quality service to the community. After all, that is the core mission.

### REFERENCES

Austin, R., and M. Smith. (2015). "Launching the Police Data Initiative." The White House Office of Science and Technology Policy (blog), May 18, 2015.

Reaves, B.A. (2013). *Local Police Departments, 2013: Equipment and Technology*. United States Department of Justice, Office of Justice Programs, Bureau of Justice Statistics.

White, M. (2015). *Police Officer Body-Worn Cameras: Assessing the Evidence*. Washington, D.C.: Office of Community Oriented Policing Services.

# 43. Report Grades Cities' Spending Transparency Websites[*]

## Mike Maciag

Whether it's reviewing credit card bills or reading reviews of the newest neighborhood restaurant, more Americans use the Internet to monitor where their money is spent. But, depending on where they live, some aren't able to do the same for taxpayer dollars.

A report published this week by U.S. Public Interest Research Group (PIRG) examines government spending transparency, grading 30 cities on how well "checkbook-level" information is presented online. The study—the first of its kind assessing local government transparency—found some cities lag far behind others.

Seventeen of the 30 governments reviewed provided public spending data online, typically via searchable databases. The remaining 13 had not yet established databases maintaining vendor payments, subsidies and other expenditures. Only five cities made copies of city contracts available online, and five others disclosed individual tax subsidies awarded.

"How governments spend the public purse is something people should have easy access to," said Phineas Baxandall, a PIRG senior analyst who co-authored the report. "Transparency is really important for good

fiscal management and checking against corruption so citizens can feel confident in how their governments spend tax dollars."

The PIRG report lauded New York City's "My Money NYC" Web portal, which relaunched this week with dashboards for more than 100 agencies. While other government transparency websites list only contract amounts, the city posts actual dollars dispersed, enabling citizens to detect cost overruns.

Other cities' websites feature their own innovative tools. Chicago's system details vendor payments issued since 1996, along with beneficiaries of tax-increment financing districts. On its website, Pittsburgh posts reports filed by mayors and council members outlining their business connections to curb potential conflicts of interest.

PIRG evaluated each city's transparency efforts by measuring a series of 12 criteria. Part of the assessment looked at the breadth of the information provided, such as vendor payments, detailed tax expenditures and budgets. The report also scored the extent to which the information was readily available, emphasizing centralized websites, searching capability and downloadable data.

In general, the nation's largest cities with

---

*Originally published as Mike Maciag, "Report Grades Cities' Spending Transparency Websites," *Governing*, January 25, 2013. Reprinted with permission of the publisher.

more resources received the highest marks. There were notable exceptions, though, with Cincinnati earning the fifth highest score overall.

New York and Chicago were awarded an "A" grade, while five cities were slapped with "Fs." PIRG scored the largest cities in the 30 most populous metro areas, as shown in the following table:

### City, Grade, Score
### (out of 100)

| | | |
|---|---|---|
| Chicago | A | 98 |
| New York | A | 98 |
| San Francisco | A– | 90 |
| Baltimore | B+ | 89 |
| Cincinnati | B+ | 87 |
| Denver | B | 85 |
| San Antonio | B | 83 |
| Washington, D.C. | B | 83 |
| Orlando | C+ | 79 |
| Pittsburgh | C+ | 79 |
| Seattle | C+ | 78 |
| Miami | C+ | 76 |
| Houston | C+ | 75 |
| Kansas City | C | 73 |
| Philadelphia | C | 72 |
| San Diego | C– | 69 |
| Los Angeles | C– | 68 |
| Dallas | D+ | 64 |
| Phoenix | D | 58 |
| Las Vegas | D | 56 |
| Tampa | D | 56 |
| Minneapolis | D– | 54 |
| Riverside | D– | 54 |
| Boston | D– | 53 |
| Portland | D– | 50 |
| Atlanta | F | 46 |
| Detroit | F | 46 |
| St. Louis | F | 46 |
| Sacramento | F | 44 |
| Cleveland | F | 41 |

City governments decide to launch online portals for a variety of reasons. Most often, Baxandall said, a politician, comptroller or other official uses his or her clout to make transparency initiatives a priority.

"Sometimes they do it because they have a vision and sense of a personal mission about it. Other times, there may be a scandal or something they're trying to overcome," he said.

For cities with limited or nonexistent transparency websites, startup costs are often a concern. But such initiatives typically don't cost too much, with most cities' price tags ranging from $25,000 to $50,000 in the report. New York City, though, spent far more—about $2.4 million—developing its transparency portal.

The good news for cities with fewer resources is that New York City plans to open source the code for its system later this year, potentially enabling cities to launch their own transparency cities at a fraction of the cost.

Other barriers preventing cities from stepping up their transparency efforts include bureaucratic hurdles and standardizing data across multiple departments, Baxandall said.

The report cited tax breaks and service requests from citizens as two data sets commonly absent from many public websites. Cities maintaining robust online portals also must ensure information is centralized and available in downloadable formats or through an application programming interface.

"As cities grapple with difficult decisions in an effort to make budgetary ends meet, transparency websites provide an important tool to allow both citizens and civil servants to make informed choices," the report concludes.

# 44. Using Technology to Increase Access and Transparency[*]

## Brian A. Moura

Today's public administrator is facing challenges to inform and engage the public about the issues that confront our cities, counties and agencies. Citizens have to balance the demands of work, family and the many life choices around them every day. Frankly, watching and attending the traditional, structured and sometimes drawn out processes of government agencies is not a priority for many people. As a result, the public often tunes in and out when it comes to the proposals and projects in their community at a time when we as public managers desire their full attention and participation. So the question is how do we compete for their attention in today's world with many competing information sources and work/life events?

### New Tools

The good news is that today public managers have many tools and technologies at our disposal to increase access to information on what's happening at City Hall and other levels of government. Many agencies have moved on from traditional methods like mailed notices, periodic printed newsletters and legal ads in newspapers to more interesting and lively approaches. Let's take a look at how one agency, the City of San Carlos, has used these tools in a "multichannel" fashion to better engage and inform the public.

### Web Sites and Email

In the mid–1990s, cities and government agencies began to develop colorful websites. These sites offered features like headlines of what's going on at the City, electronic service request forms, quick links, email and phone contacts and program and project updates, all available 24 hours a day—long before and after City Hall opened and closed each day. In short, a revolution in convenience and access. In San Carlos, the city's website at www.cityofsancarlos.org has grown from one page in 1993 to over 10,000 pages of information today—providing information on every city department and almost every city program and proposal available to the public.

During this period, cities also employed

*Originally published as Brian A. Moura, "Using Technology to Increase Access and Transparency in Local Government," http://patimes.org/technology-increase-access-transparency-local-government/, 2013. Reprinted with permission of the publisher.

email list serve software on their websites. These programs let the public select from a menu of meeting agendas and minutes, project updates, news and announcements of interest. Once the selections are made, cities can email updates knowing that the intelligence of the list serve software will direct them to interested resident subscribers in a matter of seconds. At the City of San Carlos, subscriptions to the City's eNotify email list serve have grown from 25 subscribers with 5 subscription options in its first week in the mid–1990s to more than 8,400 subscribers with more than 40 document types today. Ironically we find that more people learn about City events through email today than through other methods— even though it was one of our earliest and most basic efforts at information sharing through technology!

## Indexed Videos and Document Management

In 1999, new companies sprung up that offered cities new ways to communicate with and inform the public by offering videos of public meetings. At first these systems focused on live streaming of public meetings and events, enabling residents to watch what was "going on at City Hall" from the comfort of their own home.

The systems then added indexing so that each topic or meeting agenda item had its own time stamp or link. This made the archived video of a meeting much more relevant and friendly. Instead of watching a 3 to 5 hour public meeting, residents and interested parties could now "jump" right to the item of interest, watch that 15 to 30 minutes of discussion and skip the remainder of the meeting. The public applauded and offered kudos to cities like San Carlos that offered this service. Citizens in neighboring cities asked—and even demanded—similar services from their city.

Taking it to another level, cities worked with document management firms to link current and past meeting agendas, minutes, staff reports and attachments to the online meeting notices and archives. The result is today interested parties can not only receive a meeting agenda, but also all of the reports, maps and attachments that the City Council, Commission or Board will have at a meeting in advance of the meeting date.

Web portals like the www.epackets.net site from the City of San Carlos show how all of these technologies can be used in a compelling manner to provide full information and transparency, offering complete meeting packets for every Board, Council, Commission and Committee at the City. In some respects, this can be a mixed blessing since the City has made it so easy to learn about a meeting without attending the meeting that one could argue we are making attendance a disincentive.

## Social Media and Web 2.0

In 2006, new tools like Twitter and Facebook came on the scene. Cities soon began exploring how to use these systems as new ways to reach the public. In San Carlos, we found that the audience using Twitter and Facebook were different, requiring different approaches to writing and formatting information on each service. On Twitter, the city focuses on instant updates and short briefs while Facebook emphasizes parks and recreation and community events with colorful pictures and images. The result has been reaching residents who do not use the city website and email services. And the services continue to be popular—we've seen a jump in participation from a small group of tech fans at the start to almost 3,000 fans on Facebook and almost 4,500 followers on Twitter today.

## Web Based Services

We should also mention the growth of web based city services. In San Carlos, the most popular corner of the city website is our online recreation class and program system, www.recconnect.net. Using a vendor's recreation software and linking it to this branded portal, the city has seen online recreation registration jump from 25 percent when it was first offered to more than 79 percent today. Allowing residents to register for summer camp for their kids and sign up for courses for themselves from the comfort of home, or their desk at work, without ever setting foot in City Hall is what some residents say is "what I really want from the City."

## The Future

Additional services are coming with the advent of smartphone apps, low cost touch based tablets, laptops and computers and many other innovations. The experience in San Carlos tells us that agencies would be wise to explore, experiment and then adapt these new technologies to keeping the public aware of city information, programs and events. If you do, the result will be a better informed and engaged community. A recent citizen satisfaction survey in San Carlos showed an amazing 98 percent positive rating for the city's quality of life. This shows that sharing information and focusing on transparency leads to many happy and engaged residents, something we all aspire to have in our communities.

# 45. Unlike Zoos, Public Health Departments Don't Need National Accreditation[*]

## Mattie Quinn

In 2014, the local health department helped Toledo, Ohio, handle a crisis that left residents and businesses without tap water for days.

Libraries, universities and even zoos have national accreditation standards they must meet. But public health departments—the very agencies that oversee disease outbreaks and the sanitation of restaurants and drinking water—don't.

There is, however, a movement to change that.

A national accreditation board for state and local public health departments was officially formed in 2011, but the process is currently voluntary. Since then, 96 agencies across the country (out of 2,615) have received accreditation, with an additional 253 in the process. If all 253 attain accreditation, that still only makes 13 percent.

Some states, like Illinois and New York, have started encouraging their local public health departments to get accredited. Ohio, though, is one of the first states to make it mandatory. A law passed in 2013 requires all local public health departments to get accreditation by 2020. If they don't, they'll lose state and federal funding.

"Our system of health departments is incredibly diverse," said Rick Hodges, director of the Ohio Department of Health. "So the legislature and state health department decided that accrediting our health departments was the most basic standard we could give to Ohioans to make sure they are safe."

A big chunk of the accreditation requirements are that departments have strategic plans for potential public health problems. This includes identifying the health issues within the particular community and how they could be better addressed, the presence of a 24/7 contact line and written protocols.

The idea for a national public health accreditation board was born in 2005 when the Centers for Disease Control and Prevention (CDC) and the Robert Wood Johnson Foundation teamed up to create one. Kaye Bender, president of the Public Health Accreditation Board, said they recognized a void and filled it.

"I've worked in public health for more than 30 years, mostly in hospitals, so I was very surprised when I learned that public health departments didn't have any sort of national accreditation process. When we looked into why not, the only thing we could

*Originally published as Mattie Quinn, "Unlike Zoos, Public Health Departments Don't Need National Accreditation," *Governing*, January 5, 2016. Reprinted with permission of the publisher.

find was political will. There just didn't seem to be motivation there to get this practice standardized. We are lucky we had the backing of the CDC and Robert Wood Johnson Foundation."

At the Oklahoma Department of Health, one of the first state departments to get accredited, the process forced them to review every policy and procedure.

"We found some policies were terribly outdated and needed to be thrown out and policies that were still appropriate but needed a bit of updating," said Terry Cline, director of the Oklahoma Department of Health. "I don't know when we would have ever addressed those things if we didn't go through the accreditation process. In doing that, you learn quickly that you're not as cutting edge as you think you are."

But getting accredited isn't easy.

Bender says it can take up to 18 months and be considered costly. Accreditation fees range from $12,720 to $95,400—depending on the number of people the department serves. Most local health departments serve less than 25,000 people and tend to have fewer financial and personnel resources than departments that are larger and/ or state-run. The fees are mostly administrative, paying for a specialist, a site visit of peer review experts and support for re-accreditation, which must happen every five years.

Surveys show that limited staff, staff turnover and fees are the biggest barriers to national accreditation.

In the meantime, at least a couple of other states have taken matters into their own hands. North Carolina has a statewide standard that local health departments have been held accountable to since 2005. And like Ohio, Florida requires its local departments to attain national accreditation. But the state's system is centralized, with all local offices working as branches of the state Department of Health, which was accredited in 2014.

In Ohio, some have complained about the cost, but Hodges is confident that all departments can meet the 2020 deadline. That's because a few smaller departments in less wealthy areas have already earned accreditation, which Hodges says should serve as proof that the rest of the state can comply.

"Becoming an accredited health department is not simply of measurement of service," he said. "It's a matter of strategic planning—really showing you can plan for anything," he said.

Note: This story has been updated with information about Florida and North Carolina's accreditation policies.

# 46. Speak Out, Do the Right Thing and You're Fired!*
## Brynne VanHettinga

Public employees have one major advantage over those who work in the private sector—the protection of state and federal constitutional rights. However, these rights are not absolute. Public employees who want to know if they could lose their job if they speak out about an issue will find that the law is confusing and ambiguous. This is especially the case where the employee is pointing out malfeasance, corruption or other activity harmful to the public on the part of the public employer.

Since 1968, Pickering v. Board of Education has governed the area of free speech of public employees. Pickering, a public school-teacher, had written a letter to the local newspaper criticizing the school board's handling of bond issuance and other financial management decisions. Pickering was subsequently fired because his statements were found to have been detrimental to the efficient operations of his employer. The U.S. Supreme Court found that Pickering's free speech rights as a citizen to comment on matters of public concern (school board financial issues) outweighed the effects of his statement on school operations. The so-called Pickering test required courts to weigh the free speech rights of employees against the interests of the public employer when determining whether adverse action against the employee was lawful.

In 2006, a sharply divided U.S. Supreme Court greatly limited Pickering protections in Garcetti v. Ceballos. Ceballos, a Los Angeles County assistant district attorney, discovered that a warrant issued by the sheriff's office contained serious misrepresentations. Ceballos prepared a memo recommending that the case be dismissed. Ceballos even testified for the defense about inaccuracies in the warrant. Ceballos was denied a promotion and was reassigned to a lower position in an inconvenient location. He then filed suit, alleging retaliation for exercise of his First Amendment rights. The U.S. Supreme Court ruled that, although his speech involved a significant matter of public concern, the First Amendment did not shield him from adverse employer actions because Ceballos' communication was part of his job duties.

The irony of Garcetti is that employees whose duties involve analysis, recommendation and reporting, i.e., those who are most likely to have evidence of wrongdoing, are least likely to be protected by the First Amendment. The question of first impres-

*Originally published as Brynne VanHettinga, "Speak Out, Do the Right Thing and You're Fired!" *PA Times*, February 3, 2015. Reprinted with permission of the publisher.

sion in these cases now is what forms of employee speech are job-related (and not protected) and what forms are made pursuant to their role as citizens (which are protected).

This has created a plethora of conflicting holdings. Some courts find nearly any speech remotely connected to employer interests to be unprotected, while others find that speech is protected so long as there is no specific duty to report. This creates an obvious incentive on the part of public employers to thwart employee First Amendment rights by drafting overly broad job descriptions.

Several cases illustrate this split in court rulings. In a Texas case (Charles v. Grief, 522 F.3d 508, 5th Cir. 2008), a systems analyst for the Texas Lottery Commission sent an email to the Texas Legislature with allegations of both racial discrimination and violations of the Texas Public Information Act. When the employee was fired two days later, he sued his supervisor for violating his First Amendment rights. The court found in the employee's favor on the basis of (1) his communication was directly to the Legislature and not through an internal grievance process (which could arguably be job-related under Garcetti), and (2) his action could not be related in any conceivable way to his job duties as a computer systems analyst.

Conversely, a correctional officer in an Indiana prison (Spiegla v. Hull, 481 F.3d 961, 7th Cir. 2007) was not protected. The officer was transferred to a less desirable shift after reporting that other officers were unloading suspicious bags and circumventing the prison's vehicle search policies. The rationale for this decision was that the act of reporting security breaches was pursuant to her official job duties.

A more recent Supreme Court case (Lane v. Franks, 573 U.S., 2014) suggests that the Court is seeking a return to Pickering-style balancing of the respective rights of public employees and public employers while attempting to limit the expansion of Garcetti. Although this is encouraging, what seems to have been lost is any consideration of the public's right to the fair, honest, efficient and transparent operation of their governing institutions. Employees who call out wrongdoing by public officials—the so-called "whistleblowers"—frequently pay a high price professionally, financially and emotionally. Like First Amendment protection, public employee whistleblower protections are also complex and convoluted, requiring employees to adhere strictly to byzantine procedural sequences before statutory protections apply. Employees are not likely to consult an attorney before committing an act (in their view) of public service or moral righteousness. If the objective is to restore public trust in government, the law should not permit the punishment of public employees for telling the truth.

# 47. Dealing with Public Mistrust[*]

## Dana K. Lee

The public's mistrust of government has been on the rise since the late 1960s when Watergate and other widely publicized issues began to tarnish the image of public officials. Late last summer, in a CBS and *New York Times* survey, only 19 percent of Americans felt that they could "trust government in Washington to do what is right most or all of the time."

Thanks to the around-the-clock news cycle and numerous social media tools, people are ever more exposed to government wrongdoing and are more capable of teaming up with one another in order to attack and protest government officials. The Tea Party movement and the tax watchdog groups at the local level are indicative of the frustration and anger toward all levels of government. Stalling or even shutting down government is becoming a viable strategy for the disenfranchised, be they Tea Party activists or Occupy Wall Street protesters in Manhattan.

This article examines how elected and appointed officials will need to adapt to frustration and mistrust as well as personal attacks and the use of freedom-of-information legislation as weapons against government.

### Mistrust Grows and Consumes

One local resident decided that her local public officials were hiding something, including stealing and lying about it. She chose to bombard staff with e-mails demanding documents while also including pointed attacks on staff's integrity in those e-mails. At one point it was estimated that her freedom-of-information requests would cost $15,000 to a local Maine town over the course of a year. Her methods discouraged and upset staff and crippled their productivity.

People who mistrust government and its employees will likely never be convinced to change their views. They see corruption and incompetence at all levels of government. They see it where it exists (via television reporting, 24 hours per day), where it doesn't exist, and even where they believe it exists but just can't prove it yet. Managers can be assumed guilty by simply being associated with government, and some people have already carried out imaginary trials and convictions.

The vast majority of public servants continue to be honest, conscientious, and hardworking people, yet uncivil discourse and mistrust are sharply on the rise. It is with this contentious environment in mind that I present strategies for coping with this type of resident.

Government employees need to recognize the thinking and belief systems of the true government haters. It hurts us, of course. We are only human, and it is in our nature as

*Originally published as Dana K. Lee, "Dealing with Public Mistrust," *PM Magazine* 94, no. 1 (January/February 2012). Reprinted with permission of the publisher.

public servants to do our jobs to help society—not harm it, lie about it, steal from it, or get rich from it.

Other than espousing and living our code of ethics daily, and engaging citizens as much as possible, public servants can do precious little to reverse the growing mistrust of government. We are in unusual times given high property taxes, the rising number of foreclosures, and joblessness.

## Strategies Matter

Elected and appointed public officials need to learn strategies for compartmentalizing, minimizing, eliminating, deflecting, or otherwise ignoring the negative attacks on their integrity, motives, and competence. There is no single strategy that will work in every case. Options are needed, depending on the nature, tone, and method of attack. Here are 10 options to consider.

1. You must depersonalize the attack. You are not the position. You are a human being, and you do a job the best you can. When you think of yourself as "the city" or "the county manager," as if an equal sign exists between your name and that office, you truly risk being affected personally by the attacks. If it were not you, it would be some other person holding the office who would be under attack. It's your ego that makes it personal, and it can tie you far too closely to the position.

2. Put critics in perspective in two ways:

First, always start by having your perspective in order. What are the big chunks of beautiful blue sky that make your life grand? The spouse, kids, grandchildren, time at camp, or playing sports with buddies? Also consider all the other great relationships, hobbies, and time spent smiling.

And then there are the majority of residents—80 percent? 90 percent?—who seem pleased or content with what you do. Taken together, that's your big blue sky. Unfortunately, there are those few, tiny red holes of anger in that otherwise big beautiful sky. Does it make sense—does it work to your advantage—to focus on the tiny red holes?

Second, walk a mile in their shoes. Many of these people may have not had the upbringing, education, opportunities, and good fortune that you may have had. As noted earlier, the abused woman and the distressed widow had beliefs that, while hurtful and inappropriate, are nonetheless understandable. Isolate that thought and say to yourself, "I'm grateful that I am not them. They are very unhappy inside."

3. Never feed the beast. Don't focus on the person. Don't allow the negative words and energy to poison the office. Don't talk about him or her. Don't even discuss the latest, nuttiest attack. Anger feeds anger, and negativity feeds negativity.

4. Don't carry around a grudge at them. It's not worth it. A friend told me that a grudge was "like you drinking poison and expecting them to die." Let it go. They can carry the poison in their bellies.

5. Indifference is a nice strategy. "It takes 43 muscles to smile, 17 muscles to frown, and zero muscles to sit there with a dumb look on your face." Some of my colleagues use this strategy extremely well. They have developed a strategy to view mistrust and attacks as a minor, natural occurrence, which will not be allowed to create negative feelings for them.

6. Wait it out. Don't respond. Take time to cool down. What's the worst that happens if you choose to simply not engage the attacker? Attackers want an immediate reaction. They want to get under your skin. Deny them that joy.

7. Learn lessons from their behavior. Act as though you are an outside observer of what they are trying to express or achieve. Maybe there is a lesson to be learned in

their criticism, such as "I demand earlier posting of public meetings and agendas on the website!" It may be wise, transparent, and accountable to do that—so do it. You will not appease them in any meaningful way, but the other 80 percent—the silent majority—may appreciate it.

For the mistrustful, it would just be one item on a list of 100 top things they do not like about your office. They'll be in the town office tomorrow or at the next council meeting with a new gripe.

8. Build a support network. Your colleagues are going through this as well. Find time to have lunch and share stories with them. Support each other. Reach out to a colleague getting attacked and offer an uplifting word.

9. Ask elected officials to issue policy or guidelines allowing staff to "shut down" these folks when they are getting aggressive, time-consuming, or too personal. Make sure that elected officials "have your back" if you need to take adult control over an increasingly intolerable situation. Determine your "rights" with your supervisors about how you may choose to speak and act when an angry citizen comes through the door to chide you. In any event, never get loud or aggressive. Remain calm, but firm.

10. Finally, be aware of a rational versus an instinctive reaction. In other words, will you offer a thoughtful response or jump to a fight-or-flight reaction? You must choose to stay at a rational level and stay above the fray. A friend once told me "to never get into a mudslinging contest unless you are ready to get covered in mud." If they yell, you stay calm. They want to push your buttons; deny them that joy.

As a local government manager, you may not even be the staff member taking the most frequent and greatest abuse. Frontline staff will also need your support, your wisdom, and your strategies to mitigate the negative feelings that mistrustful people can cause.

## A Few Black Eyes

These are difficult times to be a government employee, and it is important that an individual learns to cope with attacks on character and integrity. A person must remember that the attackers are relatively few in number and that, in general, residents of a community serve a reasonably content public. Remember too that, given the number of good, conscientious government employees, only a tiny fraction commit wrongdoing and cause a black eye for the rest.

It's best to understand these attacks and maintain perspective. Also, it is best to depersonalize the attacks, and, to the maximum extent possible, leave the negativity behind. Stick by your ethics, smile, and do a good job.

# 48. When Transparency Fails to Produce Accountability[*]

## Pospere Charles

Simply stated, transparency is the act of disclosing, bringing to the open what seems to have been done in secret places. Accountability is the act of taking responsibility for actions committed. The argument is that once transparency brings secret acts to the known, accountability will follow. There seems to be a positive relationship between transparency and accountability, at least according to Transparency International and the World Bank.

Many scholars, such as Paolo De Renzio at the Overseas Development Institute and Sarah Mulley at the Global Economic Governance Programme, disagreed with this assessment. Others argue that there may be a more sinister movement taking place when exposing actors that seem to be outside of public reach. What do they mean? The following real life scenarios illustrate this debate.

The case of Eric Garner shows a cop choking a man to death. So far, right or wrong, there has been no satisfactory legal repercussions for the police officer. Although, the facts surrounding this case seem to have been well documented. Transparency was not an issue as many seem to believe they knew all the facts in this event. But apparently accountability did not follow transparency. One did not cause the other to happen automatically. What was missing?

There are those who believe that accountability has been very much in display when the Grand Jury decided not to indict the officer responsible for the death of Mr. Garner. Mr. Daniel Pantaleo, the policeman in question, submitted himself to the jurisdiction of the justice system, fulfilling his role of accountability. It was up to the justice system to render a verdict. The justice system was represented by a prosecutor and 24 unknown actors who decided the validity of this case.

Except for the prosecutor, we may never know who these citizens were. We may also never know what they discussed and how they came up with their final decision. But we know this; the final verdict did not meet the test of trust for millions of citizens. The line between transparency and accountability in this case is blurred, at best.

The case of Michael Brown in Ferguson, Missouri also surrounded a white police officer shooting a black man. According to media reports, the evidence presented to the Grand Jury was sketchy at best. A federal investigation is still ongoing. The fact

*Originally published as Pospere Charles, "When Transparency Fails to Produce Accountability," *PA Times*, January 20, 2015. Reprinted with permission of the publisher.

is that a man was killed and days of violent protestations around the nation followed suit because accountability was apparently absent in this debate.

Some argue that justice was served. They argued that the days of protestations around the nation following the verdict, were conducted by biased civil rights leaders who would have been satisfied with only a guilty verdict. Once again, the lesson learned is that the so called transparency in this case did not meet the threshold of accountability acceptable by all. Can we talk about subjectivity when referring to accountability?

In the next case, the United States revealed that the Central Intelligence Agency (CIA) tortures detainees. This case is well documented in a congressional report. The CIA itself did not totally disavow the findings. While one can argue that transparency was certainly an ingredient in the decision to publish this report, accountability so far has failed to show up. Why? Does it take time for accountability practices to catch up with transparency measures?

One of the strongest arguments that arose from the 2008 economic recession is that, although many of the players that caused the downturn are fairly known, the top individuals who led these reckless acts have not been held responsible for their actions. Expert reporting established clear links between actions of these players and consequences on the global economy, but individual accountability is still missing in action. Are these players too big to be accountable?

This is the current dilemma between transparency and accountability. One does not necessarily trigger the other. There is even a scarier thought that transparency exposes to the public what is hidden behind the veil of corruption and deception, showing how influential some actors are, and exposing the weaknesses of current systems to bring these too powerful actors to accountability. In this sense, transparency is used to intimidate people against participating in change events and bringing about the opposite effect of accountability. We should find the missing link between transparency and accountability. This will revolutionize our socio-interactions as a nation.

# 49. When Transparency Becomes the Enemy of Accountability*

## Stuart C. Gilman and Howard Whitton

Everything is connected to everything else, as in the world of ecology and in public administration. Transparency seems to have become the new panacea for all government ills and often trumps everything else from consideration—including accountability. Transparency has become the new vogue concept in public administration.

For the authors, with a combined 60 years of field experience, transparency requires a more nuanced and analytical approach than taken by many in academia and by most in politics. While it is appropriate that academic treatments of the concept lead to tenure or promotion, our concern is that much of what has been published is not particularly useful to the practitioner. To quote E.F. Schumacher from his book, *Small Is Beautiful: A Study of Economics as if People Mattered*, "an ounce of practice is generally worth a ton of theory." For today's practitioner, a more balanced and integrated approach to transparency is needed.

Meaningful accountability should be the primary focus for public administration practitioners and governments. Accountability is one of the "ends" of democracy. Transparency is not an end, but a useful but limited mechanism. Often the tool is viewed as an end in itself, leading to the belief in a self-generating accountability. As the argument goes, greater openness leads to greater involvement of citizens and therefore greater democracy. This greater democracy leads to more accountability. What could be wrong with this picture?

One recent story in the *Economist* pointed out that transparency and clarity about public budgets allow citizens "to lobby for different spending priorities" and that openness of budgets encourages lenders. Unfortunately, the article cited Morocco, Kyrgyzstan and Nigeria as models for budget transparency. Anyone who has worked in those countries would have great concerns over the accuracy and meaningfulness of those budgets. After all, Greece—with all of the scrutiny of the European Union—provided published public budgets that were artful works of fiction. From our point of view, there are three major issues that practitioners must think about in linking transparency and accountability:

### Transparency as an End in Itself

Financial disclosure systems are one of the best examples of how transparency can be

*Originally published as Stuart C. Gilman and Howard Whitton, "When Transparency Becomes the Enemy of Accountability: Reflections from the Field," http://patimes.org/transparency-enemy-accountability-reflections-field/, 2014. Reprinted with permission of the authors and publisher.

used to disguise illicit intent. Good disclosure systems have professional staff reviewing submissions regularly with the authority to ask for clarification and take action in cases of non-compliance. Too many countries view the exercise of producing disclosures and making them available to the public as enough. Even well designed disclosure systems either can exclude significant information from scrutiny and public access or may release large amounts of material relying on the public to detect problems. Collecting hundreds of thousands of disclosures was the first approach by both Argentina and the Ukraine. Both countries made the documents available to the public. Citizens and the media were so overwhelmed by the amount data that the documents were useless.

A good historical reminder is that Enron Corporation's accounts were entirely transparent. The problem was that the information provided was impossible to understand unless you were a well-qualified forensic accountant with a large research team at your disposal. Not everything significant was connected to everything else and the message was missed. After the fact, even their board of directors admitted that they could not understand the reports they were given.

### Transparency that Leads to Less Accountability

Transparency, especially at the state and local levels, can lead to 'the flight from accountability." Elected officials and senior bureaucrats often find it difficult, or not in their interests, to plan beyond the short-term. Government is not a well-oiled machine and officials are understandably reluctant to take complete responsibility for something they cannot control. Transparency in government tends to drive a focus on quarterly or annual results. There is a preference for decisions that can produce favorable,

verifiable information rather than long-term policies or programs that would be better but where easily measureable data is not readily available. Transparency can impede long-term planning, ensure that governments are less innovative and have less opportunity to plan.

Those favoring greater transparency argue that it leads to more thoughtful, considered policy choices by citizens. Although this position is attractive from a philosophical point of view, there is little empirical evidence to support it. As stated in David Primo's recent *New York Times* op-ed, "Against Disclosure," "once you account for everything available to voters, campaign-finance disclosure provides very little informational benefit."

Informational benefit is what matters. There is now good evidence that detailed and finely tuned Key Performance Indicators (one among a myriad of such measures) often leads to gaming of the system for improper advantage of various kinds, or function merely as perverse incentives to avoid accountability and responsibility.

### The Unintended Consequences of Transparency

An exclusive focus on transparency can lead to unexamined confidence in the actions of government. Open systems do not mean that information is presented in a meaningful way or that it is accurate. The innocent assumption is that the citizen or the media will be able to detect and expose this kind of wrongdoing. First, very few citizens have the ability to analyze a local government budget. Second, there are fewer and fewer traditional media players with the capacity to do investigative work. More and more newspapers employ stringers to write stories suited to broader political agendas. Combined with the tsunami of blogs of varying (and sometimes appalling) expertise and accuracy, it makes access to accurate analysis a very daunting task. The electronic media also suffer because of talking heads that have human-interest stories as their prime focus. Complex stories that take more than 60 seconds to explain do not make good television or attract audiences of the requisite size and demographic.

In the international context, simplistic evaluation of transparency (rather than accountability) allows governments to escape scrutiny, while others are unfairly labeled as corrupt. Organizations such as Transparency International produce indicators like the Corruption Perception Index (CPI). Due to the design of the CPI, if a country takes significant actions against corruption and has an open press it is possible that it will fare worse. This can lead to less transparency as the government tries to deal with the fallout of an apparently worse result in the transparency indexes.

The financial costs of transparency are often not counted. Government oversight and other transparency measures are expensive. Freedom of information regimes can have significant costs. Some experts believe the Freedom of Information Act increases expenditures of almost a billion dollars. Ironically, more senior officials around the world are making it a practice to "not take notes" or at least make them indecipherable in case there should be a freedom of information request.

The U.S. federal financial disclosure system requires the hiring of over 1000 full time and almost 9000 part-time positions to do the work. The U.S. federal budget system was initially made an annual event in order to increase transparency. However, the U.S. Congress has managed to politicize the system to the extent that citizens do not understand what is being spent. The transparency control of having only "annual" expenditures conceals the real costs of projects and encourages administrators to obligate their entire budgets before the end of the fiscal year.

## *Conclusion*

Transparency and accountability are not the same thing. They are not even the same kind of thing. Transparency is a mechanism for achieving scrutiny of meaningful information. Transparency of government information occurs in the real world of personal and political responsibility and can lead to greater accountability, but sometimes less.

The problem with transparency as a management fad is that it can lead to distraction, complacency, perverse incentives, greater costs and loss of public confidence in the integrity of government and administration. This is true in the developed world and a nightmare in the developing world. Transparency for transparency's sake is of no practical value. Accountability has to be the end. Everything is connected to everything else.

# 50. How to Embed Transparency into Collaborative Governance*

## *Jusil Lee* and *Erik W. Johnston*

What is the proper role of government transparency in collaborative governance? Is it just about improving information management practices such as processing and storing huge data sets? Otherwise, is something more than that?

In response to President Obama's Open Government Initiative, local governments have increased the level of information they disclose to the public through websites in an effort to become more transparent. This one-way top-down data push aims to inform citizens of governmental activities. Although this may increase the accountability of government by allowing public scrutiny, transparency achieved by unidirectional and hierarchal communication is not enough to achieve collaborative governance.

In *Public Participation and Collaborative Governance*, Newman et al. highlight partnerships between government and citizens designed to solve a number of "cross-cutting" policy problems. Solving complex challenges facing society requires collective intelligence widely distributed outside of government, beyond simply informing citizens. Thus, government calls for dynamic interactions with citizens to tap into "the wisdom of crowds."

Furthermore, collaborative governance more equally distributes problem-solving and decision making power among all participants from both government and the public. Citizens involved in collaborative efforts with government do not simply passively receive information and provide feedback on governmental decisions that have already occurred. Rather, citizens actively share information, express their preferences, develop common understanding and identify innovative solutions to public problems—through multi-directional interactions with government-participating in all phases of the decision-making process.

To successfully operationalize government transparency for collaborative governance, I suggest the model of "embedded" transparency. According to Oxford Dictionaries, "to embed" is to implant an idea so that it becomes ingrained within a particular context. By this definition, embedding transparency into collaborative governance implies integrating transparency into the context of collaborative governance. Since transparency concerns the disclosure of information, I define "embedded transparency" as integrating the disclosure of information into the process of government-

*Originally published as Jusil Lee and Erik W. Johnston, "How to Embed Transparency into Collaborative Governance," http://patimes.org/embed-transparency-collaborative-governancee/, 2014. Reprinted with permission of the publisher.

public collaboration activities for problem-solving.

Embedded transparency goes through four phases of "dynamic communication"–see, understand, integrate, and track—that solicit active flows of information between government and citizens. Dynamic communication makes participants informed and helps their ideation. Successfully generating embedded transparency depends on government's ability to facilitate dynamic communication.

## Dynamic Communication

**See.** The first phase of dynamic communication is see. This phase aims to build targeted information that government and citizens provide. Targeted information is a specific kind of information on a given policy problem by either government or citizens. Government and citizens build targeted information collectively by disclosing their own knowledge and perspectives to each other. In this phase, citizens can see what government is doing to address a certain policy problem, while government can see citizens' needs, preferences and perspectives about the policy problem. The targeted information consequently helps participants of the collaborative partnership realize the gap between their approaches to a given policy problem.

**Understand.** The second phase of dynamic communication is understand. This phase aims to reduce the gap between participants' approaches to a certain policy problem. In this phase, the participants build mutual understanding of why their conflicts arise. Government can identify where it fails to meet citizens' needs in addressing a given policy problem. Citizens can understand why government has dealt with the policy problem in a certain way and the obstacles to government's activity. This phase opens the chance of integrating knowledge and perspectives from diverse stakeholders into

the collaborative conversation as a starting point to develop innovative solutions to policy problems.

**Integrate.** The third phase of dynamic communication is integrate. This phase aims to develop a creative and viable solution to a given policy problem by integrating the targeted information and mutual understanding developed in the former phases. The integrated knowledge becomes a useful resource to help participants discover what they are missing to fix a certain policy problem. In this phase, the participants engage in collective action aimed at finding the substantial factors that influence a specific policy problem. The collective action of participants also includes examining their constraints and available resources in relations to a given policy problem. Such consideration helps the participants develop an innovative and feasible solution to a given policy challenge.

**Track.** The last phase of dynamic communication is track. This phase aims to enable citizens to monitor the results of collaborative communication. Government officials have a responsibility to inform citizens of how government has dealt with the suggestions by citizens in real policy decisions and actions. Through an official medium such as government websites, citizens monitor the status of processing their suggestions and the process of deciding the best idea/solution.

## The Role of Embedded Transparency

Consequently, embedded transparency in collaborative governance is "the action of creating active and multi-directional interactions between government and citizens to improve the quality of government decisions." Embedded transparency plays two distinct roles in facilitating effective collaboration.

First, transparency helps generate a "shared context" around a policy problem between government and citizens. A shared context allows participants in collaborative efforts to approach a certain policy problem in a similar way or within a similar frame. Through dynamic communication, government and citizens can see and understand the situation in which they are involved together, beyond just focusing on their own situation. Consequently, the shared context enables the participants to build more feasible solutions within a common knowledge and understanding.

Second, transparency provides citizens with a real influence on public policies. Citizens not only participate in solution-building, having their preferences and perspectives integrated into public decisions, but also track how government has dealt with their suggestions through real policy. Such public scrutiny enables the public to feel its ability to influence a policy decision; it's political efficacy. In Participation and Democratic theory, Pateman argues for political efficacy as stimulus to encourage citizen participation on the regular basis.

## Seoul City's Oasis

As local governments increasingly support the use of a variety of information and communication technologies (ICT), the possibility of realizing the model of embedded transparency increases.

Seoul City's Oasis in South Korea and provides a good example of this potential. The Oasis system of Seoul City is an open and interacting system that serves as a channel to encourage citizen participation in decision-making. Anytime and anywhere, Seoul citizens can participate in open discussions with local government officials via the Oasis website and mobile applications, integrate ideas into policies through a brainstorming process and monitor the result of their suggestions. Also, the real time feedback by public officials to questions posed by citizens can effectively address their concerns in a timely manner.

Although the Open Government Initiative advances technology as a medium of endless knowledge, its capacity is limited in creating the conditions to facilitate embedded transparency. Embedded transparency is premised on the active participation of citizens and free exchange of information among participants involved in collaborative governance. Cultivating such conditions includes creating a new relationship between government and citizens and changing the culture of governance. If so, what is the way to foster an active mindset of government officials as well as citizens for collaborative governance? What is the proper pathway of transparency toward the full realization of collaborative governance?

# 51. Corruption, Ethics and Accountability[*]

*Rod Erakovich et al.*

Good governance requires good public servants. A focus on public administration and its efforts to combat corruption are more inclusive than simply public administration and the public servant. Analysis of ethics and ethical behavior must ensure core values and standards meet public expectations. Our focus is on corruption found in public administration, those that make the wheels of government work. We define corruption as the use of a position of trust of public servants for dishonest gain. It may be a transfer to better oneself or for one or more citizens. But when the gain is received without regard to due process and public interest, it raises serious ethical concerns on the capability of a democratic government to serve all citizens.

A common practice in contemporary, democratic market-oriented countries is to hold public servants to higher ethical standards than other professions. This double standard from the vantage point of political and legal philosophy seems entirely reasonable. Our task, however, is not to suggest the entire anti-corruption strategy. We examine the role of ethical accountability in keeping in check the corruption and opportunistic behavior of public servants.

To successfully engage corruption it would seem knowing the source and cause would be useful if not imperative. Every society has a level of corruption they will tolerate and perhaps even expect. The "Bad Apple Theory" explains the most commonly held source of corruption. This is probably the train of thought most used because it is simple to grasp and provides a clear target for retaliation for what is viewed as defiant behavior. As soon as the reward exceeds the penalty and probability of being caught, the problem will resurface unless accountability and transparency policies are implemented in all levels of an operation.

Although there is a broad agreement that accountability in government is necessary to fight corruption, there is no consensus on one definition or through what mechanisms, if any, it may be achieved. In a broad sense, accountability is defined as "answerability" through a system of values, actors, expectation, actions, means and relationships. In essence, accountability in the public sector is a paradox involving external standards that pressure the moral development and internal virtues that support good administrative judgment.

Anti-corruption efforts include establish-

[*]Originally published as Rod Erakovich, William Carroll, Chelsea Smith, Tunde Campbell and Leo Wright, "Corruption, Ethics and Accountability: A Normative Approach to Control," http://patimes.org/corruption-ethics-accountability-normative-approach-control/, 2013. Reprinted with permission of the publisher.

ment of laws, codes of conduct and other legally binding documents, organization of oversight mechanisms, percent of budgets audited, percentage of recruitment of new public servants by examinations and other merit criteria and the number of financial accounting systems operating under an integrated management concept. While critical, such structural approaches are not sufficient. A critical missing part is moral accountability.

In a 2004 *Administration and Society* article titled "The Accountability Paradox in the Age of Reinvention," Philip Jos and Mark Tompkins argue that the model of administrative accountability offers a framework consisting of direction-based accountability, performance based accountability and procedure based accountability. These compliance based processes put controls over administrative behavior creating "low road" ethical choices, hindering autonomous ethical decision making, discouraging self-examination and eliminating honest moral talk. Accountability is measured in terms of outputs rather than compliance with regulation in which creativity is encouraged and formal processes are deemphasized.

What is truly important is the fact that these accountability frameworks cannot replace individual judgment. Ethics cannot be reduced to rules and formulas followed in a mechanical way. Public administrators each must have their own stable set of core values and democratic ideals that are applied consistently but meet the ever-changing external standards of their environment. The administrator with these qualities has the integrity to take responsibility for his or her own judgment and choices, even in a turbulent politically charged atmosphere. To truly stem the corruption that exists, an accountability system is needed that focuses on ethical moral development rather than those that hinder ethical decision making.

While laws, rules and formal codes of ethics offer some standards of conduct and guidelines for ethical decision-making, an added approach is to link enforcement codes with a normative approach to establishing an ethical climate that supports societal values and democratic processes. Such strategies might include:

- Develop employee ethical accountability through moral development.
- Promote participative decision-making participation by employees and citizens thereby establishing cooperation and trust.
- Within the legal and regulatory constraints of the public bureaucracy, support innovation through risk taking.

Montgomery Van Wart, in his 1998 book *Changing Public Sector Values*, sees administrators carrying out their duties in a value-laden, value-driven environment and asserts that managerial, ethical, social and political values are not separate. Public servants make decisions on a set of values that blends all considerations simultaneously. The goal is not to focus on the penalty, although we agree consequences for corrupt behavior must be present, but to focus on the process of ethical analysis in a way that defies corruption as a gain. The efforts to create ethical behavior of public officials must focus on not only structural approaches through legal and formal remedies, but also a normative approach that focuses on the due process and public interest.

# 52. Anti-Corruption Effort Targets All the States[*]

## Neal Peirce

For imprisoned governors, Illinois excels: Last Thursday, Rod Blagojevich, following in the footsteps of his predecessors George Ryan, Dan Walker and Otto Kerner, began his penitentiary time on serious corruption charges.

But now there is more heartening news. A State Integrity Investigation, 18 months in the making, was released last week, covering all 50 states—easily the most thorough look at ethics laws and susceptibility to corruption ever focused on America's state governments.

Teams of freelance journalists—at least one in each state—did the on-the-ground reporting. They didn't just look for some glaring abuse. Rather, they checked each state's anti-corruption and transparency safeguards on 330 "corruption risk indicators," ranging from accountability of governors, legislators and judges to lobbying disclosure.

What they found were open-records laws riddled with exceptions—scores of legislators suddenly becoming lobbyists, lawmakers voting on measures they'd benefit from directly and near-toothless disclosure laws.

"The depth and breadth of the loopholes we discovered in laws was stunning," says Gordon Witkin of the Center for Public Integrity, which sponsored the project along with Public Radio International and Global Integrity.

They tapped a generous budget for extensive research and fact-checking–$1.5 million from the Omidyar Network and the Rita Allen Foundation. Critics will likely have a hard time questioning the project's depth and precision. And, with luck, reformers in each state will now be armed with powerful evidence to force tighter ethics rules.

The project assigned scores (A to F) on a state's anti-corruption laws and rules (rather than a tally of actual scandals). Not a single state qualified for an A rating and only five states received a B. Each state's ranking, from ethics enforcement to political financing, is featured on the project's website—www.stateintegrity.org.

There's a big anomaly in the rankings. The five states with the best (B) rankings start with New Jersey, notorious for its wave of corrupt practices in recent years. How come? In response, its legislature has recently passed some of the nation's severest ethics and anti-corruption laws.

Others rating a B were Connecticut, Wash-

*Originally published as Neal Peirce, "Anti-Corruption Effort Targets All the States" http://www.nlc.org/media-center/news-search/columnist-anti-corruption-effort-targets-all-the-states, March 26, 2012. Reprinted with permission of the author and publisher.

ington, California and Nebraska. But check the tough investigative news reports shown on the site from reporters in those states, and imperfections crop up instantly—for example, "At least 42 Connecticut state employees took part in hurricane aid fraud." Or, "Arnold Schwarzenegger fined for campaign finance violations."

Eight states landed Fs, again with some surprises: North Dakota, South Dakota, Michigan, South Carolina, Maine, Virginia, Wyoming and Georgia.

You may well ask: Michigan, low on ethics? Well, yes, it's one of three states (with Vermont and Idaho) that have no public disclosure laws. Minnesota, despite its squeaky-clean reputation, got only a D-plus, scoring in the cellar on ethics enforcement and lobbying (lobbyists, for example, are not required to disclose which lawmakers they are lobbying or what bills they are lobbying for or against).

Plus low-population states such as Maine, Idaho, Montana, Nebraska and the Dakotas may get low scores because of a "we-all-know-each-other" self-policing ethic.

But it is not the precise scores but the new watchdog standards that the study establishes. It's important because corruption matters. As Nathaniel Heller of Global Integrity notes: "Corruption impacts people's lives." State budgets serving legitimate needs from education to public safety are depleted when special interests get tax breaks while funding politicians' campaigns. Elected leaders often act with impunity because of broken information-request systems, gutted state ethics commissions and patronage-controlled civil services.

The new accountability project's follow-through promises to be imaginative. Public Radio International, for example, will work with its 880 partner stations to inspire people to fight corruption in their own states through crowdsourcing and social media. In today's new media world, says PRI's Michael Skoler, "people, not simply reporters, can and must be watchdogs for honest government."

And there's no American monopoly on inventive anti-corruption techniques—many have been developed, proved "tried and true," in countries ranging from the Philippines to Bangladesh to India, says Heller. Examples include citizen monitoring of local governments and specific ways to track public expenditures to detect waste.

So Global Integrity plans, in the near future, to bring teams from around the world to sit down and confer with interested ethics commissions and others in U.S. states.

Roots of the state project go back to a 2009 Starbucks conversation between Heller and Bill Buzenberg, executive director of the Center for Public Integrity. Heller remarked that it was easier to find teams of qualified anti-corruption researchers in Peru than in the United States. Did Buzenberg know if anyone was checking which U.S. states are "hardwired to fail" on corruption issues?

The answer was "No—but let's fix that." And the State Integrity Investigation was born.

# 53. States Disclose Economic Development Subsidies[*]

## Mike Maciag

Assessing whether or not economic development subsidies are paying off requires examining a range of information, including lists of companies receiving money and payroll data to evaluate whether they've kept commitments. In several states, though, this crucial data isn't yet publicly available online.

A report published this morning by watchdog group Good Jobs First (GJF) reviews 246 subsidy programs in all 50 states and the District of Columbia, finding some states lag far behind others in disclosing information online.

"For most deals, taxpayers cannot even begin to weigh costs versus benefits for the tens of billions of dollars states spend in the name of jobs," the report states.

All states—with the exception of Arkansas, Delaware, Idaho and Kansas—have established some form of disclosure for their programs. But just how much information they publish online varies greatly. A few maintain easy-to-navigate portals, while others merely post PDF documents with limited information.

Illinois topped the rankings, earning an average score of 65 out of 100 points for its various programs. The state recently re-launched its Grant Tracker web portal, featuring a searchable database of awards and maps. Along with award amounts, the site lists recipients' job counts, occupational categories and average salaries.

GJF rated transparency efforts by reviewing the availability of award amounts, status, reported jobs, wages, project information and company information, along with website features. Some of the more common economic development subsidies included in the report were corporate income tax credits, grants, enterprise zones and sales tax exemptions.

After Illinois, Michigan (58) and North Carolina (48) received the highest marks (see complete list below). The group found no correlation between transparency scores and either job subsidy spending or party control of state legislatures.

One major problem area GJF identified was jobs reporting—a necessary component in assessing whether subsidies are paying off. Of the 246 programs GJF examined, only 59 (roughly a quarter) disclosed figures for jobs created or workers trained.

"Our concern is about the gaps in the reporting on outcomes," said Philip Mattera, the report's primary author. "There's such a

---

*Originally published as Mike Maciag, "Group Ranks How Well States Disclose Economic Development Subsidies," *Governing*, January 29, 2014. Reprinted with permission of the publisher.

small number of states that have good job and wage reporting."

In most cases, state agencies require companies receiving incentive awards to report job numbers.

Mattera also said states tend to do a better job posting grant disclosures than tax credits. Only about half of the reviewed film tax credits—often a source of public scrutiny—had been posted online, for example.

State economic development agencies typically report grant information, while revenue departments are mostly responsible for reporting tax credits separately.

In addition to posting the data itself, GJF advocates that states post subsidy disclosures in manner that's easy to access and download. If subsidy data is posted as PDF documents (instead of downloadable spreadsheets) or buried on little-known web pages, it's not going to be easy to track down. The report hit Georgia with a penalty, for example, because the state Department of Economic Development purges information online after just 30 days.

By and large, though, states are improving their transparency efforts.

Since the group's last study in 2010, the District of Columbia, Georgia, Massachusetts, Mississippi, Nevada, New Mexico, Oregon, South Carolina, Tennessee and Wyoming all began disclosing economic development information online. In 2007, only 23 states had some form of online disclosure.

The report identified Oregon, which did not maintain a website in 2010, as the most improved state.

Years ago, Mattera said, companies cited privacy concerns and argued publicizing subsidy information could risk divulging proprietary information. These claims have lost merit, though, as states continue disclosing more information online. "That argument just doesn't go over the way it used to," Mattera said.

Below is the 2013 ranking and scores for all tax incentive programs Good Jobs First examined in each U.S. state, including the District of Columbia. For the methodology and list of state programs, please refer to Good Jobs First, "Show Us the Subsidized Jobs" (http://www.goodjobsfirst.org/)

1. Illinois, 65
2. Michigan, 58
3. North Carolina, 48
4. Wisconsin, 46
5. Vermont, 43
6. Maryland, 42
7. Texas, 40
8. New York, 38
8. Oregon, 38
10. Louisiana, 36
10. Washington, 36
12. Kentucky, 35
13. Indiana, 34
14. Connecticut, 33
14. Missouri, 33
16. Florida, 32
17. Wyoming, 29
18. Virginia, 28
19. Iowa, 27
20. Pennsylvania, 25
21. California, 21
21. Minnesota, 21
21. Ohio, 21
24. Montana, 20
25. Colorado, 19
26. Alaska, 17
26. District of Columbia, 17
26. New Jersey, 17
29. Massachusetts, 16
29. Tennessee, 16
31. Oklahoma, 15
32. Arizona, 14
32. Rhode Island, 14
34. Mississippi, 12
34. Utah, 12
36. South Dakota, 11
37. Nebraska, 10
38. New Mexico, 7
39. West Virginia, 6
40. New Hampshire, 5

41. Georgia, 4
41. Maine, 4
41. North Dakota, 4
44. Alabama, 3
45. Hawaii, 1
45. Nevada, 1

45. South Carolina, 1
48. Arkansas, 0
48. Delaware, 0
48. Idaho, 0
48. Kansas, 0

# 54. Why It Might Finally Get Easier to Access Public Data[*]

## Liz Farmer

At a recent public finance conference at Indiana University, I found myself commiserating with a researcher who was muddling through public pension data. Governments file much of the data he needs in annual reports in PDF format. We joked about how, in such predicaments, the "Ctrl F" keyboard shortcut to find specific information in a 150-page file quickly becomes your best friend.

But that only helps so much. "Nothing is standardized," the researcher complained. Some PDFs, for example, aren't readable and the Ctrl F trick doesn't work. Or the information you are looking for may come in table form in some reports and paragraph form in others, which makes it difficult for computer programs that "read" PDF documents for data to get all the numbers right. In short, combing through these reports is extremely labor intensive and about as enjoyable as wearing wool on a hot day.

There are, however, some who want to make accessing public financial data easier. It's a push that is coming primarily from the feds, and it's rooted in a refrain heard often since the 2008 financial crisis: State and Feds Push to Make All Public Financial Data Open and municipal financial disclo-sures should be more like corporate ones. California Rep. Darrell Issa is the latest to echo this sentiment. Last month, he previewed legislation that would standardize how data is reported at the state and local level.

Issa's proposal is called the MADOFF (Making All Data Open for Financial) Transparency Act and it builds off of last year's Digital Accountability and Transparency Act, which calls for a standard way for federal agencies to report their financial data. The section of the act that would affect state and local governments requires the Municipal Securities Rulemaking Board to adopt a standard data format in which a municipality would have to submit their financial information. "So instead of submitting a PDF document," says Hudson Hollister, "they submit a data file."

Hollister is the executive director of the Data Transparency Coalition, a big proponent of standardizing government data reporting to further transparency. Such a change wouldn't necessarily require any additional tech-savviness on the part of those preparing a government's year-end reports, Hollister says. Much like TurboTax has done for the individual tax filer, he says, software

[*]Originally published as Liz Farmer, "Why It Might Finally Get Easier to Access Public Data," *Governing*, May 14, 2015. Reprinted with permission of the publisher.

companies are capable of developing similar products for municipal governments.

So what exactly would standardizing data do, other than making researchers' lives a little easier? The corporate market provides a good example. As Public Sector Credit Solutions' Marc Joffe recently noted in Governing, company financial reports have been available in textual form on the Security and Exchange Commission's website for the last 20 years. This means that analysts at firms like Yahoo Finance, MarketWatch and Morningstar can easily pull the raw data and work with it to address whatever questions they need answered. So, Joffe writes, corporate investors can readily compare the financial statistics of a safe company like Apple to an insolvent one like Radio Shack. But municipal investors who might want to perform the same exercise with Dallas and Detroit are out of luck. "The vast majority of investors and analysts lack the patience and/or technical skills needed to extract the valuable needles of insight from this haystack of disclosure," Joffe writes.

Joffe and Hollister say that making access to data easier could lower municipal borrowing costs and even reduce the market's vulnerability to negative headlines. Hollister envisions a whole industry of software built around standardizing data entry and reporting. "All of the information wrangling that state and local governments do today could be combined into a seamless process,"

he says. "That can dramatically reduce challenges for those governments while also reducing the cost of their bond financing."

All this stuff is great in theory, but in reality there's the practical matter that state and local governments are incredibly diverse in their size, operations and capabilities. That's why mandating financial reporting standards to governments can be difficult, says Lynnette Kelly, executive director of the Municipal Securities Rulemaking Board. Many wouldn't have a problem conforming; many more would. Usually the better route for these things, she says, is for governments to voluntarily adopt changes.

In fact, the Governmental Accounting Standards Board (GASB) launched an ongoing project in 2008 that explores how to improve government's electronic financial reporting. Among the project's tasks is to monitor how Extensible Business Reporting Language, a standardized digital language for business financial reporting, could be adapted for government reporting. GASB has not issued any standards related to the project but calls it a high priority issue.

Despite the slow progress, Kelly says, most governments are very much aware that there is a lot of room for improvement when it comes to reporting their financials. "I remember days of, should documents be in HTML code or PDF?" she says. "There have been conversations for a long time about data."

# 55. The Truth about Public Employees in California*

## Sylvia A. Allegretto and Jeffrey Keefe

Recently, there has been a great deal of debate and consternation over the compensation of public-sector employees across the U.S. It has been asserted that state and local government employees are overpaid compared to workers in the private sector. In California government workers have been vilified as scandals and anecdotes pass as confirming evidence of exorbitant pay. This research is especially important given the outrage over the pay of municipal officials in Bell, California. The outrage of what happened in Bell is reasonable and just. Many of the players immediately resigned and on September 21, 2010, eight city officials were arrested.

Those arrested include the former city manager of Bell, Robert Rizzo, who was making nearly $800,000 a year. Rizzo was charged with 53 counts. It is alleged that Rizzo, without approval from the City Council, actually wrote the conditions of his own contract—the case keeps growing in terms of scope and involved officials. It is clear by the arrests and scores of allegations that the scandal in Bell was not in line with usual procedures.

While anecdotes that stem from public-sector corruption capture much attention, it is a data-driven analysis of public-sector pay and compensation that is needed to answer the question: How do the pay and benefits of public sector workers compare to those in the private sector? This is a legitimate question that should not be answered anecdotally. The research in this paper investigates empirically whether California public employees are overpaid at the expense of California taxpayers.

The results from this analysis indicate that California public employees, both state and local, are not overpaid. The wages received by California public employees are about 7% lower, on average, than wages received by comparable private sector workers; however, public employees do receive more generous benefits. An apples-to-apples comparison, or one that controls for education, experience, and other factors that may influence pay, reveals no significant difference in the level of employee compensation costs on an annual or per hour basis between private and public sector workers.

Nonetheless, there are substantially different approaches to staffing and compensation between the private and public sector. Specifically, there are important workforce

*Originally published as Sylvia A. Allegretto and Jeffrey Keefe, *The Truth about Public Employees in California: They Are Neither Overpaid nor Overcompensated*, University of California, Berkeley, Center on Wage and Employment Dynamics, Policy Brief, October 2010. Reprinted with permission of the authors.

differences between the two sectors in terms of educational attainment. On average, California's public sector workers are more highly educated. Of full-time workers, 55% hold a four-year college degree in the public sector compared to 35% in the private sector. Educational attainment is the single most important predictor of earnings—thus it plays a vital role in this analysis. On average, California state and local governments pay college-educated labor less than private employers. The earnings differential is greatest for professional employees, lawyers and doctors. On the other hand, the public sector appears to set a floor on compensation. The earnings of those with a high school degree or less is higher in state and local government than it is for similar workers in the private sector.

There are other significant personnel differences between the public and private sector workforces. The age (median) of a typical worker in state and local government is 44 compared to 40 in the private sector. Furthermore, the state and local government workforce has more women (55%) compared to the private sector (40%).

In general, better educated and older, more experienced workers earn more than less educated and younger workers while women earn less than men. Thus, comparisons between the two sectors must take into account these and other differences such as race and experience when making pay comparisons. Simply comparing average pay between the two sectors, without taking into account workforce differences, would be highly misleading.

Benefits are also allocated differently between private and public sector full-time workers in California. State and Local government employees receive a higher portion of their compensation in the form of employer-provided benefits and the mix of benefits is different from the private sector. While some benefits may be more generous in the public sector, it is a serious error to imagine that comparability requires that each and every element of compensation be the same. When total compensation—both the cost of employer-provided benefits and direct pay—is taken into account state and local public sector workers in California are similarly compensated to workers in the private sector.

Public employers contribute on average 35.7% of employee compensation expenses to benefits, whereas private employers devote 30% of compensation to benefits. Public employers provide better health insurance and pension benefits. Public employers contribute 11.8% to insurance, mainly health insurance, compared to a 7.7% contribution by private employers. Retirement benefits also account for a substantially greater share of public employee compensation, 8.2% compared to 3.6% in the private sector. Most public employees also continue to participate in defined benefit plans managed by the state, while most private sector employers have switched to defined contribution plans, particularly 401(k) plans. On the other hand, public employees receive considerably less supplemental pay and vacation time, and public employers contribute significantly less to legally-mandated benefits.

Thus, the difference in workforce characteristics and benefit allocations between the public and private sectors is why a regression-adjusted analysis is employed in this research. The regression framework allows a comparison of similar workers controlling for factors which influence compensation levels. A standard wage equation produced a surprising result: full-time state and local employees are under-paid by about 7% compared to their private sector counterparts. However, a re-estimated regression equation of total compensation (which includes wages and benefits) demonstrates that there is no significant difference in total compensation between full-time state and local employees and private-sector employees.

## The Challenge of Analyzing Public Employee Compensation

To answer whether California public employees are overpaid two simple but related questions need to be asked: compared to whom? And compared to what? The standard of comparison for public employees is usually similar private sector workers, with respect to education, experience, and hours of work.

In this study we use the Integrated Public Use Microdata Series (IPUMS) of the March Current Population Survey (CPS) to obtain wage and demographic data. The CPS is a monthly U.S. household survey conducted jointly by the U.S. Census Bureau and the Bureau of Labor Statistics. The March Annual Demographic File and Income Supplement is the most widely used source of earnings data used by social scientists (King, et al. 2009). For the purpose of comparability, self-employed, part-time, agricultural, and domestic workers are excluded.

The most reliable source of benefit information in the United States is the Employer Costs for Employee Compensation (ECEC) survey, which is collected by the U.S. Department of Labor, Bureau of Labor Statistics (BLS). The ECEC includes data from both private industry and state and local government employees and provides data for private employers by firm size. Larger employers, those with over 100 employees, are significantly more likely to provide employees with benefits. This is due, in part, to their ability to spread administrative costs over a larger group. For insurance purposes, larger firms can more readily diversify risks by dint of their size. Because state and local governments resemble large private-sector firms, the compensation cost analysis will control for employer size in making comparisons.

## Education Is the Most Important Factor in Determining Earnings

Educational attainment is the single most important predictor of earnings. The strong positive association between higher levels of education and higher earnings in the labor market is a crucial factor in this analysis. There are two important issues here: (1) California public employees are substantially more educated than their private sector counterparts, and (2) the returns to education are not the same across the two sectors.

There are dissimilar distributions of education for workers in the private and public sectors. Approximately 55% of California public employees hold a Bachelors or advanced degree compared to 35% of private-sector workers. The percentages for each level of education are in comparison to workers who have not completed high school. For example, a high school graduate, all else being equal, earns on average 39% more than a worker without a high school diploma. The education premium jumps to 57% on average if the worker attended some college or 70% if the worker holds an associate's degree. Completing college with a bachelor's degree yields a 98% premium and a professional degree (law or medicine) increases average earnings by 178% compared to an individual without a high school diploma. A master's degree yields an average 128% pay premium and a doctorate produces a 159% return.

The public sector and larger private sector organizations employ more highly educated workers. Smaller private sector organizations utilize more workers with a high school degree or less compared to either larger private sector firms or state and local government. Only 3% of state and local government workers lack a high school education compared to 12% of private sector employees. The number of private-sector employees without a diploma falls to 8% within firms of 500 or more employees.

As mentioned earlier, the returns to education are not the same across the two sectors. As a result of the relatively high level of unionization, the public sector has established a floor on earnings, allowing those with a high school education or less to earn considerably more than their private sector counterparts (Asher and DeFina 1999). On the other hand, college educated private sector employees earn consider- able more than similarly educated public sector workers.

For the most part, a comparison of average earnings shows that less educated public sector workers earn more than their private sector counterparts—this differential increases when benefits are taken into account. However, just 16% of public sector workers have a high school degree or less compared to 34.1% in the private sector. The majority of public sector workers (55%) have a Bachelors degree or more compared to the private sector (35%). Public sector pay for these educated workers is considerably less than that of equivalent private sector workers. When benefits are included in the comparison public sector workers with at least a Bachelors degree are less compensated than those in the private sector.

For example, a full-time worker without a high school education earns on average 14% more when employed by state and local government ($29,640) compared to the private sector ($25,964). When the comparison is total compensation (including benefits), the public sector premium jumps to 24% for workers without a high school diploma ($41,725) compared to similarly educated private sector employees ($33,607).

Just considering wages, high school graduates approach earnings equivalency between private and public sector with public sector workers earning wages 2% less than their private sector counterparts. Nonethe-

less, when we examine total compensation, high school graduates earn $3,706 (7%) more annually in the public sector.

However, the wages and total compensation received by public sector workers at higher levels of education are less than comparable workers in the private sector. The relatively better benefits received by educated public sector workers are not enough to compensate for the pay difference. For example, government workers with a bachelor's degree earn on average 14% less than similarly educated workers in the private sector. When considering total compensation, these public-sector workers still receive 5% less.

## The Growing Role of Benefits in Employee Compensation Costs

Benefits, once referred to as fringe benefits, account for an ever-increasing portion of employee compensation costs. Benefit growth is partially fueled by the tax deductibility of health insurance payments and pension contributions which allows employers to compensate employees without either the employer or employee paying income tax at the time of compensation. Sometimes referred to as tax "efficient" compensation, the Federal government foregoes $300 billion annually in income tax revenue to subsidize these benefits (U.S. Congress, Joint Committee on Taxation 2006). Health insurance and pension benefits are particularly attractive to middle and upper income employees who face higher marginal income tax rates.

Organizational size is the single strongest predictor of employee benefit participation and compensation. For example, employee participation in retirement plans varies considerably by organization size. Organizations with 1 to 99 employees have employee pension participation rates of 38%, organizations with 100 to 499 employees have participation rates of 64% and organizations with 500 or more employees, 81% of employee participation in retirement plans. The pattern is similar for health insurance benefits. Organizations with 1 to 99 employees have employee participation rates in medical insurance of 43%, organizations with 100 to 499 employees have participation rates of 61% and organizations with at least 500 employees have a 71% participate rate in medical insurance plans. This pattern is replicated for prescription drug and dental care plans (U.S. DOL BLS September 2009, Bulletin 2731).

The Employer Costs for Employee Compensation (ECEC) survey provides the only valid and reliable estimate in the United States of benefit costs incurred by employers. It is conducted quarterly by the U.S. Bureau of Labor Statistics. The ECEC includes data from both private industry and state and local government employees and provides data for private employers by firm size. This study uses these ECEC sample estimates to calculate relative benefit costs for private and public employees in California.

Public sector employees received more of their compensation in the form of benefits than private sector workers. The positive correlation between firm size and the benefit share of total compensation is evident.

On average, benefits costs are 30% of total compensation for private firms as compared to 35.7% for state and local governments. Private sector benefits costs range from 27.2% for small private employers with less than 100 employees to 33.5% for private employers with 500 or more employees. The compensation data reveal considerable variation within the private sector and between the private sector and state and local government compensation. Public employees not only receive more of their compensation in benefits, but the mix of benefits is different among paid leave, supplemental pay, insurances, retirement security and legally mandated benefits. While overall paid leave costs are similar, private sector employees receive more vacation pay while public employees receive greater sick leave compensation (not shown). Holiday and personal time compensation is similar. Supplemental pay accounts for just 1.1% of compensation for public employees (mostly from overtime pay) but accounts for 3.5% of large firm private sector worker compensation (generally due to bonuses given by large firms).

On the other hand, public employees receive considerably more of their compensation from employer-provided insurance. Insurance accounts for 7.7% of private sector compensation but 11.8% of state and local government employee costs. Retirement benefits also account for a substantially greater share of public employee compensation, 8.2% compared to 3.6% in the private sector. As with most benefits, the differences between private and public employees' compensation costs shrink for larger private-sector firms.

Legally required benefits account for a greater share of the small employers' compensation, as organizational size increases these benefits costs decrease in relative importance. In local and state government employment, legally required benefits represent a substantially smaller share of benefit costs for several reasons. First, a nontrivial number of public employees do not participate in social security, which partially explains their higher pension costs. These employees are not eligible for Social Security benefit payments at retirement unless they chose to work in another job elsewhere which is covered by Social Security. Second, state and local governments do not participate in the federal unemployment system. Lastly, since state and local governments offer more stable employment they pay lower rates into the state unemployment insurance trust fund, because unemployment insurance contribution rates are partially experience rated.

In summary, state and local government workers receive more of their compensation in employer-provided benefits. Specifically, public employers contribute relatively more toward employee health insurance and retirement benefits costs. Public employee benefit costs, however, are relatively lower for supplemental pay and legally required benefits than those of private sector employees. To determine whether public employees are overpaid, the specific question that should be addressed is whether higher benefit costs more than offset the lower wages paid to California public employees. That is the question we turn to next.

### *Assessing Private and Public Relative Pay and Benefits*

The IPUMS-CPS data are used to assess the relative employment costs of private versus public sector workers in California. The CPS data on individuals provides information on an array of demographic characteristics including full-time status, education level, occupation, years of experience (as a function of age), gender, race, organizational size, and industry. In California, there are important differences between state and local government workers compared to those in the private sector. On average, government workers are: more experienced (22 years versus 20 years): more likely to be female (55% to 40%); work more hours (37 to 39.2); more likely to be Black (11% to 6%); less likely to be Asian (12% to 14%); and less likely to be Hispanic (25% to 35%).

California public employees work on average more hours per year than their private sector counterparts, making them unique among public sector workers throughout the country. However, the distribution of relative hours is uneven. On average public employees worked almost three days or 1.1% more than workers in the private sector.

However, public employees with a professional or Masters degree worked fewer hours, 4.7% and 3.8% less, respectively. In California, differences in the number of work hours do not appear to sharply delineate private from public employment as it does elsewhere in the country (Keefe 2010a).

What is the relative pay and total compensation of public sector workers compared to those in the private sector? The CPS data on earning with the ECEC data on benefits allow us to answer these questions. The ECEC data are employed to calculate total employer compensation costs for each employee in the sample. Each observation has an earnings and total compensation measure.

The estimates represent the earnings and total compensation premium of California state and local government workers relative to private sector workers. The annual wages of state and local California public employees are 7.77% less than comparable private sector workers (earning results are all statistically significant). The estimates in rows 2 and 3 separate out state and local workers. State workers earn 7.55% less than workers in the private sector and local government workers earn 7.86% less. Overall, the hourly wages of California's state and local employees are 6.36% less than employees in the private sector. Separately, the hourly wage gap is 8.92% for state and 5.38% for local government workers in California.

Now that it has been established that public sector workers are not overpaid what happens when benefits are considered? Results on total compensation, annual and hourly, show that the more generous benefits received by public sector workers is just enough to make up for the significant negative wage gap. Importantly, the point estimates are very small and none of the estimates are statistically different from zero. There is no measurable difference in total compensation between public and private sector workers.

## Conclusion: Are California Public Employees Overpaid? No.

The estimates from the wage analysis indicate that California public workers, both state and local, are not overpaid. An apples-to-apples comparison which accounts for education, experience, hours of work, organizational size, gender, race, ethnicity, and disability reveals no significant difference between private and public employee compensation costs.

The data analysis, however, reveals substantially different approaches to staffing and compensation between the private and public sectors. On average, California public sector workers are more highly educated than those in the private sector workforce (55% of full-time California public sector workers hold at least a four year college degree compared to 35% of full-time private sector employees).

The public sector appears to set a floor on compensation particularly improving the earnings of workers without a high school diploma compared to similarly educated workers in the private sector. This result is due in part because the earnings floor has collapsed in the private sector (Lee 1999).

Benefits are allocated differently between private and public sector full-time workers in California. State and Local government employees receive a higher portion of their compensation in the form of employer provided benefits, and the mix of benefits is different than the private sector. Public employers underwrite 35.7% of employee compensation in benefits, whereas private employers devote 30% of compensation to benefits. Public employers provide better health insurance and pension benefits. Insurance accounts for 7.7% of private sector compensation but 11.8% of state and local government employee costs. Retirement benefits also account for a substantially greater share of public employee compensation, 8.2% compared to 3.6% in the private sector. Public employees continue to participate in defined benefit plans managed by the state, while private sector employers have switch to defined contribution plans, particularly 401(k) plans. On the other hand, public employees receive considerably less supplemental pay and vacation time, and public employers contribute significantly less to legally mandated benefits.

A standard earnings equation produced a surprising result: full-time state and local workers are neither over- or under-compensated. We observed that on average public employees work slightly more hours per year than private sector employees. A re-estimated earnings equation controlling for work hours of full-time employees demonstrates that there is no significant difference in total compensation between full-time state and local employees and private sector employees.

Union status was omitted from this study of earnings and compensation comparisons, since it has been a focal point of the compensation controversy. This means that, in essence, we are statistically comparing unionized public sector workers with all private sector workers—both union and nonunion—rather than with their union counterparts. Unionized private sector workers have both better pay and higher benefits, of course, so our standard of comparison is very conservative.

It is alleged by many governors and others that public employee unions and collective bargaining have produced an over compensated work force. While this is a provocative hypothesis, its main assertion has been falsified by this analysis. The average value in total compensation received by state and local government employees is similar to that of their private-sector counterparts. This finding has now been replicated nationally in several other studies

(Keefe 2010; Schmitt 2010; Thompson and Schmitt 2010; Bender and Heywood 2010).

Alternately, high unionization rates may be a response to monopsony power (where one employer dominates) exercised by government over many critical occupations, where employees have no viable labor-market alternatives to government employment. Additionally it is well known that taxpayers do not want to pay higher taxes. Taxpayers exert considerable pressure on elected representatives to resist increases in compensation, which creates a formidable incentive and opportunity to hold government pay below market rates. Unionization represents a viable legal response to employer labor market power. The pattern of California public employee unionization is consistent with broader global patterns of unionization. For example, a study of 27 developed countries found a pattern of public employee unionization consistent with that of California (Blanchflower 2006). The study reports that union density is negatively correlated with education in the private sector and positively correlated in the public sector—just as we observe in California. Possibly, a more important question for policy makers, rather than why highly educated public employees are unionized, is why relatively less educated and low-paid private sector employees are inadequately represented by unions.

The Great Recession continues to leave a great deal of economic pain and scarring in its wake. But, the vilification of government workers sorely misplaced and has left the real culprits of this devastating downturn off the hook. Compensation received by public sector employees is neither the cause—nor can it be the solution—to the state's financial problems. Only an economic recovery can begin to plug the whole in the state's budget. Unfortunately, the current budget balancing efforts in California are anti-simulative and further act to depress demand in an economy already operating way below capacity. Budget cuts have helped to keep California's unemployment rate well into the double-digits for over a year and a half—and there is no end in sight. Thousands of California public employees have lost their jobs and many more have forgone pay through forced furloughs and their families have experience consider- able pain and disruption. All the workers who have lost their jobs or took cuts in pay or benefits were made to do so not because of their work performance, or because their services were no longer needed, nor because they were overpaid. They were simply causalities among a list of millions of hard working innocent victims of a financial system run amuck. Public sector workers help our communities to thrive and provide services that make it worthwhile to live in them—it is wrong to blame them for the fallout from the greatest economic downturn since the Great Depression.

## REFERENCES

Asher, M., and R. Defina. (1999, Summer). "The Impact of Changing Union Density on Earnings Inequality: Evidence from the Private and Public Sectors." *Journal of Labor Research* 18, no. 3.

Bender, K. A., and J. Heywood. (2010, April). "Out of Balance? Comparing Public and Private Sector Compensation over 20 Years." Center for State and Local Government Excellence and National Institute on Retirement Security.

Blanchflower, D. G. (2006, March). "A Cross-Country Study of Union Membership." Institute for the Study of Labor (IZA). Discussion Paper no. 2016. Bonn, Germany.

Johnson, S., and J. Kwak. (2010). *13 Bankers: The Wall Street Takeover and the Next Financial Meltdown*. New York: Pantheon.

Keefe, J. (2010a, July). "Are New Jersey Public Employees Overpaid?" Briefing Paper #270. Washington, D.C.: Economic Policy Institute.

Keefe, J. (2010b, September). "Debunking the Myth of the Overcompensated Public Employee." Briefing Paper #276. Washington, D.C.: Economic Policy Institute.

King, M., S. Ruggles, T. Alexander, D. Leicach, and M. Sobek. (2009). "Integrated Public Use Microdata Series, Current Population Survey: (IPUMS CPS) Version 2.0." (Machine-readable database). Minneapolis: Minnesota Population Center (producer and distributor).

Lav, I. J. (2010). "Property Tax Cap Wouldn't Improve New Jersey Policies: A Response to the Manhattan Institute." Washington, D.C.: Center on Budget and Policy Priorities.

Lee, D. S. (1999). "Wage Inequality in the U.S. During the 1980s: Rising Dispersion or Falling Minimum Wage?" *Quarterly Journal of Economics* 114(3): 941–1023.

McNichol, E., and N. Johnson. (2010, May). "Recession Continues to Batter State Budgets; State Responses Could Slow Recovery." Washington, D.C.: Center on Budget and Policy Priorities.

Munnell, A. H., and M. Soto. (2007). "State and Local Pensions Are Different from Private Plans." Cambridge, MA: Center for Retirement Research, Boston College.

Schmitt, J. (2010, May). "The Wage Penalty for State and Local Government Employees." Washington, D.C.: Center for Economic and Policy Research.

Thompson, J., and J. Schmitt. (2010, September). "The Wage Penalty for State and Local Government Employees in New England." University of Massachusetts, Amherst, Political Economy Research Institute, and Center for Economic Policy Research, Washington, D.C.

Troske, K. (1999, February). "Evidence on the Employer Size-Wage Premium from Worker-Establishment Matched Data." *The Review of Economics and Statistics* 81(1): 15–26.

U.S. Department of Labor, U.S. Bureau of Labor Statistics (2005). "New Quarterly Data from BLS on Business Employment Dynamics by Size of Firm." Washington, D.C.: Government Printing Office.

U.S. Department of Labor, U.S. Bureau of Labor Statistics (2009, September). "National Compensation Survey: Employee Benefits in the United States, March 2009." Bulletin 2731. Washington, D.C.: Government Printing Office.

U.S. Department of Labor, U.S. Bureau of Labor Statistics (2009). "Quarterly Census of Employment and Wages" (QCEW). Washington, D.C.: Government Printing Office.

U.S. Department of Labor, U.S. Bureau of Labor Statistics (2010). "Employer Costs for Employee Compensation, December 2009," with unpublished detailed compensation data for the Pacific Census division (Alaska, California, Hawaii, Oregon, Washington).

U.S. Joint Committee of Taxation (2006). "Estimates of Federal Tax Expenditures for Fiscal Years 2006–2010." Washington, D.C.: Government Printing Office.

# 56. Disclosing Public Employee Pay Troubles Some Officials[*]

## Mike Maciag

Many public officials are uncomfortable with subjecting their compensation to scrutiny as governments and transparency groups work to open the information to the public, a new Governing survey finds.

Nearly 30 percent of state and local government officials say their pay should not be considered part of the public record, while half would react negatively to names and salaries posted online. Overall, the results show public employees generally favor disclosing basic compensation information, but many feel they should not be identified by name.

"There is an underlying tension here. It's between people's desire for privacy and the public's right to know," said Daniel Schuman, policy counsel for the Sunlight Foundation.

Governing randomly surveyed more than 200 senior state and local officials across the county through its online community, Governing Exchange. Survey participants included only officials and administrators, which are not representative of all government workers.

The findings come as state and local governments push transparency initiatives aimed at making public information more readily available.

With the Internet, uncovering many public employees' compensation is only a few mouse-clicks away. A Governing review of state government websites found about half now maintain searchable compensation databases. Newspapers and watchdog groups have also contributed, launching their own public employee pay websites.

About 57 percent of survey respondents reported their salary information was posted online.

Kerry Korpi, director of research and collective bargaining for the American Federation of State, County and Municipal Employees, argued salary databases are "unneeded."

"Certainly, information about payroll overall, and how much particular jobs pay, is useful, and available virtually everywhere," Korpi said. "But it's an unwarranted invasion of privacy to associate names with a specific salary for rank-and-file employees."

About 41 percent of survey respondents said citizens should not be able to find their specific compensation with names listed online.

Knowing what specific rank-and-file workers are paid serves little policy purpose, Korpi said. Instead, she said governments

*Originally published as Mike Maciag, "Disclosing Public Employee Pay Troubles Some Officials," *Governing*, April 18, 2012. Reprinted with permission of the publisher.

should focus efforts on providing more detailed information on contracts, grants and other areas of spending.

"It seems like a custodian who works for a city is being held to different standard than a custodian who works for a contractor," Korpi said.

Withholding salary information for rank-and-file workers runs contrary to state open records laws. Typically, only corrections officers and other positions whose disclosure would pose a security risk are exempt.

"When you take on a public role, that's just the nature of the business that all of this info becomes publically available," Schuman said.

But working for the government doesn't entirely open a person's life for public view. Schuman and other transparency advocates generally do not advocate posting public employees' home phone numbers, medical records and other personal information.

## Curbing Corruption

Employee compensation records allow for public oversight of hiring practices and serve as a valuable resource for managers.

Schuman said the information also acts as a deterrent to government corruption.

Eight city officials in Bell, Calif., were charged with misappropriating public funds in 2010 after a series of reports revealed they received extravagantly large salaries. Robert Rizzo, Bell's former city manager, racked up an annual salary of nearly $800,000, while his assistant earned $376,000.

Residents of the low-income Los Angeles suburb were outraged, and the story quickly gained national attention.

In wake of the scandal, California Controller John Chiang issued an order directing all cities, counties and special districts to report compensation information. More than 85 percent of local governments complied with the order and provided salary data. Chiang's office posted this information, along with pay for state and university employees, in a searchable online database.

Now, citizens can track down pay information for most of the state's government entities.

"It's been used by everyone from your everyday voter to academic researcher to media taking a look at how much is being paid for services provided," said controller's office spokesman Jacob Roper.

Rather than list exact salaries for job titles, the database contains minimum and maximum salaries, along with wages from W-2 forms. The W-2 amounts include stipends, overtime and other pay often not accounted for in base salaries.

But names are not listed in California's database, Roper said, because the state cannot verify the unaudited records.

The majority of state and local officials surveyed said salaries and job titles should be posted online, without identifying employees by name.

## State Transparency Initiatives

Illinois, Kansas, Kentucky and New Hampshire are among states maintaining databases identifying specific employee compensation.

New Hampshire's TransparentNH database provides multiple search options, with payroll figures dating back to 2009. The state Department of Administrative Services manages the site, launched in late 2010.

Joe Bouchard, the department's assistant commissioner, said the state's top earners and employees with significant overtime generate the most buzz when the database is updated.

More importantly, the information has sparked a dialogue among lawmakers in addressing policy concerns. When data showed some corrections officers received significant overtime pay, officials began discussing whether to fill more vacancies, Bouchard said.

"The intent was that it would answer as many questions as possible," Bouchard said.

The department fielded a small number of complaints when the data was initially published, but has not since encountered many objections, Bouchard said.

## The "Creepiness" Factor

Some government workers are unaware their pay is subject to public scrutiny. Teachers and entry-level employees, for instance, rarely occupy the public spotlight.

Lucy Dalglish, executive director of the Reporters Committee for Freedom of the Press, said those closer to managing taxpayer dollars are more sensitive to the public's need for accountability. The Reporters Committee advocates for transparency issues and assists journalists, who often face obstacles in prying employee records from public agencies.

For many working in government, seeing their names and salaries displayed online is uncomfortable. Although most understand employment records are a matter of public record, asking whether they like that the information is disclosed to the public elicits a different response.

"While the balance needs to ultimately shift toward transparency, I don't think it's unrealistic to think some might be creeped out by this," Dalglish said.

Dalglish suspects there may also be a generational gap in public employee attitudes. Older, more experienced workers were often taught it was disrespectful to ask a colleague about their pay, while younger people are more used to enjoying seemingly infinite amounts of information at their fingertips.

"Anyone who knows how to spell your name and use Google can see it," Dalglish said. "That makes everyone a far more public person."

# I. Professional Code of Ethics
## *Government Finance Officers Association*

The Government Finance Officers Association of the United States and Canada is a professional organization of public officials united to enhance and promote the professional management of governmental financial resources by identifying, developing and advancing fiscal strategies, policies, and practices for the public benefit.

To further these objectives, all government finance officers are enjoined to adhere to legal, moral, and professional standards of conduct in the fulfillment of their professional responsibilities. Standards of professional conduct as set forth in this code are promulgated in order to enhance the performance of all persons engaged in public finance.

## I. Personal Standards

- Government finance officers shall demonstrate and be dedicated to the highest ideals of honor and integrity in all public and personal relationships to merit the respect, trust, and confidence of governing officials, other public officials, employees, and of the public.
- They shall devote their time, skills, and energies to their office both independently and in cooperation with other professionals.
- They shall abide by approved professional practices and recommended standards.

## II. Responsibility as Public Officials

- Government finance officers shall recognize and be accountable for their responsibilities as officials in the public sector.
- They shall be sensitive and responsive to the rights of the public and its changing needs.
- They shall strive to provide the highest quality of performance and counsel.
- They shall exercise prudence and integrity in the management of funds in their custody and in all financial transactions.
- They shall uphold both the letter and the spirit of the constitution, legislation, and regulations governing their actions and report violations of the law to the appropriate authorities.

## III. Professional Development

Government finance officers shall be responsible for maintaining their own competence, for enhancing the competence of their colleagues, and for providing encouragement to those seeking to enter the field of government finance. Finance officers shall promote excellence in the public service.

## IV. *Professional Integrity–Information*

- Government finance officers shall demonstrate professional integrity in the issuance and management of information.
- They shall not knowingly sign, subscribe to, or permit the issuance of any statement or report which contains any misstatement or which omits any material fact.
- They shall prepare and present statements and financial information pursuant to applicable law and generally accepted practices and guidelines.
- They shall respect and protect privileged information to which they have access by virtue of their office.
- They shall be sensitive and responsive to inquiries from the public and the media, within the framework of state or local government policy.

## V. *Professional Integrity–Relationships*

- Government finance officers shall act with honor, integrity, and virtue in all professional relationships.
- They shall exhibit loyalty and trust in the affairs and interests of the government they serve, within the confines of this Code of Ethics.
- They shall not knowingly be a party to or condone any illegal or improper activity.
- They shall respect the rights, responsibilities, and integrity of their colleagues and other public officials with whom they work and associate.
- They shall manage all matters of personnel within the scope of their authority so that fairness and impartiality govern their decisions.
- They shall promote equal employment opportunities, and in doing so, oppose any discrimination, harassment, or other unfair practices.

## VI. *Conflict of Interest*

- Government finance officers shall actively avoid the appearance of or the fact of conflicting interests.
- They shall discharge their duties without favor and shall refrain from engaging in any outside matters of financial or personal interest incompatible with the impartial and objective performance of their duties.
- They shall not, directly or indirectly, seek or accept personal gain which would influence, or appear to influence, the conduct of their official duties.
- They shall not use public property or resources for personal or political gain.

# II. Code of Ethics with Guidelines

*International City/County Management Association*

The ICMA Code of Ethics was adopted by the ICMA membership in 1924, and most recently amended by the membership in April 2015. The Guidelines for the Code were adopted by the ICMA Executive Board in 1972, and most recently revised in June 2015.

The mission of ICMA is to create excellence in local governance by developing and fostering professional local government management worldwide. To further this mission, certain principles, as enforced by the Rules of Procedure, shall govern the conduct of every member of ICMA, who shall:

## Tenet 1

Be dedicated to the concepts of effective and democratic local government by responsible elected officials and believe that professional general management is essential to the achievement of this objective.

## Tenet 2

Affirm the dignity and worth of the services rendered by government and maintain a constructive, creative, and practical attitude toward local government affairs and a deep sense of social responsibility as a trusted public servant.

### Guideline

*Advice to Officials of Other Local Governments.* When members advise and respond to inquiries from elected or appointed officials of other local governments, they should inform the administrators of those communities.

## Tenet 3

Be dedicated to the highest ideals of honor and integrity in all public and personal relationships in order that the member may merit the respect and confidence of the elected officials, of other officials and employees, and of the public.

### Guidelines

*Public Confidence.* Members should conduct themselves so as to maintain public confidence in their profession, their local government, and in their performance of the public trust.

*Impression of Influence.* Members should conduct their official and personal affairs in such a manner as to give the clear impression that they cannot be improperly influenced in the performance of their official duties.

*Appointment Commitment.* Members who accept an appointment to a position should not fail to report for that position. This does not preclude the possibility of a member considering several offers or seeking several positions at the same time, but once a bona fide offer of a position has been accepted, that commitment should be honored. Oral acceptance of an employment offer is considered binding unless the employer makes fundamental changes in terms of employment.

*Credentials.* An application for employment or for ICMA's Voluntary Credentialing Program should be complete and accurate as to all pertinent details of education, experience, and personal history. Members should recognize that both omissions and inaccuracies must be avoided.

*Professional Respect.* Members seeking a management position should show professional respect for persons formerly holding the position or for others who might be applying for the same position. Professional respect does not preclude honest differences of opinion; it does preclude attacking a person's motives or integrity in order to be appointed to a position.

*Reporting Ethics Violations.* When becoming aware of a possible violation of the ICMA Code of Ethics, members are encouraged to report the matter to ICMA. In reporting the matter, members may choose to go on record as the complainant or report the matter on a confidential basis.

*Confidentiality.* Members should not discuss or divulge information with anyone about pending or completed ethics cases, except as specifically authorized by the Rules of Procedure for Enforcement of the Code of Ethics.

*Seeking Employment.* Members should not seek employment for a position having an incumbent administrator who has not resigned or been officially informed that his or her services are to be terminated.

## Tenet 4

Recognize that the chief function of local government at all times is to serve the best interests of all of the people.

### Guideline

*Length of Service.* A minimum of two years generally is considered necessary in order to render a professional service to the local government. A short tenure should be the exception rather than a recurring experience. However, under special circumstances, it may be in the best interests of the local government and the member to separate in a shorter time. Examples of such circumstances would include refusal of the appointing authority to honor commitments concerning conditions of employment, a vote of no confidence in the member, or severe personal problems. It is the responsibility of an applicant for a position to ascertain conditions of employment. Inadequately determining terms of employment prior to arrival does not justify premature termination.

## Tenet 5

Submit policy proposals to elected officials; provide them with facts and advice on matters of policy as a basis for making decisions and setting community goals; and uphold and implement local government policies adopted by elected officials.

### Guideline

*Conflicting Roles.* Members who serve multiple roles—working as both city attorney and city manager for the same community, for example—should avoid participating in matters that create the appearance of a conflict of interest. They should disclose the potential conflict to the governing body so that other opinions may be solicited.

## Tenet 6

Recognize that elected representatives of the people are entitled to the credit for the establishment of local government policies; responsibility for policy execution rests with the members.

## *Tenet 7*

Refrain from all political activities which undermine public confidence in professional administrators. Refrain from participation in the election of the members of the employing legislative body.

### Guidelines

*Elections of the Governing Body.* Members should maintain a reputation for serving equally and impartially all members of the governing body of the local government they serve, regardless of party. To this end, they should not participate in an election campaign on behalf of or in opposition to candidates for the governing body.

*Elections of Elected Executives.* Members shall not participate in the election campaign of any candidate for mayor or elected county executive.

*Running for Office.* Members shall not run for elected office or become involved in political activities related to running for elected office, or accept appointment to an elected office. They shall not seek political endorsements, financial contributions or engage in other campaign activities.

*Elections.* Members share with their fellow citizens the right and responsibility to vote. However, in order not to impair their effectiveness on behalf of the local governments they serve, they shall not participate in political activities to support the candidacy of individuals running for any city, county, special district, school, state or federal offices. Specifically, they shall not endorse candidates, make financial contributions, sign or circulate petitions, or participate in fund-raising activities for individuals seeking or holding elected office.

*Elections relating to the Form of Government.* Members may assist in preparing and presenting materials that explain the form of government to the public prior to a form of government election. If assistance is required by another community, members may respond.

*Presentation of Issues.* Members may assist their governing body in the presentation of issues involved in referenda such as bond issues, annexations, and other matters that affect the government entity's operations and/or fiscal capacity.

*Personal Advocacy of Issues.* Members share with their fellow citizens the right and responsibility to voice their opinion on public issues. Members may advocate for issues of personal interest only when doing so does not conflict with the performance of their official duties.

## *Tenet 8*

Make it a duty continually to improve the member's professional ability and to develop the competence of associates in the use of management techniques.

### Guidelines

*Self-Assessment.* Each member should assess his or her professional skills and abilities on a periodic basis.

*Professional Development.* Each member should commit at least 40 hours per year to professional development activities that are based on the practices identified by the members of ICMA.

## *Tenet 9*

Keep the community informed on local government affairs; encourage communication between the citizens and all local government officers; emphasize friendly and courteous service to the public; and seek to improve the quality and image of public service.

## *Tenet 10*

Resist any encroachment on professional responsibilities, believing the member should be free to carry out official policies without interference, and handle each problem without discrimination on the basis of principle and justice.

### Guidelines

*Information Sharing.* The member should openly share information with the governing body while diligently carrying out the member's responsibilities as set forth in the charter or enabling legislation.

## Tenet 11

Handle all matters of personnel on the basis of merit so that fairness and impartiality govern a member's decisions, pertaining to appointments, pay adjustments, promotions, and discipline.

### Guideline

*Equal Opportunity.* All decisions pertaining to appointments, pay adjustments, promotions, and discipline should prohibit discrimination because of race, color, religion, sex, national origin, sexual orientation, political affiliation, disability, age, or marital status.

It should be the members' personal and professional responsibility to actively recruit and hire a diverse staff throughout their organizations.

## Tenet 12

Public office is a public trust. A member shall not leverage his or her position for personal gain or benefit.

### Guidelines

*Gifts.* Members shall not directly or indirectly solicit, accept or receive any gift if it could reasonably be perceived or inferred that the gift was intended to influence them in the performance of their official duties; or if the gift was intended to serve as a reward for any official action on their part.

The term "Gift" includes but is not limited to services, travel, meals, gift cards, tickets, or other entertainment or hospitality. Gifts of money or loans from persons other than the local government jurisdiction pursuant to normal employment practices are not acceptable.

Members should not accept any gift that could undermine public confidence. De minimus gifts may be accepted in circumstances that support the execution of the member's official duties or serve a legitimate public purpose. In those cases, the member should determine a modest maximum dollar value based on guidance from the governing body or any applicable state or local law.

The guideline is not intended to apply to normal social practices, not associated with the member's official duties, where gifts are exchanged among friends, associates and relatives.

*Investments in Conflict with Official Duties.* Members should refrain from any investment activity which would compromise the impartial and objective performance of their duties. Members should not invest or hold any investment, directly or indirectly, in any financial business, commercial, or other private transaction that creates a conflict of interest, in fact or appearance, with their official duties.

In the case of real estate, the use of confidential information and knowledge to further a member's personal interest is not permitted. Purchases and sales which might be interpreted as speculation for quick profit should be avoided (see the guideline on "Confidential Information"). Because personal investments may appear to influence official actions and decisions, or create the appearance of impropriety, members should disclose or dispose of such investments prior to accepting a position in a local government. Should the conflict of interest arise during employment, the member should make full disclosure and/or recuse themselves prior to any official action by the governing body that may affect such investments.

This guideline is not intended to prohibit a member from having or acquiring an interest in, or deriving a benefit from any investment when the interest or benefit is due to ownership by the member or the member's family of a de minimus percentage of a corporation traded on a recognized stock exchange even though the corporation or its subsidiaries may do business with the local government.

*Personal Relationships.* Member should disclose any personal relationship to the governing body in any instance where there could be the appearance of a conflict of interest. For example, if the manager's spouse works for a developer doing business with the local government, that fact should be disclosed.

*Confidential Information.* Members shall not disclose to others, or use to advance their personal interest, intellectual property, confidential information, or information that is not yet public knowledge, that has been acquired by them in the course of their official duties.

Information that may be in the public domain or accessible by means of an open records request, is not confidential.

*Private Employment.* Members should not engage in, solicit, negotiate for, or promise to accept private employment, nor should they render services for private interests or conduct a private business when such employment, service, or business creates a conflict with or impairs the proper discharge of their official duties.

Teaching, lecturing, writing, or consulting are typical activities that may not involve conflict of interest, or impair the proper discharge of their official duties. Prior notification of the appointing authority is appropriate in all cases of outside employment.

*Representation.* Members should not represent any outside interest before any agency, whether public or private, except with the authorization of or at the direction of the appointing authority they serve.

*Endorsements.* Members should not endorse commercial products or services by agreeing to use their photograph, endorsement, or quotation in paid or other commercial advertisements, marketing materials, social media, or other documents, whether the member is compensated or not for the member's support. Members may, however, provide verbal professional references as part of the due diligence phase of competitive process or in response to a direct inquiry.

Members may agree to endorse the following, provided they do not receive any compensation: (1) books or other publications; (2) professional development or educational services provided by nonprofit membership organizations or recognized educational institutions; (3) products and/or services in which the local government has a direct economic interest.

Members' observations, opinions, and analyses of commercial products used or tested by their local governments are appropriate and useful to the profession when included as part of professional articles and reports.

# III. Proposed Code of Ethics for Municipal Officials

## State of Connecticut

### Section 1. Definitions (Effective January 1, 2016)

The following terms, when used in this part, have the following meanings unless the context otherwise requires:

(1) "Blind trust" means a trust established by a municipal official or municipal employee or member of his or her immediate family for the purpose of divestiture of all control and knowledge of assets.

(2) "Business with which he is associated" means any sole proprietorship, partnership, firm, corporation, trust or other entity through which business for profit or not for profit is conducted in which the municipal official or municipal employee or member of his or her immediate family is a director, officer, owner, limited or general partner, beneficiary of a trust or holder of stock constituting five per cent or more of the total outstanding stock of any class, provided, a municipal official or municipal employee, or member of his or her immediate family, shall not be deemed to be associated with a not for profit entity solely by virtue of the fact that the municipal official or municipal employee or member of his or her immediate family is an unpaid director or officer of the not for profit entity. "Officer" refers only to the president, executive or senior vice president or treasurer of such business.

(3) "Candidate for municipal office" means any individual who has filed a declaration of candidacy or a petition to appear on the ballot for election as a municipal official, or who has raised or expended money in furtherance of such candidacy, or who has been nominated for appointment to serve as a municipal official.

(4) "Board" means the Citizen's Ethics Advisory Board established in section 1–80.

(5) "Gift" means anything of value, which is directly and personally received, unless consideration of equal or greater value is given in return. "Gift" does not include:

(A) A political contribution otherwise reported as required by law or a donation or payment as described in subdivision (9) or (10) of subsection (b) of section 9–601a;

(B) Services provided by persons volunteering their time, if provided to aid or promote the success or defeat of any political party, any candidate or candidates for municipal office or the position of convention delegate or town committee member or any referendum question;

(C) A commercially reasonable loan made on terms not more favorable than

196

loans made in the ordinary course of business;

(D) A gift received from (i) an individual's spouse, fiancé or fiancée, (ii) the parent, brother or sister of such spouse or such individual, or (iii) the child of such individual or the spouse of such child;

(E) Goods or services (i) that are provided to a municipality (I) for use on municipal property, or (II) that support an event or the participation by a municipal official or municipal employee at an event, and (ii) that facilitate municipal action or functions. As used in this subparagraph, "municipal property" means property owned by a municipality or property leased to a municipality;

(F) A certificate, plaque or other ceremonial award costing less than one hundred dollars;

(G) A rebate, discount or promotional item available to the general public;

(H) Printed or recorded informational material germane to municipal action or functions;

(I) Food or beverage or both, costing less than fifty dollars in the aggregate per recipient in a calendar year, and consumed on an occasion or occasions at which the person paying, directly or indirectly, for the food or beverage, or his representative, is in attendance;

(J) A gift, including, but not limited to, food or beverage or both, provided by an individual for the celebration of a major life event, provided any such gift provided by an individual who is not a member of the family of the recipient does not exceed five hundred dollars in value;

(K) Admission to a charitable or civic event, including food and beverage provided at such event, but excluding lodging or travel expenses, at which a municipal official or municipal employee participates in his or her official capacity, provided such admission is provided by the primary sponsoring entity;

(L) Anything of value provided by an employer of (i) a municipal official, (ii) a municipal employee, or (iii) a spouse of a municipal official or municipal employee, to such official, employee or spouse, provided such benefits are customarily and ordinarily provided to others in similar circumstances;

(M) Anything having a value of not more than ten dollars, provided the aggregate value of all things provided by a donor to a recipient under this subdivision in any calendar year does not exceed fifty dollars;

(N) Training that is provided by a vendor for a product purchased by a municipality that is offered to all customers of such vendor; or

(O) Expenses of a municipal official, paid by the party committee of which party such official is a member, for the purpose of accomplishing the lawful purposes of the committee. As used in this subdivision, "party committee" has the same meaning as provided in subdivision (2) of section 9–601, and "lawful purposes of the committee" has the same meaning as provided in subsection (g) of section 9–607.

(6) "Immediate family" means any spouse, children or dependent relatives who reside in the individual's household.

(7) "Individual" means a natural person.

(8) "Member of a municipal advisory board" means any individual (A) appointed by a municipal official as an advisor or consultant or member of a committee, commission or council established to advise, recommend or consult with a municipal official or branch of government or committee thereof, (B) who receives no municipal funds other than per diem payments or reimbursement for his or her actual and necessary expenses incurred in the performance of his or her official duties, and (C) who has no authority to expend any municipal funds or to exercise the power of the municipality.

(9) "Municipal employee" means any employee of a municipality or political subdivision thereof, whether in the classified or unclassified service, permanent or temporary, and whether full or part-time.

(10) "Municipal official" means any elected officer or officer-elect of a municipality, including a district officer elected pursuant to section 7–327 of the general statutes, any person appointed to any office of the municipality or political subdivision thereof, but does not include a member of a municipal advisory board.

(11) "Municipality" means any town, city, borough, consolidated town and city, consolidated town and borough and includes any special district contained therein.

(12) "Person" means an individual, sole proprietorship, trust, corporation, limited liability company, union, association, firm, partnership, committee, club or other organization or group of persons.

(13) "Political contribution" has the same meaning as in section 9–601a except that for purposes of this part, the provisions of subsection (b) of said section shall not apply.

(14) "Necessary expenses" means a municipal official's or municipal employee's expenses for an article, appearance or speech or for participation at an event, in his official capacity, which shall be limited to necessary travel expenses, lodging for the nights before, of and after the appearance, speech or event, meals and any related conference or seminar registration fees.

(15) "Trust" means a trust in which any municipal official or municipal employee or member of his immediate family has a present or future interest which exceeds ten per cent of the value of the trust or exceeds fifty thousand dollars, whichever is less, but does not include blind trusts.

(16) "Legal defense fund" means a fund established for the payment of legal expenses of a municipal official or municipal employee

incurred as a result of defending himself or herself in an administrative, civil, criminal or constitutional proceeding concerning matters related to the official's or employee's service or employment with the municipality.

(17) "Special district" means "district" as defined in section 7–324 of the general statutes.

## Section 2. Existing municipal ethics boards may complete pending matters. (NEW) (Effective from passage)

Notwithstanding the provisions of this part, a board, commission, council, committee or other agency that has been established to investigate allegations of unethical conduct within a municipality may decide and dispose of any matters that have been submitted for its consideration and disposition prior to January 1, 2016.

## Section 3. Duties of board and Office of State Ethics. Regulations. Advisory opinions. (NEW) (Effective January 1, 2016)

(a) The board and general counsel and staff of the Office of State Ethics shall:

(1) Compile and maintain an index of all reports and statements filed by and with the Office of State Ethics under the provisions of this part, advisory opinions and informal staff letters issued by the board with regard to the requirements of this part, and memoranda issued by the board in accordance with subsection (b) of section 3 of this act, to facilitate public access to such reports, statements, advisory opinions, informal staff letters and memoranda promptly upon the filing or issuance thereof;

(2) Preserve advisory opinions and

informal staff letters, permanently; preserve memoranda issued in accordance with subsection (b) of section 3 of this act and statements and reports filed by and with the board for a period of five years from the date of receipt;

(3) Upon the concurring vote of a majority of the board present and voting, issue advisory opinions with regard to the requirements of this part, upon the request of any person subject to the provisions of this part, and publish such advisory opinions in the Connecticut Law Journal. Advisory opinions rendered by the board, until amended or revoked, shall be binding on the board and shall be deemed to be final decisions of the board for purposes of appeal to the superior court, in accordance with the provisions of section 4–175 or 4–183. Any advisory opinion concerning the person who requested the opinion and who acted in reliance thereon, in good faith, shall be binding upon the board, and it shall be an absolute defense in any criminal action brought under the provisions of this part, that the accused acted in reliance upon such advisory opinion;

(4) Respond to inquiries and provide advice regarding the code of ethics either verbally or through informal letters;

(5) Provide yearly training to all municipal officials and municipal employees regarding the code of ethics;

(b) The Citizen's Ethics Advisory Board shall adopt regulations, in accordance with chapter 54, to carry out the purposes of this part. Such regulations shall not be deemed to govern the conduct of any judge trial referee in the performance of such judge trial referee's duties pursuant to this chapter.

(c) The Office of State Ethics shall report annually, prior to February fifteenth, to the Governor summarizing the activities of the Office of State Ethics.

## Section 4. Complaints. Procedure. Time limits. Investigation; notice; hearings. Attorneys' fees. Damages for complaints without foundation. (NEW) (Effective January 1, 2016)

(a)(1) Upon the complaint of any person on a form prescribed by the board, signed under penalty of false statement, or upon its own complaint, the ethics enforcement officer of the Office of State Ethics shall investigate any alleged violation of this part. Not later than five days after the receipt or issuance of such complaint, the board shall provide notice of such receipt or issuance and a copy of the complaint by registered or certified mail to any respondent against whom such complaint is filed and shall provide notice of the receipt of such complaint to the complainant. When the ethics enforcement officer of the Office of State Ethics undertakes an evaluation of a possible violation of this part prior to the filing of a complaint, the subject of the evaluation shall be notified not later than five business days after an Office of State Ethics staff member's first contact with a third party concerning the matter.

(2) In the conduct of its investigation of an alleged violation of this part, the Office of State Ethics shall have the power to hold hearings, administer oaths, examine witnesses and receive oral and documentary evidence. The Office of State Ethics may subpoena witnesses under procedural rules adopted by the Citizen's Ethics Advisory Board as regulations in accordance with the provisions of chapter 54 to compel attendance before the Office of State Ethics and to require the production for examination by the ethics enforcement officer of the Office of State Ethics of any books and papers which the Office of State Ethics deems relevant in any matter under investigation or in question, provided any such subpoena is

issued either pursuant to a majority vote of the Citizen's Ethics Advisory Board or pursuant to the signature of the chairperson of such board. The vice-chairperson of such board may sign any such subpoena if the chairperson of such board is unavailable. In the exercise of such powers, the Office of State Ethics may use the services of the state police, who shall provide the same upon the office's request. The Office of State Ethics shall make a record of all proceedings conducted pursuant to this subsection. The ethics enforcement officer of the Office of State Ethics may bring any alleged violation of this part before a judge trial referee assigned by the Chief Court Administrator for such purpose for a probable cause hearing. Such judge trial referee shall be compensated in accordance with the provisions of section 52–434 from such funds as may be available to the Office of State Ethics. Any witness summoned before the Office of State Ethics or a judge trial referee pursuant to this subsection shall receive the witness fee paid to witnesses in the courts of this state. During any investigation conducted pursuant to this subsection or any probable cause hearing conducted pursuant to this subsection, the respondent shall have the right to appear and be heard and to offer any information which may tend to clear the respondent of probable cause to believe the respondent has violated any provision of this part. The respondent shall also have the right to be represented by legal counsel and to examine and cross-examine witnesses. Not later than ten days prior to the commencement of any hearing conducted pursuant to this subsection, the Office of State Ethics shall provide the respondent with a list of its intended witnesses. Any finding of probable cause to believe the respondent is in violation of any provisions of this part shall be made by a judge trial referee not later than thirty days after the ethics enforcement officer brings such alleged violation before such judge trial ref-

eree, except that such thirty-day limitation period shall not apply if the judge trial referee determines that good cause exists for extending such limitation period.

(b) If a judge trial referee determines that probable cause exists for the violation of a provision of this part, the board shall initiate hearings to determine whether there has been a violation of this part. Any such hearing shall be initiated by the board not later than thirty days after the finding of probable cause by a judge trial referee and shall be concluded not later than ninety days after its initiation, except that such thirty or ninety-day limitation period shall not apply if the judge trial referee determines that good cause exists for extending such limitation period. A judge trial referee, who has not taken part in the probable cause determination on the matter shall be assigned by the Chief Court Administrator and shall be compensated in accordance with section 52–434 out of funds available to the Office of State Ethics and shall preside over such hearing and rule on all issues concerning the application of the rules of evidence, which shall be the same as in judicial proceedings. The trial referee shall have no vote in any decision of the board. All hearings of the board held pursuant to this subsection shall be open. At such hearing the board shall have the same powers as the Office of State Ethics under subsection (a) of this section and the respondent shall have the right to be represented by legal counsel, the right to compel attendance of witnesses and the production of books, documents, records and papers and to examine and cross-examine witnesses. Not later than ten days prior to the commencement of any hearing conducted pursuant to this subsection, the Office of State Ethics shall provide the respondent with a list of its intended witnesses. The judge trial referee shall, while engaged in the discharge of the duties as provided in this subsection, have the same authority as is provided in section 51–

35 over witnesses who refuse to obey a subpoena or to testify with respect to any matter upon which such witness may be lawfully interrogated, and may commit any such witness for contempt for a period no longer than thirty days. The Office of State Ethics shall make a record of all proceedings pursuant to this subsection. During the course of any such hearing, no ex-parte communication shall occur between the board, or any of its members, and: (1) The judge trial referee, or (2) any staff member of the Enforcement Division of the Office of State Ethics, concerning the complaint or the respondent. The board shall find no person in violation of any provision of this part except upon the concurring vote of six of its members present and voting. No member of the board shall vote on the question of whether a violation of any provision of this part has occurred unless such member was physically present for the duration of any hearing held pursuant to this subsection. Not later than fifteen days after the public hearing conducted in accordance with this subsection, the board shall publish its finding and a memorandum of the reasons therefor. Such finding and memorandum shall be deemed to be the final decision of the board on the matter for the purposes of chapter 54. The respondent, if aggrieved by the finding and memorandum, may appeal therefrom to the Superior Court in accordance with the provisions of section 4–183.

(c) If a judge trial referee finds, after a hearing pursuant to this section, that there is no probable cause to believe that a municipal official or municipal employee has violated a provision of this part, or if the board determines that a municipal official or municipal employee has not violated any such provision, or if a court of competent jurisdiction overturns a finding by the board of a violation by such respondent, the state shall pay the reasonable legal expenses of the respondent as determined by the Attorney General or by the court if appropriate. If any complaint brought under the provisions of this part is made with the knowledge that it is made without foundation in fact, the respondent shall have a cause of action against the complainant for double the amount of damage caused thereby and if the respondent prevails in such action, he may be awarded by the court the costs of such action together with reasonable attorneys' fees.

(d) No complaint may be made under this section later than five years after the violation alleged in the complaint has been committed.

(e) No person shall take or threaten to take official action against an individual for such individual's disclosure of information to the board or the general counsel, ethics enforcement officer or staff of the Office of State Ethics under the provisions of this part. After receipt of information from an individual under the provisions of this part, the Office of State Ethics shall not disclose the identity of such individual without such individual's consent unless the Office of State Ethics determines that such disclosure is unavoidable during the course of an investigation. No person shall be subject to civil liability for any good faith disclosure that such person makes to the Office of State Ethics.

## Section 5. Confidentiality of complaints, evaluations of possible violations and investigations. Publication of findings. (NEW) (Effective January 1, 2016)

(a) Unless a judge trial referee makes a finding of probable cause, a complaint alleging a violation of this part shall be confidential except upon the request of the respondent. An evaluation of a possible violation of this part by the Office of State Ethics prior to the filing of a complaint shall be confidential except upon the request of the subject of the evaluation. If the evaluation is confidential, any information supplied to or received from the Office of State Ethics shall not be disclosed to any third party by a subject of the evaluation, a person contacted for the purpose of obtaining information or by the ethics enforcement officer or staff of the Office of State Ethics. No provision of this subsection shall prevent the Office of State Ethics from reporting the possible commission of a crime to the Chief State's Attorney or other prosecutorial authority.

(b) An investigation conducted prior to a probable cause finding shall be confidential except upon the request of the respondent. If the investigation is confidential, the allegations in the complaint and any information supplied to or received from the Office of State Ethics shall not be disclosed during the investigation to any third party by a complainant, respondent, witness, designated party, or board or staff member of the Office of State Ethics.

(c) Not later than three business days after the termination of the investigation, the Office of State Ethics shall inform the complainant and the respondent of its finding and provide them a summary of its reasons for making that finding. The Office of State Ethics shall publish its finding upon the respondent's request and may also publish a summary of its reasons for making such finding.

(d) If a judge trial referee makes a finding of no probable cause, the complaint and the record of the Office of State Ethics' investigation shall remain confidential, except upon the request of the respondent and except that some or all of the record may be used in subsequent proceedings. No complainant, respondent, witness, designated party, or board or staff member of the Office of State Ethics shall disclose to any third party any information learned from the investigation, including knowledge of the existence of a complaint, which the disclosing party would not otherwise have known. If such a disclosure is made, the judge trial referee may, after consultation with the respondent if the respondent is not the source of the disclosure, publish the judge trial referee's finding and a summary of the judge trial referee's reasons therefor.

(e) The judge trial referee shall make public a finding of probable cause not later than five business days after any such finding. At such time the entire record of the investigation shall become public, except that the Office of State Ethics may postpone examination or release of such public records for a period not to exceed fourteen days for the purpose of reaching a stipulation agreement pursuant to subsection (c) of section 4–177. Any such stipulation agreement or settlement shall be approved by a majority of those members present and voting.

## Section 6. Prohibited activities. (NEW) (Effective January 1, 2016)

(a) No municipal official or municipal employee shall, while serving as such, have any financial interest in, or engage in, any business, employment, transaction or professional activity, which is in substantial conflict with the proper discharge of his duties or employment in the public interest and of his responsibilities as prescribed in the laws of this state, as defined in section 9 of this act.

(b) No municipal official or municipal employee shall accept other employment which will either impair his independence of judgment as to his official duties or employment or require him, or induce him, to disclose confidential information acquired by him in the course of and by reason of his official duties.

(c) No municipal official or municipal employee shall wilfully and knowingly disclose, for financial gain, to any other person, confidential information acquired by him in the course of and by reason of his official duties or employment and no municipal official or municipal employee shall use his public office or position or any confidential information received through his holding such public office or position to obtain financial gain for himself, his spouse, child, child's spouse, parent, brother or sister, his employer other than the municipality or a business with which he is associated.

(d) No municipal official or municipal employee or employee of such municipal official or municipal employee shall agree to accept any employment, fee or other thing of value, or portion thereof, for appearing, agreeing to appear, or taking any other action on behalf of another person before any municipal board, commission, council or department of the municipality in which such municipal official or municipal employee holds a public office or position or the subject matter over which municipal official or municipal employee has authority or control; provided this shall not prohibit any such person from making inquiry for information on behalf of another before any such municipal board, commission, council or department if no fee or reward is given or promised in consequence thereof. Notwithstanding the provisions of this subsection to the contrary, a municipal official or municipal employee may be or become a member or employee of a firm, partnership, association or professional corporation which represents clients for compensation before any municipal board, commission, council or department of the municipality in which such member or officer holds public office, provided the member or officer shall take no part in any matter involving any such municipal board, commission, council or department and shall not receive compensation from any such matter. Receipt of a previously established salary, not based on the current or anticipated business of the firm, partnership, association or professional corporation involving municipal board, commission, council or department, shall be permitted. Nothing in this subsection shall prohibit or restrict a municipal official or municipal employee from appearing before any municipal board, commission, council or department in his own individual interest or the individual interest of an immediate family member, or being a party in any action, proceeding or litigation brought by or against the municipal official or municipal employee to which the municipality is a party.

(e) No person shall offer or give to a municipal official or municipal employee or candidate for municipal office or his spouse, his parent, brother, sister or child or spouse of such child or a business with which he is associated, anything of value, including, but not limited to, a gift, loan, political contribution, reward or promise of future employment based on any understanding that the vote, official action or judgment of the municipal official, municipal employee or candidate for municipal office would be or had been influenced thereby.

(f) No municipal official or municipal employee or candidate for municipal office shall solicit or accept anything of value, including but not limited to, a gift, loan, political contribution, reward or promise of future employment based on any understanding that the vote, official action or judgment of the municipal official or municipal employee or candidate for municipal office would be or had been influenced thereby.

(g) Nothing in subsection (e) or (f) of this section shall be construed (1) to apply to any promise made in violation of subdivision (6) of section 9–622, or (2) to permit any activity otherwise prohibited in section 53a-147 or 53a-148.

(h) No municipal official or municipal employee or member of the official or employee's immediate family or a business with which he is associated shall enter into any contract with the municipality in which such municipal official or municipal employee holds a public office or position, valued at five hundred dollars or more, other than a contract (A) of employment as a municipal employee, or (B) pursuant to a court appointment, unless the contract has been awarded through an open and public process, including prior public offer and subsequent public disclosure of all proposals considered and the contract awarded. In no event shall an executive head of a municipal department, or the executive head's immediate family or a business with which he is associated enter into any contract with that department. Nothing in this subsection shall be construed as applying to any municipal official who is appointed as a member of a municipal board, commission, council or department and who receives no compensation other than per diem payments or reimbursement for actual or necessary expenses, or both, incurred in the performance of the municipal official's duties unless such municipal official has authority or control over the subject matter of the contract. Any contract made in violation of this subsection shall be voidable by a court of competent jurisdiction if the suit is commenced not later than one hundred eighty days after the making of the contract.

(i) No municipal official or municipal employee shall accept a fee or honorarium for an article, appearance or speech, or for participation at an event, in the municipal official's or municipal employee's official capacity, provided a municipal official or municipal employee may receive payment or reimbursement for necessary expenses for any such activity in his or her official capacity. If a municipal official or municipal employee receives such a payment or reimbursement for lodging or out-of-state travel, or both, the municipal official or municipal employee shall, not later than thirty days

thereafter, file a report of the payment or reimbursement with the Office of State Ethics, unless the payment or reimbursement is provided by the federal government or state government. If a municipal official or municipal employee does not file such report within such period, either intentionally or due to gross negligence on the municipal official's or municipal employee's part, the municipal official or municipal employee shall return the payment or reimbursement. If any failure to file such report is not intentional or due to gross negligence on the part of the municipal official or municipal employee, the municipal official or municipal employee shall not be subject to any penalty under this chapter. When a municipal official or municipal employee attends an event in this state in the municipal official's or municipal employee's official capacity and as a principal speaker at such event and receives admission to or food or beverage at such event from the sponsor of the event, such admission or food or beverage shall not be considered a gift and no report shall be required from such municipal official or municipal employee or from the sponsor of the event.

(j) No municipal official or municipal employee shall knowingly accept, directly or indirectly, any gift, as defined in subdivision (4) of section 1 of this act, from any person the municipal official or municipal employee knows or has reason to know: (1) Is doing business with or seeking to do business with the municipal board, commission, council or department in which the municipal official or municipal employee holds a public office or position; or (2) is engaged in activities which are directly regulated by such board, commission, council or department. No person shall knowingly give, directly or indirectly, any gift or gifts in violation of this provision. Any person prohibited from making a gift under this subsection shall report to the Office of State Ethics any solicitation of a gift from such person by a municipal employee or municipal official.

(k) (1) No municipal official or municipal employee or member of the immediate family of a municipal official or municipal employee shall knowingly accept, directly or indirectly, any gift costing one hundred dollars or more from a municipal official or municipal employee who is under the supervision of such municipal official or municipal employee.

(2) No municipal official or municipal employee or member of the immediate family of a municipal official or municipal employee shall knowingly accept, directly or indirectly, any gift costing one hundred dollars or more from a municipal official or municipal employee who is a supervisor of such municipal official or municipal employee.

(3) No municipal official or municipal employee shall knowingly give, directly or indirectly, any gift in violation of subdivision (1) or (2) of this subsection.

(l) No municipal official or municipal employee shall intentionally counsel, authorize or otherwise sanction action that violates any provision of this part.

## Section 7. Certain activities restricted after leaving public office or employment. (NEW) (Effective January 1, 2016)

(a) No former municipal official or municipal employee shall disclose or use confidential information acquired in the course of and by reason of his official duties, for financial gain for himself or another person.

(b) No former municipal official or municipal employee shall represent anyone other than the municipality, concerning any particular matter (1) in which he participated personally and substantially while in municipal service or employment, and (2) in which the municipality has a substantial interest.

(c) No former municipal official or municipal employee shall, for one year after leaving municipal service or employment, represent anyone, other than the municipality, for compensation before the municipal board, commission, council or department in which he served at the time of his termination of service or employment, concerning any matter in which the municipality has a substantial interest.

(d) No former municipal official or municipal employee who participated substantially in the negotiation or award of a municipal contract valued at an amount of twenty-five thousand dollars or more, or who supervised the negotiation or award of such a contract, shall seek or accept employment with a party to the contract other than the municipality for a period of one year after his resignation from his municipal office or position if his resignation occurs less than one year after the contract is signed. No party to such a contract other than the municipality shall employ any such former municipal official or municipal employee in violation of this subsection.

## Section 8. Donation of goods or services to municipality. (NEW) (Effective January 1, 2016)

Nothing in this part shall prohibit the donation of goods or services, as described in subparagraph (E) of subdivision (4) of section 1 of this act, to a municipality, the donation of the use of facilities to facilitate municipal action or functions or the donation of real property to a municipality.

## Section 9. Conflicts of Interest— Substantial and Direct. (NEW) (Effective January 1, 2016)

A municipal official or municipal employee has an interest which is in substantial conflict with the proper discharge of his duties or employment in the public interest and of his responsibilities as prescribed in the laws of this state, if he has reason to believe or expect that he, his spouse, a dependent child, his employer other than the municipality or a business with which he is associated will derive a direct monetary gain or suffer a direct monetary loss, as the case may be, by reason of his official activity. A municipal official or municipal employee does not have an interest which is in substantial conflict with the proper discharge of his duties in the public interest and of his responsibilities as prescribed by the laws of this state, if any benefit or detriment accrues to him, his spouse, a dependent child, his employer other than the municipality or a business with which he, his spouse or such dependent child is associated as a member of a profession, occupation or group to no greater extent than any other member of such profession, occupation or group. A municipal official or municipal employee who has a substantial conflict may not take official action on the matter.

## Section 10. Conflicts of Interest— Potential. (NEW) (Effective January 1, 2016)

Any municipal official or municipal employee who, in the discharge of such official's or employee's official duties, would be required to take an action that would affect a financial interest of such official or employee, such official's or employee's spouse, parent, brother, sister, child or the spouse of a child, employer other than the municipality or a business with which such official or employee is associated, other than an interest of a de minimis nature, an interest that is not distinct from that of a substantial segment of the general public or an interest in substantial conflict with the performance of official duties as defined in section 8 of this act has a potential conflict of interest.

Under such circumstances, such official or employee shall, if such official or employee is a member of a municipal regulatory board, council or commission, either excuse himself or herself from the matter or prepare a written statement signed under penalty of false statement describing the matter requiring action and the nature of the potential conflict and explaining why despite the potential conflict, such official or employee is able to vote and otherwise participate fairly, objectively and in the public interest. Such municipal official or municipal employee shall deliver a copy of the statement to the Office of State Ethics and enter a copy of the statement in the journal or minutes of the board, council or commission. If such official or employee is not a member of a municipal regulatory board, council or commission, such official or employee shall, in the case of either a substantial or potential conflict, prepare a written statement signed under penalty of false statement describing the matter requiring action and the nature of the conflict and deliver a copy of the statement to such official's or employee's immediate superior, if any, who shall assign the matter to another employee, or if such official or employee has no immediate superior, such official or employee shall take such steps as the Office of State Ethics shall prescribe or advise.

## Section 11. Legal defense fund established by or for a municipal official or municipal employee. Reports. Contributions. (NEW) (Effective January 1, 2016)

(a) Any municipal official or municipal employee who establishes a legal defense fund, or for whom a legal defense fund has been established, shall file a report on said fund with the Office of State Ethics not later than the tenth day of January, April, July and October. Each such report shall include the following information for the preceding calendar quarter: (1) The names of the directors and officers of the fund, (2) the name of the depository institution for the fund, (3) an itemized accounting of each contribution to the fund, including the full name and complete address of each contributor and the amount of the contribution, and (4) an itemized accounting of each expenditure, including the full name and complete address of each payee and the amount and purpose of the expenditure. The municipal official or municipal employee shall sign each such report under penalty of false statement.

(b) (1) In addition to the prohibition on gifts under subsection (j) of section 5 of this act, no municipal official or municipal employee shall accept, directly or indirectly, any contribution to a legal defense fund established by or for the municipal official or municipal employee, from (A) a member of the immediate family of any person who is prohibited from giving a gift under subsection (j) of section 5 of this act, or (B) a person who is appointed by said municipal official or municipal employee to serve on a paid, full-time basis. No person described in subparagraph (A) or (B) of this subdivision shall make a contribution to such a legal defense fund, and no such person or any person prohibited from making a gift under subsection (j) of section 5 of this act shall solicit a contribution for such a legal defense fund.

(2) A municipal official or municipal employee may accept a contribution or contributions to a legal defense fund established by or for the municipal official or municipal employee from any other person, provided the total amount of such contributions from any such person in any calendar year shall not exceed one thousand dollars. No such person shall make a contribution or contributions to said legal defense fund exceed-

ing one thousand dollars in any calendar year.

(3) Notwithstanding the provisions of subdivision (2) of this subsection, a municipal official or municipal employee may accept a contribution or contributions, in any amount, to a legal defense fund established by or for the municipal official or municipal employee from a relative of the municipal official or municipal employee or a person whose relationship with the municipal official or municipal employee is not dependent on the official's or employee's status as a municipal official or municipal employee. The factors that the board shall consider in determining whether a person's relationship is so dependent shall include, but not be limited to, whether the person may be able to benefit from the exercise of official authority of the municipal official or municipal employee and whether the person made gifts to the municipal official or municipal employee before the official or employee began serving in such office or position.

### Section 12. Consultants and independent contractors. Prohibited activities. (NEW) (Effective January 1, 2016)

(a) No person hired by a municipality as a consultant or independent contractor shall:

(1) Use the authority provided to the person under the contract, or any confidential information acquired in the performance of the contract, to obtain financial gain for the person, an employee of the person or a member of the immediate family of any such person or employee;

(2) Accept another municipal contract which would impair the independent judgment of the person in the performance of the existing contract; or

(3) Accept anything of value based on an understanding that the actions of the

person on behalf of the municipality would be influenced.

(b) No person shall give anything of value to a person hired by a municipality as a consultant or independent contractor based on an understanding that the actions of the consultant or independent contractor on behalf of the municipality would be influenced.

## Section 13. Aggrieved persons. Appeals. (NEW) (Effective January 1, 2016)

Any person aggrieved by any final decision of the board, made pursuant to this part, may appeal such decision in accordance with the provisions of section 4–175 or section 4–183.

## Section 14. Authority of board after finding violation. (NEW) (Effective January 1, 2016)

(a) The board, upon a finding made pursuant to section 3 of this act that there has been a violation of any provision of this part, shall have the authority to order the violator to do any or all of the following: (1) Cease and desist the violation of this part; (2) file any report, statement or other information as required by this part; and (3) pay a civil penalty of not more than ten thousand dollars for each violation of this part.

(b) Notwithstanding the provisions of subsection (a) of this section, the board may, after a hearing conducted in accordance with sections 4–176e to 4–184, inclusive, upon the concurring vote of six of its members, present and voting impose a civil penalty not to exceed ten dollars per day upon any individual who fails to file any statement or other information as required by this part. Each distinct violation of this subsection shall be a separate offense and in case of a continued violation, each day thereof shall be deemed a separate offense. In no event shall the aggregate penalty im-

posed for such failure to file exceed ten thousand dollars.

(c) The board may also report its finding to the Chief State's Attorney for any action deemed necessary. The board, upon a finding made pursuant to section 3 of this act that a member or member-elect of the legislative body of a municipality has violated any provision of this part, shall notify such legislative body, in writing, of such finding and the basis for such finding.

(d) Any person who knowingly acts in such person's financial interest in violation of section 5, 8, 9, 10 or 11 of this act or any person who knowingly receives a financial advantage resulting from a violation of any of said sections shall be liable for damages in the amount of such advantage. If the board determines that any person may be so liable, it shall immediately inform the Attorney General of that possibility.

## Section 15. Violations; penalties. Disciplinary powers of municipal legislative bodies, boards, commissions, councils and departments. Civil action for damages. (NEW) (Effective January 1, 2016)

(a) Any person who intentionally violates any provision of this part shall (1) for a first violation, be guilty of a class A misdemeanor, except that, if such person derives a financial benefit of one thousand dollars or more as a result of such violation, such person shall be guilty of a class D felony, and (2) for a second or subsequent violation, be guilty of a class D felony, provided no person may be found guilty of a violation of subsection (e) or (f) of section 5 of this act and bribery or bribe receiving under section 53a-147 or 53a-148 upon the same incident, but such person may be charged and prosecuted for all or any of such offenses upon the same information.

(b) The penalties prescribed in this part shall not limit the power of the legislative body of a municipality to discipline its own members, and shall not limit the power of municipal boards, commissions, councils or departments to discipline their officials or employees.

(c) The Attorney General may bring a civil action against any person who knowingly acts in the person's financial interest in, or knowingly receives a financial advantage resulting from, a violation of section 5, 8 or 9 of this act. In any such action, the Attorney General may, in the discretion of the court, recover any financial benefit that accrued to the person as a result of such violation and additional damages in an amount not exceeding twice the amount of the actual damages.

## Section 16. Statements of financial interests. Filing requirements. (NEW) (Effective January 1, 2016)

(a) (1) A municipality may require, upon consent of the legislative body of the municipality or, in the case of a municipality in which the legislative body is a town meeting, the board of selectmen, the filing of a statement of financial interests with the Office of State Ethics, as provided in subdivision (2) of this subsection.

(2) All elected officers of a municipality, appointed members of the legislative body of a municipality, members of a municipal land use agency or commission, members and employees of any municipal board, commission, council or department who exercise (A) significant policymaking, regulatory or contractual authority, (B) significant decision-making and/or supervisory responsibility for the review and/or award of municipal contracts, or (C) significant decision-making and/or supervisory responsibility over staff that monitor municipal contracts, shall file, under penalty of false statement, a statement of financial interests for the pre-

ceding calendar year with the Office of State Ethics on or before the May first next in any year in which they hold such an office or position. If, in any year, May first falls on a weekend or legal holiday, such statement shall be filed not later than the next business day. Any such individual who leaves his or her office or position shall file a statement of financial interests covering that portion of the year during which such individual held his or her office or position. The Office of State Ethics shall notify such individuals of the requirements of this subsection not later than thirty days after their departure from such office or position. Such individuals shall file such statement not later than sixty days after receipt of the notification.

(b) The statement of financial interests shall include the following information for the preceding calendar year in regard to the individual required to file the statement and the individual's spouse and dependent children residing in the individual's household: (1) The names of all businesses with which associated; (2) all sources of income, including the name of each employer, with a description of each source, in excess of one thousand dollars, without specifying amounts of income; (3) the name of securities in excess of five thousand dollars at fair market value owned by such individual, spouse or dependent children or held in the name of a corporation, partnership or trust for the benefit of such individual, spouse or dependent children; (4) the existence of any known blind trust and the names of the trustees; (5) all real property and its location, whether owned by such individual, spouse or dependent children or held in the name of a corporation, partnership or trust for the benefit of such individual, spouse or dependent children; (6) the names and addresses of creditors to whom the individual, the individual's spouse or dependent children, individually, owed debts of more than ten thousand dollars; and (7) any leases or contracts with the municipality held or entered into by the individual or a business with which he or she was associated.

(c) The statement of financial interests filed pursuant to this section shall be a matter of public information, except the list of names, filed in accordance with subdivision (6) of subsection (b) of this section shall be sealed and confidential and for the use of the Office of State Ethics only after a complaint has been filed under section 3 of this act and such complaint has been determined by a vote of the board to be of sufficient merit and gravity to justify the unsealing of such list or lists and not open to public inspection unless the respondent requests otherwise. If the board reports its findings to the Chief State's Attorney in accordance with subsection (c) of section 13 of this act, the board shall turn over to the Chief State's Attorney such relevant information contained in the statement as may be germane to the specific violation or violations or a prosecutorial official may subpoena such statement in a criminal action. Unless otherwise a matter of public record, the Office of State Ethics shall not disclose to the public any such subpoena which would be exempt from disclosure by the issuing agency.

(d) Any individual who is unable to provide information required under the provisions of subsection (b) of this section by reason of impossibility may petition the board for a waiver of the requirements.

## Section 17. Citizen's Ethics Advisory Board. Qualifications. Restrictions. Subsection (b) of section 1–80 of the general statutes is repealed and the following is substituted in lieu thereof (Effective January 1, 2016)

(b) All members shall be electors of the state. No member shall be a state or municipal employee. No member or employee of said board shall (1) hold or campaign for any public office, including municipal office; (2) have held public office, including municipal office, or have been a candidate for public office or a candidate for municipal office for a three-year period prior to appointment; (3) hold office in any political party or political committee or be a member of any organization or association organized primarily for the purpose of influencing legislation or decisions of public agencies; or (4) be an individual who is a registrant as defined in subdivision (17) of section 1–91. For purposes of this subsection, "public office" does not include the offices of justice of the peace or notary public.

## Section 18. Citizen's Ethics Advisory Board. Qualifications. Restrictions. Subsection (d) of section 1–80 of the general statutes is repealed and the following is substituted in lieu thereof (Effective January 1, 2016)

(d) The board shall elect a chairperson who shall, except as provided in subsection (b) of section 1–82, [and] subsection (b) of section 1–93 *and subsection (b) of section 3 of this act*, preside at meetings of the board and a vice-chairperson to preside in the absence of the chairperson. Six members of the board shall constitute a quorum. Except as provided in subdivision (3) of subsection (a) of section 1–81, subsections (a) and (b) of section 1–82, subsection (b) of section 1–88, subsection (e) of section 1–92, subsections (a) and (b) of section 1–93, [and] subsection (b) of section 1–99, *subdivision (3) of subsection (a) of section 2 of this act, subsections (a) and (b) of section 3 of this act and subsection (b) of section 13 of this act* a majority vote of the members shall be required for action of the board. The chairperson or any three members may call a meeting.

## Section 19. Citizen's Ethics Advisory Board. Qualifications. Restrictions. Subsection (e) of section 1–80 of the general statutes is repealed and the following is substituted in lieu thereof (Effective January 1, 2016)

(e) Any matter before the board, except hearings held pursuant to the provisions of subsection (b) of section 1–82, [or] subsection (b) of section 1–93 or subsection (b) of section 3 of this act, may be assigned by the board to two of its members to conduct an investigation or hearing, as the case may be, to ascertain the facts and report thereon to the board with a recommendation for action.

## Section 20. Citizen's Ethics Advisory Board. Qualifications. Restrictions. Subsection (l) of section 1–80 of the general statutes is repealed and the following is substituted in lieu thereof (Effective January 1, 2016)

(l) No member of the board may hold any other position in state or municipal employment for a period of one year following the end of such member's service on the board, including, but not limited to, service as a member on a state or municipal board or commission, service as a judge of the Superior Court or service as a state agency commissioner.

## Section 21. Subdivision (10) of subsection (c) of section 7–148 of the general statutes is repealed and the following is substituted in lieu thereof (Effective January 1, 2016)

(10) (A) Make all lawful regulations and ordinances in furtherance of any general

powers as enumerated in this section, and prescribe penalties for the violation of the same not to exceed two hundred fifty dollars, unless otherwise specifically provided by the general statutes. Such regulations and ordinances may be enforced by citations issued by designated municipal officers or employees, provided the regulations and ordinances have been designated specifically by the municipality for enforcement by citation in the same manner in which they were adopted and the designated municipal officers or employees issue a written warning providing notice of the specific violation before issuing the citation;

[(B) Adopt a code of ethical conduct;]

[(C)] *(B)* Establish and maintain free legal aid bureaus;

[(D)] *(C)* Perform data processing and related administrative computer services for a fee for another municipality;

[(E)] *(D)* Adopt the model ordinance concerning a municipal freedom of information advisory board created under subsection (f) of section 1–205 and establish a municipal freedom of information advisory board as provided by said ordinance and said section.

## Section 22. Section 7–148h of the general statutes is repealed (Effective January 1, 2016)

[(a) Any town, city, district, as defined in section 7–324, or borough may, by charter provision or ordinance, establish a board, commission, council, committee or other agency to investigate allegations of unethical conduct, corrupting influence or illegal activities levied against any official, officer or employee of such town, city, district or borough. The provisions of subsections (a) to (e), inclusive, of section 1–82a shall apply to allegations before any such agency of such conduct, influence or activities, to an investigation of such allegations conducted prior to a probable cause finding, and to a finding of probable cause or no probable cause. Any board, commission, council, committee or other agency established pursuant to this section may issue subpoenas or subpoenas duces tecum, enforceable upon application to the Superior Court, to compel the attendance of persons at hearings and the production of books, documents, records and papers.

(b) Notwithstanding the provisions of any special act, municipal charter or ordinance to the contrary, an elected official of any town, city, district or borough that has established a board, commission, council, committee or other agency under subsection (a) of this section, has an interest that is in substantial conflict with the proper discharge of the official's duties or employment in the public interest and of the official's responsibilities as prescribed by the laws of this state, if the official has reason to believe or expect that the official, the official's spouse or dependent child, or a business with which he is associated, as defined in section 1–79, will derive a direct monetary gain or suffer a direct monetary loss, as the case may be, by reason of the official's official activity. Any such elected official does not have an interest that is in substantial conflict with the proper discharge of the official's duties in the public interest and of the official's responsibilities as prescribed by the laws of this state, if any benefit or detriment accrues to the official, the official's spouse or dependent child, or a business with which he, his spouse or such dependent child is associated as a member of a profession, occupation or group to no greater extent than to any other member of such profession, occupation or group. Any such elected official who has a substantial conflict may not take official action on the matter.]

# IV. Transparency in Government Procurement

## *National Institute of Governmental Purchasing*

### *Preamble*

Procurement[1] in the public sector plays a unique role in the execution of democratic government. It is at once focused on support of its internal customers to ensure they are able to effectively achieve their unique missions while serving as stewards of the public whose tax dollars bring to life the political will of its representative governing body. The manner in which the business of procurement is conducted is a direct reflection of the government entity that the procurement department supports.

In a democratic society, public[2] awareness and understanding of government practice ensures stability and confidence in governing systems. Awareness and understanding of government practices relies greatly on the public's ability to access the information relevant to its interests. Ease of information access and understanding is more succinctly referred to as "transparency." In his 2009 inaugural address, President Obama emphasized the importance of transparency in government practice and its value in holding government accountable for its actions *"...And those of us who manage the public's dollars will be held to account, to spend wisely, reform bad habits, and do our business in the light of day, because only then can we restore the vital trust between a people and their government."*

Today's democracies enjoy the benefits of evolved information technology systems that aggregate and communicate government information to those who would benefit by it. Unfortunately, not all government entities are financially able to equally provide their publics with the technology-based information systems that maximize transparency. Though perhaps unintended, the consequence is a community less able to ensure that its government is acting in a manner that effectively balances the needs of all its constituents.

In this brief treatise on the importance and role of transparency in the public procurement process, the National Institute of Governmental Purchasing highlights the historical importance of transparency in a democracy and the contemporary tools available that enable greater transparency, and offers a series of recommendations governments can adopt to achieve transparency in practice, without undue burden.

### *Transparency in Government Procurement Operations*

#### Introduction

In a democratic society, citizens rightfully demand judicious and prudent use of their tax dollars. Businesses are accountable to owners and citizens should not expect

213

any less from their government. Thomas Jefferson is credited with saying, "We might hope to see the finances as clear and intelligible as a merchant's books, so that every member of Congress, and every man of every mind in the Union should be able to comprehend them, to investigate abuses, and consequently, to control them."

Annual government expenditures for goods and services are a major factor in the U.S. economy. In FY 2007, federal government civilian agencies purchased over $129 billion in goods and services and the department of defense purchased over $330 billion in goods and services.[3] Spending at the state and local government level for FY 2007 totaled $3.14 trillion.[4] With the size and scope of government spending activity it is critical that all stakeholders have confidence in the process.

Recent federal legislation reflects recognition of the fundamental nature and value of transparency in democratic governance. On September 26, 2006, President George W. Bush signed into law the Federal Funding Accountability and Transparency Act of 2006. The intent of the act is to empower every American with the ability to hold the government accountable for each spending decision. The FFATA legislation requires information on federal awards, including contracts, subcontracts, purchase orders, task orders, and delivery orders to be made available to the public via a single, searchable website.

In 2008, the Transparency in Government Act was adopted. Title V of the act directs the Administrator of General Services to establish and maintain a database of information regarding integrity and performance of federal contracts.

Shortly after taking office, President Obama signed a memorandum outlining the commitment of his administration to openness and transparency, signaling the importance of this continuing initiative. Government agencies have willingly complied with open record or "Sunshine Laws," but with the advantages offered by modern technology, a higher quality and diversity of information is available.

The Association of Government Accountants (AGA) commissioned the Harris Interactive research firm to conduct a survey of public attitudes towards government transparency and accountability. According to the study, 90% of American adults believe that, as taxpayers, they are entitled to transparent financial management information. The survey found that the public believed the government could better serve them and improve accountability through better *reporting* (open disclosure, easy-to-read reports), a change in *attitude in communications* (honesty and transparency) and better *information in the right channels* (websites, through the press).[5]

Thomas Jefferson remarked on the importance of transparency in government 200 years ago. Today, transparency in government operations is discussed at all levels of government. Accountability, understanding of spending priorities, economic conditions, identification of businesses opportunities, and political scandals all drive the demand for information.

## Transparency Legislation

While transparency is not a new concept in the area of public procurement, many of the transparency measures recently implemented are associated with public contracting.

### Federal

At the federal level, the Federal Funding Accountability and Transparency Act of 2006 requires full disclosure to the public by all entities or organizations receiving federal funds. The Office of Management and Budget is responsible for establishing and maintaining a website that complies with this mandate.

In 2009, the United States' Federal CIO Council shepherded the creation and launch of the *Data.gov* Website. The site's mission is "to increase public access to high value, machine readable datasets generated by the executive branch of the federal government." The site offers "raw" datasets (such as those exported from ERP systems) that individuals may utilize, manipulate and interpret. Datasets are offered through keyword searchable catalogs and are provided in multiple file formats to maximize accessibility and software compatibility.

The Data.gov site serves also as a blueprint for similar sites created at the state and local level. Data.gov provides an interactive map that links to the state and local data sites that have been launched. [http://www.data.gov/statedatasites]. As of January, 2010, California, Michigan, Utah, Massachusetts, and the District of Columbia have such sites.

### STATE AND LOCAL

At the state level, a number of states have implemented a form of transparency law.

- Mississippi has legislative mandates to provide taxpayers access to financial activities. The Mississippi Department of Finance and Administration is responsible for providing access and updating financial data regularly. Information includes budget appropriations, revenues, payroll information and contracts (Mississippi Accountability and Transparency Act of 2008).
- The State of Alaska provides budget and financial information online.
- California offers online access to a summary of contracts awarded by state agencies.
- Texas provides contract information on the state website.
- The State of Kansas shares expenditure information by vendor as a result of its transparency initiative to provide access to the State's financial activity.

- The State of Illinois recently enacted legislative action that requires greater transparency in the procurement process and provides a structure in an attempt to shelter procurement officials from the political influences. Public Act 96–0975 of the State of Illinois requires not only greater transparency in the procurement process, but also requires that conversations held with vendors associated with a particular contract or procurement action be captured in written form and made available for public inspection. State officials required to oversee implementation of these provisions will need to wrestle with the absence of adequate resources and the investment necessary to see that all state agencies are in compliance with the new law that went into effect on July 1, 2010.

Various cities, including Chicago, IL, and Fort Collins, CO, have adopted transparency legislation and make transactions available on their web sites. Chicago introduced the Chicago Transparency in Government initiative in 2003, making final contracts available to the public via its Web site. It also made available other information such as a freedom of information directory, an online permit center, public safety and community e-mail alerts, 3–1–1 online service requests, and other information of interest to stakeholders.

## Technology: Critical to Transparency in Government

Information maintained by the government is a public asset and must be disclosed rapidly in forms the public can readily find and use. Implementing transparency measures and providing information about government operations to the public in a timely manner relies heavily on technology-based solutions. Of course, technology-centric information systems require substantial initial investment and ongoing financial and human resource allocation. As governments are perpetually challenged to adequately fund all public services, public officials must necessarily balance transparency mandates with limited available resources. Absent adequate technology support, transparency initiatives depend on labor-intensive, ineffective, and time-consuming processes to make documents available. For transparency initiatives to achieve their great potential for success, investment in technology is essential.

As technology solutions are founded upon and must integrate with the operating practices of the entity, procurement officials must continue to find ways to creatively streamline processes, become more efficient, promote accountability, preserve process integrity and provide information regarding contracting activities and decisions that build and strengthen public trust. Efficient, well-defined systems processes and rules contribute to reducing the cost of the technology investment.

### Evolution of Technology

Prior to the late 1980s, aggregating data into centralized, "mine-able" repositories was much more difficult than it is today. With the advent of sophisticated network architectures and a commonly accessible Internet, the capacity for broadly sharing volumes of useful data is realistic. Public and corporate bodies rely on enterprise-wide technology solutions to support their data acquisition, processing and distribution needs. These Enterprise Resource Planning (ERP) systems have intentionally and substantially eroded information "silos" and organizational "shadow systems" that would otherwise prevent easy access to sought-after information. This is not to say that these barriers have altogether vanished; simply that ERPs have substantially weakened information domains that now require more deliberate effort to maintain.

## Elements of Technology Solutions

At its simplest, transparency in procurement is about public access to information. However, anticipating and meeting the broad variety of public information needs is not so simple. Individual citizens may want information about how their tax dollars are spent, while a business may want current and historical information related to an upcoming bid or proposal.

### What and How

State and local regulations determine 'what' information is to be provided to the public. However, 'how' information is provided to the public is frequently left up to the discretion of the state or local jurisdiction.

Ease of public access to government-generated data, i.e., *transparency*, greatly depends on the jurisdiction's use of technology-oriented operations.

Many procurement entities are high on the *transparency* curve with easy access to procurement information online, electronic bid notification and on-line bidding and award notification. Others are somewhere further down the *transparency* curve and may be posting bids on-line, registering suppliers on-line, and/or posting financial data and award information on-line. Unfortunately, many organizations are technologically challenged and function entirely in a paper environment. Paper is the least transparent form of information and may make it difficult for the public to find the desired information or do business with government.

### Business Environment

Transparency-in-government initiatives may strongly influence procurement practices and, perhaps unintentionally, transform governments into better customers for their suppliers. Customers who appear easy to do business with are more desirable to suppliers and are more likely to secure better business terms than entities relying on archaic methodologies and systems. Governments committed to being 'easy to do business with' may invite supplier and vendor feedback to determine their success in providing a transparent procurement process.

Factors that reflect how easy it is to do business with a procurement entity:

- Clearly expressed, readily available regulations, policies and procedures
- Standardization of documents
- Completeness of information
- Equal access and opportunity

**Regulations, policies and procedures.** NIGP works in cooperation with the American Bar Association's (ABA) Section of Public Contract Law to improve state and local procurement. The ABA's Model Procurement Code includes "best practices" that promote transparency in procurement. Adopted by 17 states and many hundreds of local jurisdictions, the Model Procurement Code addresses a broad range of issues arising in the procurement of supplies, services and construction. *[Source ABA Section of Public Contact Law web page for Model Procurement Code]* While public purchasing entities may not need the Model Procurement Code to be "easy to do business with," they do need well defined regulations and policies that promote fair and open competition. Confusing regulations, policies or procedures can make it hard doing business with any public procurement entity.

**Standardization of Documents.** Vendors must wade through a wide array of documents when attempting to do business with public procurement entities. Vendors are confronted with literally hundreds of different formats for bids, quotes, proposals and registrations. This lack of standardization increases the time and effort that vendors must spend in order to do business with a government activity. Some public procurement activities have developed standardized templates and documents that provide the public with easier access to information as well as making it simpler for vendors to do business with them.

**Completeness of Information.** This sounds simple, but maintaining the integrity of information and data so that the public can access complete information can be very challenging. The harder it is for an activity to generate complete information to the public, the less transparent that activity is. The use of electronic data and word processing makes the maintenance of information integrity much easier.

**Equal Access and Opportunity.** There should be no "insiders" when it comes to accessing public procurement information or the opportunity to do business with government. An example of "insiders" would be a department holding a pre-meeting with selected vendors prior to a bid or request for proposals being issued. Other "insider" examples include refusing to meet with some vendors or failing to answer bid/proposal questions to all by addendum. Competitive acquisitions should be "fair and open," an expression that has long been a standard axiom for procurement professionals. It is relatively easy to write bid specifications or requirements that limit competition. However, it can be difficult to develop specifications and requirements that do not limit competition. Under no circumstances should a competing vendor be allowed to write the bid specifications for your procurement. Transparency in procurement means conducting "fair and open" acquisitions throughout the acquisition process.

**Example** Websites of government entities supporting transparency in process:

- http://citydocs.fcgov.com/
- http://www.fcgov.com/openbook/
- http://www.fcgov.com/purchasing/
- http://www.cpa.state.tx.us/comptrol/expendlist/cashdrill.php (State of Texas)

- http://www.window.state.tx.us/comptrol/expendlist/cashdrill.php
- http://milwaukeecounty.headquarters.com/
- http://mapyourtaxes.mo.gov/MAP/Portal/Default.aspx
- Watchdog group website http://www.fiscalaccountability.org/featured-website-open-book-city-fort-a884

## Identifying Solutions

Any solution that will remain viable over the long term must strike a balance between available resources and transparency. Affordability often forces government to balance resources against desired or mandated levels of transparency.

The American Bar Association's model procurement code focuses on promoting transparency, fairness, and competitiveness in state and local government procurement to encourage broad participation and yield best value procurements. Unfortunately, legacy technology systems and inconsistent data collection standards frequently undermine realization of the ABA model's ideal. At minimum, in the absence of technology investments, incremental improvements can be achieved through standardization of documents and simplification of process.

The best systems solution provides for the appropriate scale of technology investment and the inclusion of procurement staff in the solution development process. The return on investment for implementing new technology solutions are transparency, streamlined workflows and improved decision-making. Yet, in addition to acquiring the necessary technology, government staff must be willing to learn and adopt new or more efficient ways of conducting procurement transactions. A focused change management plan must be in place.

Successful implementation of technology-based solutions requires preparation and vision. Organizations must be willing to undertake an assessment of its existing processes to identify opportunities for streamlining and standardization. Engaging procurement staff in the organizational assessment enhances the likelihood of achieving a broader set of possible solutions and more enthusiastic adoption of the final product.

In addition to achieving greater transparency, integrating new processes and technology often achieves a broader range of benefits for the entity.

- Standardized documents
- Efficiency gains and adopted best practices
- Simplified information requirements that result in higher quality responses
- Reduced FOIA or other forms of public records requests (frees resources for redirection to other priorities)
- Broader pool of vendors; increased competition; improved prices for the agency
- Improved vendor-related documentation
- Improved audit process
- Easier procurement planning and strategic sourcing
- Access to federal grant programs that have transparency-related evaluation criteria

## Recommendations

Ultimately, the goal of transparency is to provide sufficient information to allow private citizens to view and/or monitor government spending. Access to information is the best way to protect taxpayers' dollars against abuse and fraud.

To this end, the NIGP recommends that entities:

1. Identify existing and proposed legislation guiding transparency-related requirements
2. Allocate the financial and human resources necessary to undertake an

entity assessment of its "transparency friendliness"

3. Allocate the financial and human resources necessary to establish a systems solution that supports transparency

4. Establish Web-based reporting of entity data that includes, at minimum, current bid opportunities, bid results, current contracts, and solicitation schedules

5. Model entity portals after the data.gov or nyc.gov data mines

6. Establish recommended raw data format (such as .txt for statistical data)

7. Establish a Public-Procurement Liaison link on the government procurement site as a method for providing data not immediately available through the Website

8. Establish and post Terms of Use to discourage fraud and misuse of information

9. Establish and post an entity *statement of commitment* to the NIGP Code of Ethics

## Conclusion

The ideal of transparency in government practice is fundamental to successful democratic process. Transparency has been a recurring topic of focus for leaders of democracies throughout history. The manner in which government conducts itself in its business transactions immediately affects public opinion and the public's trust in its political leaders. In addition to garnering the public's good will and strengthened trust, the more practical, measurable business benefits of transparency are increased competition and better value goods and

services. Standardization of process, simplified information requirements, and availability of information, all make doing business with government much more attractive to the supplier community.

Today, democracies enjoy the benefits of database and networking technologies that support achievement of the transparency ideal. For many government entities, however, identifying the financial resources for enhanced information systems is a challenge. Nevertheless, with awareness that the enabling knowledge and tools exist, it is a challenge political leaders have the capacity to overcome. Through their budget debates, they can demonstrate their commitment to a principle operating tenet of democracy. In so doing, they grasp the opportunity to improve the financial performance of their government, strengthen their personal platform for continued leadership, and establish a legacy of trust for all government constituents.

## Notes

1. Throughout this paper, we will use the term ***procurement*** to capture the many functionalities associated with the process of acquiring goods and services, including description of requirements, solicitation and selection of sources, preparation and award of contract, all phases of contract administration, inventory control, and salvage and disposal operations.

2. ***Public*** refers to both the private individuals and corporate entities in a jurisdiction.

3. Federal Procurement Report FY 2007, Federal Procurement Data System.

4. U.S. Census Bureau's State and Local Government Finances by Level of Government 2006–2007.

5. "Survey Report on Perceptions of Government Financial Management—Verbatim Survey Results," Slide 6, Association of Government Accountants, http://www.agacgfm.org/harrispoll 2008.aspx, February 2008.

# V. Glossary of Anti-Corruption Practices

*Joaquin Jay Gonzalez III*

**Background check**: a verification of a person's character and/or criminal record

**Campaign finance reform**: initiatives to limit the influence of money in political campaigns

**Check and balance system**: structural arrangement that keeps power equal among the branches of government

**Civil service commission**: government agency tasked with developing policies and guidelines ensuring employees are selected and promoted based on merit rather than relationships

**Civil service exam**: a test taken to determine eligibility to serve in the government

**Closed-circuit television camera (CCTV)**: live video monitoring and recording of government transactions to prevent illicit behavior and actions

**Compliance officer**: person tasked with enforcing rules and procedures

**Conflict of interest law**: legislation that prohibits competing professional or personal interest that would make it difficult for the public official to fulfill his or her duties impartially

**District attorney, city attorney**: the legal counsel of a city or municipal jurisdiction

**eGovernment transaction**: online or electronic government transactions provide citizens with convenience, efficiency, and accuracy

**Election**: an opportunity to vote upright, ethical, and accountable politicians and public officials

**Ethics commission**: a commission established to investigate dishonest or unethical practices

**FBI sting operation**: a special operation designed to catch a person committing an unethical act.

**Form 700: Statement of Economic Interest**: a submission by every elected official and public employee who makes or influences governmental decisions declaring the person's financial interests and any conflicts of interest

**Grand jury**: an independent legal body that is empowered to investigate potential criminal conduct and to determine whether criminal charges should be brought against an elected or appointed official

**Inspector general**: an investigative official or office

**Internal affairs unit**: an internal department within a law enforcement agency that is tasked to do an impartial investigation of alleged misconduct by one of its officers

**Internal and external audit**: a formal examination of a government agency's financial accounts by an inside department or outside organization

**Law enforcement officer**: a public official whose main responsibility is to enforce the law in an ethical and accountable manner

**Media exposé**: an investigative report of government wrongdoing

**Merit-based system**: recruitment, selection, promotion, and retention based on testing and other competitive performance measures

**Oath of office**: an oath or pledge to uphold the public trust that a person makes before assuming an elective or appointive office.

**Ombudsman**: an independent office created to investigate public authorities

**1-800 toll free anonymous tip hotline**: a toll-free phone number used by citizens to report misbehavior and abuse by government officials and contractors

**Open bidding system**: Open to the public unsealing and examination of sealed bids or proposals received in response to a government agency's request for bids or proposals

**Openness and transparency**: two key principles that ensure public trust and accountability in democratic societies

**Sunset law**: a law that provides that public programs or policies shall terminate after a specific date, unless further legislative action is taken to extend it

**Sunshine law**: a legislation requiring certain government proceedings be open to the public

**Watchdog group**: a nonpartisan, nongovernmental organization (NGO) who monitor public officials and agencies for graft and corruption

**Whistleblower**: a person who exposes any kind of information or activity that is deemed illegal and unethical in public agencies

# About the Editors and Contributors

*All positions are as of the time of writing*

Tom **Arrandale** writes the *Sustainability* newsletter and reports on environmental issues.

Dulce Pamela **Baizas** is an auditor with the U.S. Department of Energy and also the director of finance for the Young Government Leaders' Northern California Chapter.

Chelsea A. **Binns** is an assistant professor in the Department of Criminal Justice, Legal Studies, and Homeland Security at St. John's University, New York City.

Paul **Blumenthal** is the senior writer at the Sunlight Foundation.

Troy **Brown** is city manager of Tracy, California.

**California City Management Foundation** is an advocacy and support organization for city managers.

Tunde **Campbell** is a student in the MPA program at Upper Iowa University.

John J. **Carroll** is an assistant professor of public administration at Nova Southeastern University in Fort Lauderdale, Florida.

William **Carroll** is a student in the MPA program at Upper Iowa University.

Pospere **Charles** received his doctoral degree in public policy and administration from Walden University.

Arne **Croce** is city manager of San Mateo, California.

G. Edward **DeSeve** is a *Governing* contributing writer.

Kevin **Duggan** is ICMA West Coast regional director and former city manager of Mountain View, California.

Alan **Ehrenhalt** is senior editor of *Governing*.

Rod **Erakovich** is an adjunct professor of public administration at Upper Iowa University.

Liz **Farmer** is *Governing*'s finance reporter, covering state and local budgets, pensions and other public-sector fiscal issues.

Paul **Figueroa**, a lifelong resident of Oakland, California, serves as the assistant chief of police for the City of Oakland Police Department.

Patrick **Fitzgerald** is partner at Skadden, Arps, Slate, Meagher & Flom and was formerly U.S. attorney for the Northern District of Illinois.

H. George **Frederickson** is Edwin O. Stene Distinguished Professor of Public Administration at the University of Kansas in Lawrence.

Mark **Funkhouser** is publisher of *Governing*.

Stuart C. **Gilman**, Ph.D., is a senior partner in the Global Integrity Group, which works with governments around the world on issues of governance and anti-corruption.

Joaquin Jay **Gonzalez** III is Mayor George Christopher Professor of Government and Russell T. Sharpe Professor of Business at Golden Gate University.

Josh **Goodman** is a former *Governing* staff writer.

Michael **Gordon** is a contributing writer for *The Charlotte Observer*.

Andrea **Headley** is a doctoral student at Florida International University in the Department of Public Administration, with a major in criminal justice.

**International City/County Management Association** was founded in 1914 to combat rampant corruption plaguing U.S. local governments and to promote the value of professional management.

Dan **Ivers** is Newark reporter for NJ Advance Media.

Erik W. **Johnston** is an associate professor and director of the Center for Policy Informatics in the School of Public Affairs at Arizona State University.

Jeffrey **Keefe** is an associate professor of labor and employment relations at the School of Management and Labor Relations at Rutgers University.

Elizabeth **Kellar** is president and chief executive officer of the Center for State and Local Government Excellence at the International City/County Management Association.

Roger L. **Kemp** is a distinguished adjunct professor at the Edward S. Ageno School of Business of Golden Gate University and was a city manager for 25 years in California, New Jersey, and Connecticut.

Dana K. **Lee** is a principal with Lee Facilitation Service in Mechanic Falls, Maine.

Jusil **Lee** is a doctoral student in the School of Public Affairs at Arizona State University.

Penelope **Lemov** is a *Governing* correspondent.

Kevin **Litten** is a state politics reporter based in Baton Rouge.

Mike **Maciag** is data editor of *Governing*.

Michael W. **Manske** was a pre-law advisor and associate professor at Washburn University in Topeka, Kansas.

Michael **McGrath** is chief information officer and editor of the *National Civic Review*.

Ken **Miller** is a management expert and author of *Extreme Government Makeover*.

Jim **Morrill** is a contributing writer for *The Charlotte Observer*.

Brian A. **Moura** was a long-time, award-winning assistant city manager of San Carlos, California.

Zach **Patton** is executive editor of *Governing*.

Neal **Peirce** is editor-in-chief and founder of Citiscope and is a specialist in the changes in how cities govern themselves and prepare to face challenges.

Martha **Perego** is ethics director at the International City/County Management Association.

Jan **Perkins** is an International City/County Management Association senior adviser and local government consultant with Management Partners of Laguna Beach, California.

Mattie **Quinn** is a *Governing* staff writer covering health.

Alicia **Schatteman** is an assistant professor in the School of Public Affairs, Department of Public Administration and the Center for NGO Leadership and Development at Northern Illinois University.

Dick **Simpson** is a professor of political science at the University of Illinois, Chicago.

Chelsea **Smith** is a student in the MPA program at Upper Iowa University.

JoAnne **Speers** is executive director of the Institute for Local Government in Sacramento, California.

Jim **Sullivan** is a *Governing* contributor.

Bob **Stone** is a *Governing* contributing writer.

Ravi **Subramanian** is a deputy administrative officer at the Santa Clara Valley Water District and has worked for public and private sector organizations for 30 years.

Brynne **VanHettinga** is an independent writer whose career has been in representing middle and working class employees and families, regulating and prosecuting financial entities, and legislative analysis and lobbying.

Daniel C. **Vock** is a staff writer with *Governing*.

Mark **Washburn** is a contributing writer for *The Charlotte Observer*.

Robert **Wechsler** is director of research at City Ethics, Inc., a nonprofit, nonpartisan organization that provides information and advice on local government ethics nationwide.

Howard **Whitton** is an associate of the Centre for Governance and Public Policy at Griffith University (Australia) and a specialist consultant in public sector ethics and integrity projects for governments and international NGOs.

Leo **Wright** is a student in the MPA program at Upper Iowa University.

# Index